William C. Jones

Elements and Science of English Versification

William C. Jones

Elements and Science of English Versification

ISBN/EAN: 9783743344341

Manufactured in Europe, USA, Canada, Australia, Japa

Cover: Foto ©ninafisch / pixelio.de

Manufactured and distributed by brebook publishing software (www.brebook.com)

William C. Jones

Elements and Science of English Versification

ELEMENTS AND SCIENCE OF
ENGLISH VERSIFICATION.

ELEMENTS AND SCIENCE

OF

ENGLISH VERSIFICATION

BY

WILLIAM C. JONES

BUFFALO:
THE PETER PAUL BOOK COMPANY.
1897.

COPYRIGHT, 1897, BY
THE PETER PAUL BOOK COMPANY.

PRINTED AND BOUND BY
THE PETER PAUL BOOK COMPANY
BUFFALO, N. Y.

INSCRIBED TO

Rev. William G. Williams, LL. D.

WRIGHT PROFESSOR OF
GREEK LANGUAGE AND LITERATURE,
OHIO WESLEYAN UNIVERSITY,
DELAWARE, OHIO.

PREFACE.

IT IS the desire of the author to create a greater love for poetry. I do not think it is possible to make great poets any more than it is possible to create great musicians, sculptors, artists, or orators. All must be born with the spark of genius inherent within the soul. I believe, however, that even those possessed of great genius may profit by the research of others, and frequently are induced to follow their art by suggestions and rules pointed out to them. To such who possess real genius from a poetic standpoint this work may be of benefit. Another class to be benefited are readers who love poetry and make a study of it, and yet fail to receive the benefits or see the beauties of true poetry simply because they fail to understand the technique.

It is a pleasure to be able to scan critically that which we read. If, however, we are unable to criticise for ourselves the merits of a poem from every standpoint, we necessarily lose much of the real pleasure of the reading. To be able to tell the measure, the rhythm, and the number of feet a verse contains is in every sense a satisfaction to the reader of a poem; yet, not one-third of those who read poetry know anything whatever about measure, feet, or rhythm. They realize there is a certain jingle to the stanza that pleases them, and that is all they know about it. Few readers ever stop to consider whether the poem is composed

The aim of the true poet is always high. He should not only rely upon those resources with which nature has equipped him, but he, too, should study appropriate models, until he becomes a sufficient master of the art to be able in turn to leave models for others who may follow after.

W. C. J.

Robinson, Illinois.

TABLE OF CONTENTS.

PART FIRST.

	PAGE
POETRY AS AN ART,	1
ACCENT AND QUANTITY,	6
OF VERSE,	10
HEMISTICH,	10
DISTICH,	10
TRISTICH,	11
TETRASTICH,	11
FORMS OF THE QUATRAIN,	12
OF METER,	18
THE TROCHEE,	23
THE IAMBUS,	23
THE DACTYL,	24
THE ANAPEST,	24
OF RHYTHM,	30
OF SCANSION,	33
POETIC PAUSES,	36
OF RHYME,	40
ALLITERATION,	42
ASSONANTAL,	44
CONSONANTAL,	45
MASCULINE AND FEMININE,	45
TRIPLE,	46

	PAGE
MIDDLE,	46
SECTIONAL,	48
INVERSE,	49
TASK, OR ODD,	50
CENTO VERSES,	54
ACROSTIC,	56

SELECTION OF WORDS, . . . 58

FOREIGN WORDS AND EXPRESSIONS, . . 60

THE CONSTRUCTION OF THE STANZA, . . 63

RHYTHMIC COMBINATIONS,	65
THE FIVE LINE STANZA,	69
THE SIX LINE STANZA,	75
THE SEVEN LINE STANZA,	82
THE EIGHT LINE STANZA,	92
THE NINE LINE STANZA,	98
THE TEN LINE STANZA,	102
THE SONNET,	107
THE BALLADE,	116
THE CHANT ROYAL,	118
THE RONDEAU,	120
THE RONDEL,	123
THE ROUNDEL,	124
THE SESTINA,	126
THE TRIOLET,	129
THE VIRELAY,	130
THE PANTOUM,	131
BLANK VERSE,	133

MEASURES EXEMPLIFIED, ... 136

TROCHAIC,	136
Monometer,	137
Dimeter,	138
Trimeter,	139
Tetrameter,	140

TABLE OF CONTENTS. xi

	PAGE
Pentameter,	142
Hexameter,	143
Heptameter,	144
Octometer,	146

IAMBIC, ... 147

Monometer,	148
Dimeter,	150
Trimeter,	151
Tetrameter,	152
Pentameter,	155
Hexameter,	157
Heptameter,	158
Octometer,	159

DACTYLIC, ... 160

Dimeter,	160
Tetrameter,	163
Hexameter,	164

ANAPESTIC, ... 165

Monometer,	165
Dimeter,	166
Trimeter,	167
Tetrameter,	168
Hexameter,	170

IMITATION OF CLASSICAL MEASURES, . 171

POETICAL LICENSES, . . . 177

PART SECOND.

FIGURES OF SPEECH COMMON TO POETRY, 187

FIGURES OF ETYMOLOGY, ... 187
    Apheresis, ... 187
    Apocope, ... 188

Epenthesis,	188
Paragoge,	189
Prosthesis,	190
Syncope,	190
Synæresis,	190
Tmesis,	191

FIGURES OF SYNTAX, . . . 191

Ellipsis,	191
Enallage,	193
Hyperbaton,	197
Pleonasm,	198
Syllepsis	198

FIGURES OF RHETORIC, . 199

Allegory,	199
Apostrophe,	200
Anaphora,	201
Antithesis,	202
Epanalepsis,	203
Epigram,	203
Epizeuxis,	204
Erotesis,	205
Ecphonesis,	206
Euphemism,	207
Hearing,	208
Hyperbole,	208
Irony,	210
Litotes,	211
Metonymy,	212
Echo,	218
Onomatopœia,	218
Paraleipsis,	220
Personification,	220
Refrain,	221
Simile,	222
Synecdoche,	223
Trope,	223
Vision,	226

PART THIRD.

	PAGE
OF THE VARIOUS KINDS OF POETRY,	229
THE EMPIRE OF POETRY,	229
CLASSIFICATION OF POETRY,	235
OBJECTIVE AND SUBJECTIVE POETRY,	236
THE LYRIC,	237
SECULAR SONGS,	238
SACRED SONGS,	248
OTHER METERS,	250
THE ODE,	254
The Sacred Ode,	255
The Moral Ode,	255
The Amatory Ode,	256
The Heroic Ode,	257
THE BALLAD,	258
THE ELEGY,	262
THE EPITAPH,	278
THE PASTORAL,	281
THE DIDACTIC,	285
Philosophical,	286
Meditative,	288
THE EPIC,	288
The Mock Epic,	289
Metrical Romance,	291
Metrical History,	293
THE DRAMA,	293
The Tragedy,	296
The Comedy,	296
The Divisions of the Drama,	296
The Farce,	297
The Travesty,	297
The Melodrama,	297
The Burletta,	297
The Prologue,	297

	PAGE
The Epilogue,	298
The Envoy,	298
The Subjective Drama,	299
The Opera,	299
THE SATIRE,	299
THE DIALECTIC,	303
German Dialect,	304
Irish Dialect,	306
Western Dialect,	3'8
Chinese Dialect,	311
Southern Dialect,	311
Yankee Dialect,	315
Scotch Dialect,	318
Child Dialect,	319
NONSENSE,	320
THE VERSICLE,	323
CONCLUSION,	327
INDEX OF AUTHORS,	329
INDEX OF SUBJECTS,	337

THE ART OF POETRY.

PART FIRST.

CHAPTER I.

POETRY AS AN ART.

POETRY is an art. Like music, painting and sculpture, it is a divine art. The poetic principle burns within those who are gifted by nature with the true and the ideal. It is a part of their existence, a part of their being. There are those who love music, and spend their best days in its study and composition. It is their joy and their sorrow. The world drinks in that which their souls pour out. Music, to the master mind, is his heart's gratification. He lives and breathes in its atmosphere. To him it is a greater solace than the pleasures of fashion, pomp or power.

He who is master of the art of painting enjoys satisfaction in consummating that art. He gives his life daily to the task of bringing it into perfection. His art is his love, and throughout life he admires her charms.

The sculptor spends days and years in modeling and chiseling the rough marble into the perfect image. He, too, finds true enjoyment in giving his days in bringing his art to the highest degree of excellence.

The true poet finds delight in the rhythmical creation of beauty. His word-pictures are paintings, his ideals are modeled with the care of a sculptor. He sees beauty in the tinting of the flowers, the waving of the grain, the cluster of the trees, the babbling of the brooks, the ripple of the rivers, the rifting of the clouds, the twinkling of the stars. The birds sing for him, and the winds sigh unto him. The calm, still ocean furnishes a picture of desolation, while its deep surf and mighty waves thunder back its power and destruction as they swell and surge the sands upon the shore.

The moss upon the rock, the violet and the rose, the hum of the bee, the heather and the hyacinth, all have for him some charm.

He can picture the beauty of woman as well as he who paints her upon the canvas. He can sing to her in song as well as he who trills before the harp. He finds the gems and true graces of womanhood. He idolizes the luster of her eye, the soft melody of her voice—the sigh, the laughter, the tear. He worships at the shrine of her faith, in the strength of her purity, in the sweetness of her love.

All that is true and beautiful he sees with the eye of the sculptor, feels with the touch of the painter, and hears with the ear of the musician.

The mysteries of nature are unfolded unto him, and he finds a pleasure in singing, in painting and in picturing her charms and her grandeurs. It is only those who possess the inherent power and a perfect art that can do this. Nature presents to us strength in the rough stone. Art brings to us beauty in the polished diamond.

> True ease in writing comes from art, not chance.

This verse is from Pope, a master of the art of versification. Born an invalid and possessed of a frail constitution throughout life, he devoted his time to his art. Educated and refined, with a vigor of mind possessed by few, he found time to eclipse Dryden, his chosen master and model. Mr. Walsh, who was regarded by Dryden as the best critic in all London, encouraged Pope to become the critical writer he afterwards became. "For," said Mr. Walsh, "there is one way of excelling. Although we have several great poets, we have never had any one great poet that was correct." How well Pope succeeded, Cowper tells us:

> But he (his musical finesse was such),
> So nice his ear, so delicate his touch,
> Made poetry a mere mechanic art;
> And every warbler has his tune by heart.

The act, art or practice of composing poetic verse is versification. The word "verse," in our language, means a line of poetry. A piece of poetry is often incorrectly termed a verse.

> This *verse* be thine.
> *Pope.*
>
> Virtue was taught in *verse.*
> *Prior.*

A verse may be defined as a succession of articulate sounds, consisting of words arranged in measured lines, constituting an order of accented and unaccented syllables, disposed of according to the rules of the species of poetry which the author intends to compose. Verse is merely the dress which poetry assumes. All verse is not poetry, nor is all poetry verse, as one can see by an examination of Ossian's poems, and "Leaves of Grass" by Walt Whitman. A large portion of the Holy Scriptures is poetical. Many parts are called songs, and the elevation of style clearly indicates the poetical construction of others. We give a quotation from the forty-fourth chapter ot Isaiah :

> For I will pour water upon him that is thirsty,
> And floods upon the dry ground ;
> I will pour my Spirit upon thy seed,
> And upon thine offspring my blessing profound.

Josephus affirms that the "Songs of Moses" were heroic verse, while the songs of David were composed in trimeters and pentameters.

> Sing unto the Lord with the harp ; with the harp ;
> And the voice of a psalm ;
> With trumpets and sound of cornet make a joyful noise
> Before the Lord, the King.
> "Psalm xcvii."

Some souls in this world fancy they have no love for poetry. They are mistaken. They love poetry, but they do not understand it. Every one fancies the true and the ideal. Who loves the natural world around and about us? Is it only the man of cultivation and leisure? All love nature. Every beautiful landscape that is visible to our eye is a poem. The everyday occurrences of life are poems. Yet it is only when the master mind perceives and tells to us their hitherto untold beauties, that we pause and listen. It is related of Robert Burns that he knew "The Cotter's Saturday Night" was a success, when told that the scenes he had so faithfully depicted "were common, very common; such as might be witnessed in Scotland at all times in the dwellings of the poor."

Who would now remember "Sheridan's Ride," were it not for a Thomas Buchanan Read? Who would now remember John Howard Payne, were it not for "Home,

Sweet Home"? Ages still preserve, and will, our best poems. This world of ours, with its rivers and lakes, its country and cities, its prairies and mountains, its almost every little nook and dell, is being painted with word accents by someone who sees a special beauty in the little things about him. The polite literature of poetry is keeping almost as many records of heroic events, and the heroes ; of inventions, and the inventors ; of art, and the artists ; of social, domestic, religious and political life, and the actors —as her sister prose. Life's histories of love, adventure, romance, grief, joy, adversity, hope and pleasure—all are woven together and told with unerring skill by the master.

CHAPTER II.

ACCENT AND QUANTITY.

ENGLISH poetry depends upon accent, and accent upon time. Let us illustrate: English poetry has four principal or primary meters. These meters or measures are known as iambic, trochaic, anapestic, and dactylic. All English poetry is written in one of these measures. Again, we have what is known as rhythm. The rhythm of verse is its relation of quantities or time. Take for example an iambic word, or a line of iambuses. The word "běfōre" is an iambus. Why? Because the accent falls on the second syllable, the first being unaccented. Hence, should we select an iambic verse, the accent would fall on the second syllable of each foot or measure of the line.

    'Twăs văin : thĕ lōud wăveś lāshed thĕ shōre,
     Rĕtūrn ŏr āid prĕvēntĭng :—
    Thĕ wātĕrs wĭld wĕnt ō'er hĭs chĭld,—
     Ănd hē wăs lēft lămēntĭng.
       Campbell—"Lord Ullin's Daughter."

Here we have word accent applied to poetry; every other word or syllable in the verse or line being accented. A long syllable is termed an accented syllable. Now the quantity of a syllable is the relative portion of time occupied in uttering it. In English poetry every syllable must be reckoned long or short, and a long syllable is usually equal to two short or unaccented syllables.

All words that have not a fixed accent, or in other words, all monosyllables are reckoned in the first instance as being unaccented or short. While this is true, monosyllables when used in English poetry may be used as accented or long, or, as unaccented or short even in the same line, when it becomes necessary in order to make the meter and rhythm. Take the first line of the stanza just quoted :

'Twăs vaīn : thĕ loūd wavĕs lāshed thĕ shōre.

Here we have a line of iambuses. Here we have a line of four iambic feet. Here we have a line that ticks like a clock :

Tĭck-tŏck, tĭck-tŏck, tĭck-tŏck, tĭck-tŏck.

Here we have a line in iambic rhythm. The rhythm here being determined by the accent, viz : The accent falling upon the second syllable of the foot, and the number of syllables in the foot or measure being two. There are four feet in this line. Each foot has two syllables, one accented and one not accented.

Now, let us take another word, and another line. Take the word "lōvelў." Here the accent falls upon the first syllable. In other words it would be termed long, while the "lў" would be unaccented or short syllable. Now, this word is termed a trochee. It is one of the primary feet in English poetry ; a foot where the accent falls upon the first syllable. Here is a stanza familiar to all, a stanza by one of the greatest and most charming of poets,

> Līves ŏf greāt mĕn āll rĕmīnd ŭs
> Wē căn māke oŭr līves sŭblīme,
> Ānd, dĕpārtĭng leāve bĕhīnd ŭs,
> Foōtprĭnts ōn thĕ sānds ŏf time.
> *Longfellow*—"A Psalm of Life."

Here we have another stanza of word accents. The accents all fall on the first syllable or unemphatic word of each foot or measure of the line or verse. The trochaic and iambic measures are termed dissyllabic, for the reason that two monosyllables, or two syllables or a word of two syllables, compose a foot or measure.

Now, we have the same old clock ticking, but we will elevate one side of it and put a chip under it. We now have it ticking just the reverse of what it did before. It ticks a little livelier. It now ticks—

> Tōck-tĭck, tōck-tĭck, tōck-tĭck, tōck-tĭck.

Its measure is trochaic, because composed of trochees. Its rhythm is trochaic, because it thus signifies or denotes the kind and character of the feet employed, and arranged into measures. If the line then is composed of four trochaic feet, viz: a trochaic tetrameter, the rhythm must necessarily be trochaic.

What has been said of iambic meter, and trochaic meter, is equally true of anapestic and dactylic meter. These are termed trisyllablic feet. These measures or feet may be also distinguished from the dissyllabic measures. The anapestic foot having one accented and two unaccented syllables, the first two being unaccented the last being accented, hence, it necessarily follows, the time meter and rhythm must be different. The clock would now tick,—

Tĭck, tĭck-tōck, tĭck, tĭck-tōck, tĭck, tĭck-tōck.

On the other hand, dactylic measure being composed of dactyls, words of three syllables, having the accent upon the first syllable, the last two being unaccented, the clock being elevated slightly again, would tick a little faster, thus

Tōck, tĭck-tĭck, tōck, tĭck-tĭck, tōck, tĭck-tĭck.

The quantity of a syllable, whether long or short, in other words, accented or unaccented, does not depend upon the long or short sound of the vowel, or diphthong, but upon the intensity with which the syllable is uttered, whereby a greater or less portion of time is employed in uttering it.

Rhythmus in the widest sense is a division of time into short portions by regular succession of emotions, impulses, and sounds producing agreeable effect. We speak of the rhythmus of the dance, the rhythmus of music, the rhythmus of the poem. The language of the true-born poet is rhythmical, and its rhythmic nature distinguishes it from ordinary speech. To the lover of true poetry and art there is a peculiar charm and grateful satisfaction attaches to and delights the ear when reading a beautiful poem of a peculiar or particular rhythm. The rhythmic accent marks off given periods of time, and the natural or trained ear is thus enabled to say, as each measure passes in review before it, whether the time value of that particular measure is correct.

CHAPTER III.

OF VERSE.

A VERSE being a metrical line of a length and rhythm determined by rules which usage has sanctioned, it will be therefore necessary to ascertain the divisions of verse.

First, we have the Half Verse or Hemistich, it being a half poetic line or verse not complete:

>   ANAPESTIC TETRAMETER.
>
>   Heavĕn's firĕ ĭs ăroŭnd thĕe, tŏ blāst ănd tŏ būrn;
>   Rĕtūrn tŏ thў dwĕllĭng! * * *
>   *Campbell*—"Lochiel's Warning."

Second, we have the Couplet or Distich, two verses or a pair of rhymes:

>   DACTYLIC DIMETER.
>
>   Ălās! fŏr thĕ rārĭtў
>   Ŏf Chrĭstiăn chārĭtў.
>   *Hood*—"The Bridge of Sighs."

>   TROCHAIC TETRAMETER.
>
>   Fŏr thĕ heărt whŏse wŏes arĕ lĕgiŏn
>   'Tis ă peācefŭl, soŏthĭng rēgiŏn.
>   *Poe*—"Dreamland."

IAMBIC PENTAMETER.

Whŏ hāth nŏt paūsed whīle Bĕautў's pĕnsivĕ ĕye
Askĕd frŏm hĭs heārt thĕ hŏmăge ŏf ă sĭgh?
  Campbell—"Pleasures of Hope."

Third, the Triplet or Tristich, three verses rhyming together:

IAMBIC PENTAMETER.

Ă sēntĭnĕl āngĕl sĭttĭng hīgh ĭn glōrў
Heărd thīs shrĭll wāil rĭng oūt frŏm Pūrgătōrў:
Hăve mērcў, mīghtў āngĕl, heār mў stōrў!
  Hay—"A Woman's Love."

Ănd whăt's ă life?—ă wēarў pĭlgrĭmāge,
Whŏse glōrў in onĕ dāy dŏth fĭll thĕ stāge
Wĭth chĭldhoŏd, mānhoŏd, ănd dĕcrēpĭt āge.
  Quarles—"What is Life."

Fourth, the Stanza or Tetrastich, a regular division of a poem, consisting of two or more lines or verses. They are formulated according to usage, and the taste of the writer, and may be of every conceivable variety. Stanzas of the same poem should be uniform, and constitute a regular division of a poem. Stanzas are often incorrectly termed verses.

A verse is one line of a poem; a stanza, two or more. Stanzas are frequently known by the name of those using them most; as, the stanza of Spenser, the stanza of Burns, the stanza of Chaucer.

The Couplet is the simplest form of the stanza; as,

Whĕre dĭd yŏu cōme frŏm, bābў dēar?
Oŭt ŏf thĕ ĕvĕrўwhēre ĭntō thĕ hēre.
  George Macdonald—"The Baby."

> Ălās! fŏr lōve, ĭf thōu ărt āll,
> Ănd naŭght bĕyŏnd, Ŏ Eārth!
> *Hemans*—"The Graves of a Household."

Any two lines of poetry that make complete sense when taken together, whether they rhyme or do not rhyme may be termed a couplet; and this form of stanza is frequently employed in poems of considerable length; as, Whittier's "Barbara Frietchie;" Tennyson's "Locksley Hall;" Edwin Arnold's "Secret of Death."

The couplet is also employed in combination to form other stanzas.

The next form of stanza is the Triplet, which is three lines rhyming together.

The following example is a trochaic tetrameter:

> Bĕar thrŏugh sŏrrŏw, wrŏng, ănd rūth,
> Ĭn thy̆ hĕart thĕ dĕw ŏf yōuth,
> Ŏn thy̆ līps thĕ smīle ŏf trūth.
>
> Ănd thăt smīle, līke sŭnshĭne, dărt
> Ĭntŏ mány ă sŭnlĕss hĕart,
> Fŏr ă smīle ŏf Gōd thŏu ārt.
> *Longfellow*—"Maidenhood."

Like the couplet, the triplet is used in combination to form other stanzas.

The next form is a four-line stanza called a Quatrain. The quatrain is also used in combination to form other stanzas. Quatrains are a very common form of stanzas, and we shall give examples of many of them. Let us take the following iambic:

I.

His wăs thĕ trŏublĕd līfe,
 Thĕ cōnflĭct ānd thĕ pāin,
Thĕ grīef, thĕ bīttĕrnĕss ŏf strīfe,
 Thĕ hŏnŏr wĭthŏut stāin.
    Longfellow—"Charles Sumner."

The first, second and fourth lines are iambic trimeter, composed of three iambuses. An iambus consists of a foot of two syllables, the first syllable is unaccented, the second accented. The third line is iambic tetrameter, composed of four iambic feet. In this stanza, the first and third lines rhyme, the second and fourth.

From S. T. Coleridge we have the following :

II.

Shĕ līstenĕd wĭth ă flīttĭng blŭsh,
 Wĭth dōwncăst eyēs ănd mōdĕst grāce ;
Fŏr wĕll shĕ knēw, Ĭ coŭld nŏt choōse
 Bŭt gāze ŭpŏn hĕr fāce.
    "Genevieve."

In this stanza, the second and fourth lines rhyme. The first three lines are iambic tetrameter, the fourth, iambic trimeter.

III.

Mў dāys ăre īn thĕ yĕllŏw lēaf,
 Thĕ flowērs ănd frŭits ŏf lŏve arĕ gōne ;
Thĕ wŏrm, thĕ cānkĕr, ānd thĕ grīef,
 Arĕ mīne ălonē.
    Lord Byron—(Composed on his 36th birthday.)

The first three lines are iambic tetrameter, the fourth, iambic dimeter.

IV.

A keēpsăke, măybē,
Thĕ gift ŏf ănōthĕr, pĕrhāps ă brōthĕr,
Ŏr lōvĕr, whŏ knōws? hĭm hĕr heărt chōse,
Ŏr wās hĕr heărt-frēe?
N. G. Shepherd—"Only the Clothes She Wore."

This stanza is iambic, the first and fourth lines rhyming. The first and fourth lines dimeter, the second and third, tetrameter. The second and third have line rhymes.

V.

Clĕŏn hāth ă mīlliŏn ācrĕs, ne'ĕr ă onē hăve Ī ;
Clĕŏn dwēllĕth in ă pălăce, ĭn ă cōttăge Ī ;
Clĕŏn hāth ă dōzĕn fōrtŭnes, nōt ă pĕnnȳ Ī ;
Yĕt thĕ poōrĕr ŏf thĕ twāin ĭs Clĕŏn, ănd nŏt Ī.
Charles Mackay—"Cleon and I."

This stanza is thirteen syllabled, heptameter, trochaic measure.

VI.

Līke Diăn's kīss, ŭnāsked, ŭnsōught,
Lŏve gīves ĭtsēlf, bŭt ĭs nŏt bōught ;
Nŏr voĭce, nŏr soūnd bĕtrāys
Ĭts dēep, ĭmpāssiŏned gāze.
Longfellow—"Endymion."

The first two lines are iambic tetrameter, the third and fourth, trimeters.

VII.

Rĕvīle hĭm nōt,—thĕ Tēmptĕr hāth
Ă snāre fŏr āll ;
Ănd pĭtyĭng tēars, nŏt scōrn ănd wrāth,
Bĕfīt hĭs fāll !
Whittier—"Ichabod."

The first and third lines are iambic trimeters, the second and fourth dimeters. The lines rhyme alternately.

VIII.

Tŏ shōw ă heārt griĕf-rēnt ;
Tŏ stārve thȳ sīn,
Nŏt bīn,—
Ănd thāt's tŏ keēp thȳ Lēnt.
Herrick— " True Lent."

This is a quatrain of iambics.

IX.

Whăt mōre ? wĕ toōk oŭr lāst ădieū,
Ănd ūp, thĕ snōwȳ Splūgĕn drēw,
Bŭt ēre wĕ reāched thĕ hīghĕst sūmmĭt
Ĭ plūck'd ă dāisȳ, Ĭ gāve ĭt yoū.
Tennyson—"The Daisy."

This is a tetrameter stanza of iambuses.

X.

Ănd thĕ night shăll bĕ fĭlled wĭth mūsĭc,
Ănd thĕ cāres, thăt ĭnfēst thĕ dāy,
Shăll fōld theĭr tēnts, lĭke thĕ Ārăbs,
Ănd ăs sīlĕntlȳ stēal ăwāy.
Longfellow—"The Day is Done."

This is an anapest.

XI.

Ŏ hēard yĕ yŏn pībrŏch sŏund sād ĭn thĕ gāle,
Whĕre ă bănd cŏmĕth slōwlȳ wĭth weēpĭng ănd wāil ?
'T ĭs thĕ chiĕf ŏf Glĕnārā lămēnts fŏr hĭs dēar ;
Ănd hĕr sīre, ănd thĕ pĕoplĕ, ăre cālled tŏ hĕr biĕr.
Campbell—"Glenara."

This is an excellent anapestic tetrameter quatrain.

XII.

Thĕn shoōk thĕ hĭlls wĭth thŭndĕr rĭvĕn,
Thĕn rūshed thĕ steēds tŏ băttlĕ drĭvĕn,
Ănd loūdĕr thăn thĕ bōlts ŏf heāvĕn,
Făr flāshed thĕ rēd ărtĭllĕrȳ.
Campbell—"Hohenlinden."

This stanza is composed of a triplet and an odd line. It is a tetrameter. The last syllables of the first three lines are redundant.

XIII.

Ĭnhûmăn măn! Cŭrse ōn thȳ bărbaroŭs ărt,
Ănd blăstĕd bē thȳ mŭrdĕr-āimĭng ēye!
Mău nĕvĕr pĭty soōthe theĕ wĭth ă sīgh,
Nŏr ēvĕr plēasŭre glăd thȳ crŭĕl heārt!
Burns—"On Seeing a Wounded Hare."

The stanza is an iambic pentameter.

XIV.

Ăs Ī loŏk ŭp ĭntō yoŭr ēyes, ănd wāit
Fŏr sōme rĕspōnse tŏ mȳ fŏnd gāze ănd toŭch,
Ĭt seēms tŏ mē thĕre īs nŏ săddĕr făte
Thăn tŏ bĕ doōmed tŏ lŏvĭng ōvĕrmŭch.
Ella Wheeler Wilcox—"The Common Lot."

This is a ten-syllabled iambic pentameter, the first and third, and the second and fourth lines rhyming.

XV.

Whĭthĕr, mĭdst fălling dĕw,
Whĭle glŏw thĕ heāvens wĭth thĕ lăst stĕps ŏf dāy,
Făr, throūgh theĭr rōsȳ dĕpths, dŏst thoū pŭrsūe
Thȳ sōlĭtărȳ wăy.
Bryant—"To a Waterfowl."

This stanza is iambic. The first and fourth lines are trimeter, the second and third, hexameter.

We have given many forms of the quatrain. We have also given the measure of the stanzas selected. We have endeavored to present different forms with a view to show at a glance the numerous ways the quatrain may be formed. It is a fine form of the stanza, and is more in use than any other style of poetry. Employed with the couplet, and the triplet, as well as the single line of verse, the quatrain is capable of producing many other forms of beautiful stanzas.

CHAPTER IV.

OF METER.

WHILE we may learn to distinguish measures by sound, if we happen to have a good ear for music, or time, still, until one acquaints himself with the art of versification and understands the rules or laws governing the formation of stanzas, he cannot tell or give the reasons why any particular stanza is written in any particular meter. Meter is derived from the Greek word *metron*, and denotes a measure. Measure or meter is a succession of groups of accented and unaccented syllables in which poetry is written. In the classic languages, the measure depended upon the way the long and short syllables were made to succeed one another. Our modern verse depends, as we have seen, not upon the distinction of long and short syllables, but upon that of accented and unaccented syllables.

The accents should occur at regular intervals; and the groups of syllables thus formed, each constitute a measure.

In the classic verse these groups of long and short syllables composing the measure, were called feet, each foot having a distinctive name. Meter in poetry, being similar to measures or musical bars in music, received the name of feet because the measure was regulated by the foot of the director of the Greek choirs.

> Keeping time, time, time.
> *Poe*—"The Bells."

The same names are applied to the modern that were applied to the classic measures, from which they are all taken. An accented syllable in modern verse being held equivalent to a long syllable in classic verse. It is designated by a (—) macron ; an unaccented syllable is equal to a short syllable, and designated by a (⌣) breve.

'T ĭs dĭstānce lēnds ĕnchāntmĕnt tō thĕ viēw,
Ănd rōbes thĕ mōuntāin īn ĭts āzŭre hūe.
  Campbell—"Pleasures of Hope."

The first word is unaccented and is marked with a breve, the second accented, and marked with a macron, denoting the character of the measure, which is iambic pentameter.

Each measure contains one accented syllable, and either one or two unaccented syllables.

In poetry monosyllables receive accent. Most monosyllables in our language are variable in quantity,. and can be used as long or short, as strong or weak sounds suit the sense or rhythm.

Every emphatic word, and every accented syllable, in verse forms a long or accented syllable. Monosyllabic unemphatical words constitute short or unaccented syllables. Words of greater length usually have-fixed accents. Accented syllables are always long. Syllables immediately before or after an accented syllable are usually short. To determine the kind of verse, it is always safe to look, first, to the words that have a fixed accent ; second, to words that are emphatic that are unaccented.

The number of feet in a stanza must always be reckoned by the number of accented syllables constituting each line or verse.

A syllable is a whole word or each part of a word that is

uttered by one impulse of the mouth. A word usually has as many syllables as it has principal parts. A word of but one principal part is termed a monosyllable; as, God. Such words are pronounced with but one impulse of the voice.

A word of two syllables is termed a dissyllable; as, God-ly. Such words require two articulations. Words of three syllables or principal parts are trisyllables, as God-li-ness, Un-god-ly, and require as many articulations as they have syllables.

Accent in poetry is defined as the uttering or pronouncing of a word, noting the particular stress or force of the voice upon certain words and syllables of words.

The acute accent is marked thus — or thus /

All words of more than one syllable are accented, as,

   Hō-lỹ, Hō-lĭ-nĕss, Ŭn-hō-lỹ.

Compound words may have two accents; as,

   ēv-ĕr-chāng-ĭng, ē-vĕn-mīnd-ĕd.

Accent is the peculiar stress we lay upon some word or syllable of a word, as,

Fŏr-give,	Beaū-tĭ-fŭl,
Hōld-ĭng,	Rĕ-wārd-ĭng,
Rĕs-ŏ-nănce,	Wĭnd-ĭng-sheēt,
Cŏn-fū-sĭon,	Bō-nă-fĭ-dĕ,
Fĭn-ăn-ciĕr,	Rĕ-gārd,
Rōgue-haŭnt-ĕd,	Hāp-pỹ,
Rĕ-wārd,	Ăb-sĕn-teē,
Scārce-lỹ,	Cŏn-sĭgn-eē,

These words have all fixed accents.

We believe that accent is the sole principle that regulates our English rhythm. It is therefore necessary to observe certain principles that govern accent. In words of two or more syllables, there is one syllable which receives a stronger verbal accent than the others. That is called the primary accent. When the word contains three or more syllables, there is a secondary accent.

Poets have in all ages, where the primary accent fell upon the first syllable, in words of three syllables, taken the liberty of giving a secondary accent to the third syllable, where the rhythm required it. Words of four syllables have a secondary accent, unless the primary accent falls on one of the middle syllables, it is then governed by the same as the trisyllable. Words of five syllables, if accented on the first, seldom have less than three accented syllables and never have less than two.

When a pause separates two syllables, each syllable may receive the accent. In that case the pause fills the place of a syllable.

When a verse, or a section of a verse, begins with an accent, that accent should be a strong, not a weak one.

There is no word, however, so unimportant, that it may not be accented if the rhythm requires it. The article may, and does, receive accent. The rule, however, is that qualifying words, as adjectives, adverbs, and others of the same class, receive a fainter accent than the words qualified.

In Will Carleton's "The Burning of Chicago," we have a fine illustration. Notice the fine effect of the compound words and how nicely the accent falls. The measure is anapestic. The first four lines of the stanza are anapestic trimeter. The remaining ten lines are anapestic hexameter. We give the third stanza as follows :

'T wăs nīght ĭn thĕ sĭn-bŭrdĕned cĭtȳ,
Thĕ tūrbŭlĕnt, vĭce-lădĕn cĭtȳ,
Thĕ sĭn-cŏmpăssed, rōgue-hăuntĕd cĭtȳ,
Thŏugh Queēn ŏf thĕ Nŏrth ănd thĕ Wĕst.
And lōw ĭn thĕir cāves ŏf pŏllūtiŏn greăt beāsts ŏf hŭmānĭtȳ growled ;
And ŏvĕr hĭs mŏnĕy-strĕwn tăblĕ thĕ gāmblĕr bĕnt fiĕrcelȳ, ănd scōwled ;
And mĕn wĭth nŏ seēmĭng ŏf mănhoŏd, wĭth coūntĕnănce flāmĭng ănd fĕll,
Drănk deĕp frŏm thĕ fīre-lădĕn foūntăins thăt sprĭng frŏm thĕ rīvĕrs ŏf hêll ;
And mĕn wĭth nŏ seēmĭng ŏf mănhoŏd, whŏ dreādĕd thĕ cōmĭng ŏf dāy,
Prŏwled, căt-līke, fŏr bloŏd-pŭrchăsed plŭndĕr frŏm mĕn whŏ wĕre bĕttĕr thăn thĕy ;
And mĕn wĭth nŏ seēmĭng ŏf mănhoŏd, whŏse deārĕst-crăved glōrȳ wăs shāme,
Whŏse jōys wĕre thĕ sŏrrŏws ŏf ŏthĕrs, whŏse hārvĕsts wĕre ācrĕs ŏf flāme,
Slŭnk whīspĕrĭng ănd lŏw, ĭn thĕir cŏrnĕrs, wĭth bōwĭe ănd pĭstŏl tĭght-prĕssed,
Ĭn rōgue-hăuntĕd, sĭn-cŭrsed Chĭcāgŏ, thŏugh Queēn ŏf thĕ Nŏrth ănd thĕ Wĕst.

The stanza is mixed by the introduction of an iambus in the first foot of each verse.

The words selected and accented in the preceeding chapter were selected for a two-fold purpose ; first, to show their fixed accents ; second, to illustrate meter, or measure.

Every primary measure in English poetry contains one syllable accented, and either one or two, that are unaccented. Accent may be on either the first, second or third syllable of the group, hence there are four complete and distinct primary meters in our modern poetic forms. In chapter two they were mentioned as iambic, trochaic, anapestic and dactylic measures. Let us further illustrate and define them.

THE TROCHEE.

Two are composed of dissyllables; as an example, the word hō-lў. Here we have the accent falling upon the first syllable, the second being unaccented. This word in poetry is called a trochee, and the verse composed in it would be termed trochaic. It is a classic foot and simply means a foot of two syllables, the first accented, the second unaccented.

THE IAMBUS.

Let us next take the word rĕ-wārd. Here we find the accent is placed upon the second syllable, instead of the first. In poetry this word is termed an iambus, a classic foot, signifying a foot of two syllables, the first unaccented, the second accented. Verse written in this measure is termed iambic.

The songs and satires of the ancient classics were written in this measure. We have, then, two dissyllabic meters, the trochaic and the iambic. The greater part of our entire verse is written in one or the other of these measures.

The iambic measure is suited for grave and dignified subjects. The poetry written in this measure cannot well be enumerated. Three-fourths of our modern verse, we feel safe in saying, is written in iambic meter. The trochaic is an elegant foot. It has a faster movement than the iambic. It moves lightly and with a brisk trip. It is not encumbered by an extra syllable, as its sister foot, the dactyl. The trochee and iambus are interchangeable.

THE DACTYL.

Of trisyllabic feet we have two that are primary. The first is the dactyl, the second the anapest. Both are classic feet. Let us take the word bēau-tĭ-fŭl. Here the accent falls upon the first syllable, the second and third being unaccented. This is the dactyl. This meter or foot is called the dactylic, and signifies a meter having the first foot accented, and the other feet unaccented.

THE ANAPEST.

Let us next take the word fĭn-ăn-ciēr. Here we have a word with the accent falling upon the final syllable. This is termed in verse an anapest. Verse written in this measure is termed anapestic. It signifies in poetry a measure having the first two syllables unaccented, the last accented.

The trisyllabic measures are often substituted one for another and like the dissyllabic they are interchangeable. They are also interchangeable with the spondee.

These four primary measures are those most in use. The trisyllabic measures are more difficult to use than the dissyllabic, although the dactyl is termed the flowing measure of poetry. It is capable of many results, and much beautiful verse is written in the dactylic.

We have then four separate and distinct measures, which are termed primary, as follows:

The Trochaic,	— ᴗ
The Iambic,	ᴗ —
The Dactylic,	— ᴗ ᴗ
The Anapestic,	ᴗ ᴗ —

The substitution of these feet denominated primary, where one foot is substituted for another frequently, gives rise to what is known and termed mixed measure.

We shall now illustrate the four measures by a specimen of verse written in each kind. The following is a trochaic. The stanza is the eight and seven syllabled trochaic verse; a twelve line stanza, the second, fourth, sixth and eighth lines rhyming.

> Whĕn thĕ hūmĭd shădŏws hŏvĕr
> Ŏvĕr āll thĕ stārrў sphēres,
> Ānd thĕ mēlănchōlў dărknĕss
> Gēntlў weĕps ĭn rāinў tēars,
> Whāt ă blĭss tŏ prēss thĕ pĭllŏw
> Ŏf ă cōttăge-chămbĕr bĕd,
> Ānd tŏ lĭstĕn tō thĕ pāttĕr
> Ŏf thĕ sōft răin ōvĕrhēad !
> *Coates Kinney*—"Rain on the Roof."

Our next stanza is an iambic six line stanza.

> Yĕs ! beār thĕm tō thĕir rēst ;
> Thĕ rōsў bābe, tĭred wĭth thĕ glāre ŏf dāy,
> Thĕ prăttlĕr, fāllĕn ăsleĕp e'ĕn ĭn hĭs plāy ;
> Clăsp thĕm tŏ thў sŏft breāst,
>   Ŏ night !
> Blĕss thĕm ĭn dreāms wĭth ā deĕp, hūshed dĕlīght.
> *G. W. Bethune*—"Hymn to Night."

This stanza contains six lines, the first and fourth are iambic trimeters ; the second, third, and sixth iambic lines of ten syllables, or pentameters, and the fifth a fine specimen of the iambic monometer, a verse of two syllables.

The next stanza is composed of dactyls, and known as dactylic measure :

> Cōme tŏ mĕ, deārĕst, Ĭ'm lōnelў wĭthōut theĕ,
> Dāy-tĭme ănd nīght-tĭme, Ĭ'm thīnkĭng ăbōut theĕ ;
> Nīght-tĭme ănd dāy-tĭme, ĭn dreāms Ĭ bĕhōld theĕ ;
> Ŭnwēlcŏme thĕ wākĭng whĭch ceāsĕs tŏ fōld thee.

Cōme tŏ mĕ, dārling, mȳ sōrrŏws tŏ līghtĕn.
Cōme ĭn thȳ bēautȳ tŏ blĕss ănd tŏ brīghtĕn ;
Cōme ĭn thȳ wōmănhoŏd, mēeklȳ ănd lōwlȳ,
Cōme ĭn thȳ lōvĭngnĕss qūeenlȳ ănd hōlȳ.
   Joseph Brennan—" Come to Me, Dearest."

This is a stanza of eight lines, dactylic tetrameter, with the exception of the fourth verse, which is a pure line or verse of amphibrachic tetrameter, a secondary foot substituted for the dactylic, with a truly pleasing effect.

Our next stanza is anapestic.

'T ĭs thĕ voīce ŏf thĕ slŭggărd ; Ĭ hēard hĭm cŏmplāin,
Yoŭ hăve wăk'd mĕ toŏ soŏn, Ĭ mŭst slŭmbĕr ăgaīn.
Ăs thĕ doōr ŏn ĭts hīngĕs, sŏ hĕ ŏn hĭs bĕd,
Tŭrns hĭs sīdes, ănd hĭs shoŭldĕrs, ănd hĭs hĕavȳ hēad.
   Dr. Isaac Watts—" The Sluggard."

A four line stanza of anapestic tetrameter.

In addition to the measures which we have termed primary, the ancients had other measures denominated secondary measures. They are frequently introduced into verse to relieve monotony, as well as allowing the writer freer scope. They are also unconsciously introduced by writers fervent with the passion of the subject or theme, and give grace and style. They are three in number.

The Spondee, a foot of two accented syllables ; as, prāise Gōd, vāin wōrld, poōr mān. A verse in this foot or meter is termed spondaic.

An Amphibrach is a poetic foot consisting of three syllables, the first and last syllables unaccented, the middle accented ; as, cŏnsīdĕr, trănspōrtĕd.

A Cretic, or Amphimacer, a poetic foot, the first syllable accented, the second unaccented, and the third, accented ; as, wīn-dŏw-sāsh, wīnd-ĭng-sheēt, līfe-ĕs-tāte.

The dissyllabic feet then, are three in number, as follows:

The Trochee — ◡
The Iambus ◡ —
The Spondee — —

The trisyllabic are four in number, as follows:

The Anapest ◡ ◡ —   The Amphibrach ◡ — ◡
The Dactyl — ◡ ◡   The Cretic — ◡ —

Coleridge, in "A Lesson for a Boy," exemplified these seven feet:

Trōcheĕ trīps frŏm lōng tŏ shŏrt;
Frŏm lōng tŏ lōng ĭn sōlĕmn sōrt
Slōw Spōndeĕ stālks; strōng foŏt! yĕt ĭll-ăblĕ
Ĕvĕr tŏ cōme ŭp wĭth Dāctȳl trĭsȳllăblĕ.
Ĭāmbĭcs mārch frŏm shŏrt tŏ lōng :—
Wĭth ă leāp ănd ă boūnd thĕ swĭft Ānăpĕsts thrŏng;
Onĕ sȳllăblĕ lōng, wĭth ŏne shŏrt ăt ĕach sīde,
Ămphĭbrăchȳs hāstes wĭth ă statēlȳ strĭde;
Fīrst ănd lāst bēĭng lōng, mĭddlĕ shŏrt, Āmphĭmācĕr
Strīkes hĭs thūndĕrĭng hoŏfs, lĭke ă proūd hĭgh-brĕd rācĕr.

Where a verse or line consists wholly of one kind of feet, it is termed pure. If a verse consists of nothing but iambuses, it would be a pure iambic verse; if no foot but the trochee, a trochaic; if no foot but the anapest, anapestic; if dactyls compose the entire line, the line is termed dactylic rhythm.

Thĕ prōpĕr stūdȳ ŏf mănkind ĭs mān.
Pope.

This verse, as will be seen by scansion, is iambic pentameter; *viz*, a ten syllabled line of iambuses.

> Blĕssĭngs ŏn theĕ, lĭttlĕ mān,
> Barēfoŏt bŏy, wĭth cheĕk ŏf tān!
> *Whittier*—"The Barefoot Boy."

This poem is seven syllabled trochaic rhythm:

In "Why should the Spirit of Mortal be Proud," by William Knox we have a poem written in pure anapestic rhythm save the first foot, which is an iambus.

> Thĕ hānd ŏf thĕ kīng, thăt thĕ scēptrĕ hăth bōrne;
> Thĕ brōw ŏf thĕ prīest, thăt thĕ mītrĕ hăth wōrn;
> Thĕ ĕye ŏf thĕ sāge, ănd thĕ heārt ŏf thĕ brāve,—
> Arĕ hīddĕn ănd lōst ĭn thĕ dēpths ŏf thĕ grāve.

These two lines from the same poem are pure anapestic tetrameter:

> Tŏ thĕ life wĕ arĕ clīngĭng, thĕy, ālsŏ, wŏuld clīng;
> Bŭt ĭt speēds fŏr ŭs āll, lĭke ă bīrd ŏn thĕ wīng.

The anapestic measure is a very capable one, smooth flowing and strong. It is alike suitable for the more serious thoughts of life, as well as, some that are exceedingly mirthful. Brete Harte has adopted this meter in very many of the quaint, mirth-provoking poems which he has written.

For an illustration of the dactylic, we have taken a stanza from Tennyson's "Charge of the Light Brigade:"

> "Fōrwărd, thĕ Līght Brĭgāde!"
> Wăs thĕre ă mān dĭsmāyed?
> Nŏt thŏugh thĕ sōldiĕr knĕw
>   Sōme onĕ hăd blūndĕred:
> Thēirs nŏt tŏ māke rĕplȳ,
> Thēirs nŏt tŏ rēasŏn whȳ,
> Thēirs bŭt tŏ dō ănd dīe:
> Ĭntŏ thĕ vāllĕy ŏf Deāth,
>   Rŏde thĕ sĭx hūndrĕd.

This is a fine specimen of dactylic dimeter, mixed with trochees and anapests.

The more pure these several measures are preserved, the more complete and perfect the chime of the verse, which should in every instance be as pure and smooth flowing as it is in the power of the writer to make it. Where, however, verse becomes monotonous, it is well to substitute some other foot. Verse is truly beautiful where these substitutions are made, as—

>   Knŏw yĕ thĕ lānd whĕre thĕ cȳprĕss ănd mȳrtlĕ
>   Ărĕ ēmblĕms ŏf deēds thăt ăre dōne ĭn thĕir clīme—
>   Whĕre thĕ rāge ŏf thĕ vūltŭre, thĕ lōve ŏf thĕ tūrtlĕ,
>   Nŏw mēlt ĭntŏ sōftnĕss, nŏw māddĕn tŏ crīme?
>   Knōw yĕ thĕ lānd ŏf thĕ cēdăr ănd vīne,
>   Whĕre thĕ flōwĕrs ĕvĕr blōssŏm, thĕ beāms ĕvĕr shīne,
>   Ănd thĕ līght wĭngs ŏf zēphȳr, ŏpprēssed wĭth pĕrfūme,
>   Wăx fāint ŏ'er thĕ gārdĕns ŏf Gūl ĭn hĕr bloōm?
>   Whĕre thĕ cītrŏn ănd ōlĭve ăre fāirĕst ŏf frūit,
>   Ănd thĕ vōice ŏf thĕ nīghtĭngăle nēvĕr ĭs mūte?
>   Whĕre thĕ vīrgĭns ăre sōft ăs thĕ rōsĕs thĕy twīne,
>   Ănd āll, săve thĕ spīrĭt ŏf mān, ĭs dĭvīne?
>   'T ĭs thĕ lānd ŏf thĕ Eāst—'t ĭs thĕ clīme ŏf thĕ sūn—
>   Căn hĕ smīle ŏn sŭch deēds ăs hĭs chīldrĕn hăve dōne?
>   Ŏh, wĭld ăs thĕ āccĕnts ŏf lōvĕrs' fărewēll,
>   Ăre thĕ heārts thăt thĕy beār, ănd thĕ tāles thăt thĕy tĕll.
>   *Byron*—" Bride of Abydos."

Few prettier lines have ever been written in trisyllabic verse than these lines. Note how smoothly flowing the rhythm; how the measures mix and commingle together. It will be seen that the first line is dactylic; second, anapestic, first foot being iambic; third, anapestic. The stanza is anapestic rhythm, that being the prevailing primary foot.

CHAPTER V.

OF RHYTHM.

POETRY being the polite literature of the world, much of its beauty necessarily depends upon how it is written. No matter how beautiful the thought, it must still depend upon how that thought is arranged. To be able to tell at a glance the measure and rhythm of poetry is worth the effort of all classes, especially all readers who enjoy and love that literature that springs from the cathedral of the human heart. Musical notes properly arranged by the hand of a master, give joy to the listener. There is music that lulls to rest. There is music that curdles the blood. There is music that is awe inspiring. There is music that breathes of love. There is rhythm in music. There is rhythm in poetry, the kindred art. How much poetry depends upon rhythm let James Montgomery, a master spirit tell us : " How much the power of poetry depends upon the nice inflections of rhythm alone, may be proved by taking the finest passages of Milton or Shakespeare, and merely putting them into prose with the least possible variation of the words themselves. The attempt would be like gathering up dewdrops which appear jewels and pearls on the grass, but run into water in the hands ; the essence and the elements remain, but the grace, the sparkle and the form are gone."

Poetry originates in the enjoyment of equality and fitness. Rhythm, meter, rhyme, stanza, alliteration, and other analogous effects are employed in the moods of verse. Many fail to make any distinction between meter and rhythm. Meter is the arrangement of poetic feet, or of accented and unaccented syllables into verse. Rhythm signifies the character of the feet thus arranged, as,

> Ōh ! ĭt wăs pĭtĭfŭl !
> Nĕar ă͜whŏle cĭtў fŭll,
> Hōme shĕ hăd nōne.
> *Hood*—" The Bridge of Sighs."

This is termed dactylic rhythm, a dactylic dimeter, it being a line or measure consisting of two dactyls; thus, a line composed of iambuses, anapests, trochees, and dactyls, being primary feet, would be termed iambic rhythm, anapestic rhythm, trochaic rhythm, dactylic rhythm.

Every reader of poetry has observed that it seldom happens that verse proceeds uniformly with a succession of absolutely equal feet; namely, with a regular succession of trochees, iambuses, spondees, dactyls, amphibrachys, cretics or anapests only. The most musical lines are often interrupted in the succession and are varied by the introduction of other feet. Trochees are substituted for iambuses; anapests, amphibrachys, dactyls; spondees and cretics are substituted one for an other. These feet may be termed equivalents, for the feet are of the same length, in ˙other words, where they are of the same number of accented and unaccented syllables.

We find trochees at the beginning of a verse we term iambic, where the iambus is the prevailing foot, denoting that the rhythm is in its character iambic. We also frequently find anapests in a line that is iambic rhythm;

trochees are interrupted by the dactyl; dactyls are interrupted or interspersed with the amphibrachys or some other trisyllabic foot. It is allowable thus to vary the verse, if the time and melody of the line be preserved. The time and the melody of the verse are often rendered more harmonious by the substitution of the trisyllabic foot for the dissyllabic, or the dissyllabic foot for the trisyllabic; or, in other words, the substitution of one foot for another, where there is still preserved harmony in the sound, or where the substituted foot is equal to, or amounts to an equivalent. Pure dactylic stanzas are rare. Anapestic stanzas are seldom pure; and even the trochaic and iambic rhythms, although purer than other rhythms are interspersed with spondees, anapests, dactyls, or some other foot.

The classics were pleased to term the substitution of the trisyllabic for the dissyllabic foot, an irrational foot.

In the iambic measure we more frequently find a spondee or an anapest substituted for the iambus; in a trochaic foot we more frequently find the dactyl as a substitute; in the dactylic foot, the trochee, the spondee, the amphibrach and the cretic. In these substitutions equality should be maintained.

CHAPTER VI.

OF SCANSION.

SCANNING or scansion of verse, is critically to examine and resolve it into poetic feet. Should there be a syllable wanting to complete the measure of a line, the foot is imperfect, and the line is said to be catalectic.

Where there is a syllable over at the end of the line it is said to be hypermeter, or redundant. When, however, the line is found to be neither deficient nor redundant, it is said to be acatalectic. We have seen that meter is a system employed in the formation of verses. Meter depends not only on the character of the feet employed, but likewise on the number of feet employed in the formation of the line or verse. We have, therefore, several varieties of meter or measure, determined by the number of poetic feet the line contains, as :

A monometer, or a line composed of one foot.

'Tĭs tīme !

A dimeter, a line of two feet.

Thĕ twīlĭght fālls.

A trimeter, a line of three feet.

Thĕ ēvenĭng shādes ăppēar

A tetrameter, a line of four feet.
> Nŏ lĭttlĕ stărs shīne oūt tŏ-nīght.

A pentameter, a line of five feet.
> Hŏw glād tŏ feĕl thăt jōyoŭs nīght ĭs hēre.

A hexameter, a line of six feet.
> Cŏme hāste! Ănd 'mĭd thĕ dārknĕss fleē ăwāy, ăwāy!

A heptameter, a line of seven feet.
> Erĕ soōn ăgāin thĕ līght ŏf stĭll ănōthĕr tēll-tăle dāy.

An octometer, a line of eight feet.
> Ĭ hēar thĕ soūnd ŏf hoŏf ăfār! Tŏ ārms! Tŏ ārms! 'Tĭs wār! 'Tĭs wār!

Lines in this measure, written in trochees or in iambuses are usually too lengthy for the ordinary page, hence, are frequently written in tetrameter.

It is more important in writing poetry to preserve the same number of accents in lines of like measure than the same number of syllables. An exception to this rule is in our ballad measure, where feet of three syllables are sometimes intermingled with the ordinary feet of two syllables. The redundant syllable in that case should be unaccented and devoid of stress, and capable of being pronounced rapidly. The time of the trisyllabic foot and the time of the dissyllabic foot should be equal. Each syllable should be pronounced distinctly, but with greater rapidity. Our best writers prefer the use of words in their natural state, to words used as follows: flowers to flow'rs, silvery to silv'ry, glistening to glist'ning, murmuring to murm'ring, th' for the, i' for in, a' for an. We have here a stanza from Whittier.

And I, ŏbēdĭĕnt tŏ thў will,
Hăve cōme ă sīmplĕ wrēath tŏ lāy,
Sŭpĕrflŭoŭs, ōn ă grāve thăt still
Ĭs sweēt wĭth āll thĕ flōwers ŏf Māy.
"Summer."

From Longfellow:

Thōu hăst taūght mĕ, Sĭlĕnt Rĭvĕr!
Mănŷ ă lĕssŏn, deēp ănd lōng;
Thōu hăst beēn ă gēnerŏus gĭvĕr;
Ĭ căn gīve theĕ bŭt ă sōng.
"To the River Charles."

From Willis :

Brĭght flăg ăt yōndĕr tāperĭng māst!
Flĭng ōut yŏur fĭĕld ŏf āzurĕ blūe;
Lĕt stār ănd strīpe bĕ wĕstwărd cāst,
Ănd poĭnt ăs freēdŏm's eaglĕ flēw!
Străin hōme! Ŏh, lithe ănd quīverĭng spārs!
Poĭnt hōme, mў coūntrў's flăg ŏf stārs!
"Lines on Leaving Europe."

From Tennyson :

Bĕgīns thĕ clāsh ănd clăng thăt tĕlls
Thĕ jōy tŏ ēverў wăndering breēze;
Thĕ blīnd wăll rŏcks, ănd ōn thĕ treēs
Thĕ dēad lĕaf trĕmblĕs tō thĕ bĕlls.
"In Memoriam."

In the first stanza, the words ŏbēdĭĕnt, sŭpērflŭoŭs and flowers are used by the writer making lines of nine syllables, instead of syncopating the words; in the second stanza, mănŷ a, and gēnerŏŭs, not gen'rous ; in the third, tāperĭng and quīverĭng are used and not syncopated ; in the fourth stanza, ēverў and wănderĭng are used in their full form instead of being contracted to the forms ev'ry and wand'ring as is often the case in some poems. Elision and syncope, as a rule is no longer in use where it can be avoided, nevertheless, it is true, in some cases it is a help to the writer, and lends a charm to the rhythm.

Time is essentially the basis of all true rhythm, and true rhythm is in fact frequently destroyed to the cultivated ear by the syncopation of words that properly belong in the line, and that only need to be spoken in quicker time, which the ear is always ready to recognize. Not only is the ear offended, but the eye, that other organ that enables us to perceive the beauty of written verse.

POETIC PAUSES.

In addition to the regular pauses that occur in the verse or line of poetry, there are other pauses, known as the cesural, and the final pause. The Cesural pause is a natural suspension of the voice, which occurs in the verse, and is readily perceived when the verse is properly read. It is found in long lines, and usually occurs about the middle of the line. The art of the poet is shown in making these pauses occur where the thought requires them. Iambic pentameters usually have the cesural pause come after the fourth or fifth syllables. In Alexandrine, or iambic hexameter, the cesural pause usually occurs after the third foot. Two or more cesurals may sometimes occur in the same line. The cesura is indicated by two parallel lines ; thus, ||.

The final pause occurs at the end of every poetic line, and should always be observed in reading, even when not required by the grammatical construction.

We have selected the following lines from Pope, to illustrate the position of the cesura. Pope's ear was exceedingly accurate in matters of euphony, and the cesural pause usually occurs after the fourth or fifth syllable in his verse or line. Observe their position in the following lines : -

But most by numbers || judge a poet's song,
And smooth or rough, || with them, is right or wrong ;
These equal syllables || alone require,
Tho' oft the ear || the open vowels tire ;
While expletives || their feeble aid do join ;
And ten long words || oft creep in one dull line :
While they ring round || the same unvaried chimes,
With sure returns || of still recurring rhymes ;
Where 'er you find || 'the cooling western breeze,'
In the next line || it ' whispers through the trees : '
If crystal streams || 'with pleasing murmurs creep,'
The reader's threat'ned ||—not in vain—with ' sleep.'
Then at the last || and only couplet, fraught
With some unmeaning thing || they call a thought,
A needless Alexandrine || ends the song,
That, like a wounded snake, || drags its slow length along.
Leave such to tune || their own dull rhymes, to know
What's roundly smooth, || or languishingly slow;
And praise the easy vigor || of a line
Where Denham's strength || and Waller's sweetness join.
True ease in writing || comes from art, not chance,
As those move easiest || who have learned to dance.
'T is not enough || no harshness gives offense,
The sound must seem an echo || to the sense.
"Essay on Criticism."

Let us take next an iambic hexameter by William Wordsworth.

The dew was falling fast, || the stars began to blink ;
I heard a voice; it said, || " Drink, pretty creature, drink ! "
And, looking o'er the hedge, || before me I espied
A snow-white mountain lamb, || with a maiden at its side.

It will be observed the pause occurs after the third foot. It is difficult to lay down absolute rules for the use of the cesura in English poetry. In a decasyllable line, it may occur after any foot, and it is by shifting its place, that verse is rendered less monotonous. In shorter poems, especially of the amatory or lyric nature, it generally falls midway in the line or verse. The cesura should not divide a word; neither should it separate an adjective and its noun; nor an adverb and verb, when in either case, the latter immediately follows the former. The cesura is also counted a foot in poetry.

A single emphatic syllable is used frequently in variegated forms of verse, and when thus taken by itself it is termed a cesura. To illustrate, let us take a stanza in iambic rhythm —iambic trimeter:

> Breāk, breāk, breāk.
> Ŏn thy̆ cōld gră̆y stōnes, Ŏ sēa!
> Ănd Ĭ woūld thăt my̆ tōngue coŭld ūttĕr
> Thĕ thōughts thăt ă̆rīse ĭn mē.
>   *Tennyson*—" Break, Break, Break."

We select the following stanza. It is trochaic rhythm, one of the best of a fastidious poet's productions. Nothing in its line has ever excelled it. We give the second stanza:

> Hĕar thĕ mēllŏw wĕddĭng bĕlls,
>   Gōldĕn bĕlls!
> Whăt ă̆ wōrld ŏf hă̆ppĭnĕss theĭr hārmŏny̆ fŏretĕlls!
> Throūgh thĕ bālmy̆ āir ŏf nĭght,
> Hŏw thĕy rĭng ŏut theĭr dĕlīght!
> Frŏm thĕ mōltĕn gōldĕn nōtes,
>   Ănd ăll ĭn tūne,
> Whăt ă̆ lĭquĭd dĭtty̆ flŏats

Tŏ thĕ tūrtlĕ-dōve thăt lĭstĕns, whīle shĕ glōats
    Ŏn thĕ moōn!
Ōh, frŏm ōut thĕ sōundĭng cēlls,
Whāt ă gūsh ŏf eūphŏnў vŏlūmĭnōuslў wĕlls!
    Hōw ĭt swēlls!
    Hōw ĭt dwēlls
    Ŏn thĕ Fūtūre! hŏw ĭt tēlls
    Ŏf thĕ rāptūre thāt ĭmpēls
Tŏ thĕ swīngĭng ănd thĕ rīngĭng
    Ŏf thĕ bēlls, bēlls, bēlls.
Ŏf thĕ bēlls, bēlls, bēlls, bēlls,
    Bēlls, bēlls, bēlls, —
Tŏ thĕ rhӯmĭng ănd thĕ chīmĭng ŏf thĕ bĕlls.
                            Poe—"The Bells."

CHAPTER VII.
OF RHYME.

Sŏme rhȳme ă neīghbŏr's nāme tŏ lăsh;
Sŏme rhȳme [văin thōught!] fŏr neĕdfŭ' căsh;
Sŏme rhȳme tŏ cōurt thĕ coūntrў clăsh,
    Ănd māke ă pūn;
Fŏr mē, ăn āim Ĭ nĕvĕr făsh—
    Ĭ rhȳme fŏr fūn.
                    Burns—"To James Smith."

RHYME in poetry is of ancient origin. It was brought in by the Gothic conquerors during the middle ages. Some Latin poetry rhymed as early as 500 A. D. It can hardly be considered the invention of any race or age. It is universal, like music, painting, and the sister arts. Since its first use it has steadily gained favor, until it is now the popular form of poetic expression. Alliteration was the common form of the Anglo-Saxon poetry; it had no other ornament. Although no longer a regular constituent of English verse, alliteration is of frequent occurrence in modern poetry. In its most usual sense, rhyme is a correspondence of sound in the last syllables of two or more lines, succeeding each other immediately, or at no great distance. It is used to mark the ends of lines, or verses, of poetry. Rhyme depends upon the sound, and not upon the spelling. To make a perfect rhyme it is necessary that the syllables be both accented. It is also necessary that the vowel sounds be the same ; that the sounds following the vowel sounds be the same ; that the sounds preceding the vowel sounds be different. Good and stood, talk and walk, code and ode, dodge and lodge, plod and odd, toil and boil, all are perfect rhymes. We give a stanza from the famous national hymn of France ·

> Yĕ sōns ŏf Frānce, ăwāke tŏ glōrȳ !
> Hărk ! Hărk ! Whăt mȳrĭads bĭd yoŭ rīse !
> Yoŭr chĭldrĕn, wīves, ănd grāndsīres hōarȳ,
> Bĕhōld thĕir tēars ănd hēar thĕir crīes.
>   *Rouget de Lisle*—" The Marseilles Hymn."

Here the first and third lines have a redundant syllable. Here the first and third lines have the common sound of "ory," in the first line being preceded by the consonants "gl," in the third by the consonant "h." The second and fourth lines have the common sound "ise," the second line being preceded by the consonant "r," and the fourth by the consonants "cr." Rhyme is not always the correspondence of sounds in the terminating or final syllables of two lines or verses. The lines may end with words that are spelled differently, and that may be entirely different in their meaning, yet, they may have an exact correspondence of sound ; as peak, pique, and peek ; also raze, raise, and rays. These words would not form rhymes, there being a sameness of the initial consonants. Should the initial consonants be changed, we shall have words that make perfect rhymes, as the following :

> Fōr thĕ strūctŭre thăt wĕ rāise,
> Tīme ĭs wĭth mătērĭăls fĭlled ;
> Ōur tŏ-dāys ănd yēstĕrdāys
> Āre thĕ blōcks wĭth whĭch wĕ build.
>   *Longfellow* —" The Builders."

The common sound "aise," "ays" here have the initial consonants "r" and "d" different, and hence form a perfect rhyme. It is an absolute rule that no syllable should rhyme with itself. Rhyme always speaks to the ear and not to the eye. Perfect rhymes are pleasing to the ear and not a mere ornament. All people who have adopted an accented rhythm have adopted rhyme. Rhyme marks and helps us find the accent, and strengthens and supports rhythm.

We have in poetry various kinds of rhymes. They may be denominated, alliteration, assonantal, consonantal, masculine, feminine, triple, middle, sectional, inverse and task or odd rhymes.

ALLITERATION.

As we have already seen, alliteration was an old form of Anglo-Saxon verse, which was simply rhyme at the beginning of the word instead of at its ending. It was the distinctive characteristic of all the Gothic meters. Poems continued to be written in English, the verse of which was merely alliterative, down to the time of the sixteenth century. The taste, however, that introduced rhyme rejected alliteration to a very great extent, and its use began to decline. Chaucer was the first English poet particularly to discard it for rhyme, and hence, might be termed the father of English rhyme. While the recurrence of the same sound gave pleasure and satisfaction to the sense, slight, it is true, still one that was perceptible enough ; yet, there can be but little doubt, that the affectation displayed in crowding every line with alliteration, by which inappropriate words were often introduced, not unfrequently obscuring the sense and offending the taste, led to its disuse. Alliteration is, however, still much used in modern verse. There is a tendency in our nature to form recurring sounds; hence alliteration is frequently produced without any set design; and it is frequently so sparingly and unobtrusively introduced, that many readers of poetry are gratified by the graceful use of alliteration, though not aware to what source their gratification is owing.

We give the following from a poem of Thomas W. Parsons:

>September strews the woodland o'er
>   With many a brilliant color;
>The world is brighter than before,
>   Why should our hearts be duller?
>Sorrow and the scarlet leaf,
>   Sad thoughts and sunny weather.
>Ah me! This glory and this grief
>   Agree not well together.
>
> "A Song for September."

This is an iambic tetrameter, the second, fourth, sixth and eighth lines redundant.

We give the following, an iambic tetrameter:

>Warm broke the breeze against the brow,
>   Dry sang the tackle, sang the sail:
>The Lady's-head upon the prow
>   Caught the shrill salt, and sheered the gale.
>The broad seas swelled to meet the keel,
>   And swept behind: so quick the run,
>We felt the good ship shake and reel,
>   We seemed to sail into the Sun!
>
> *Tennyson*—"The Voyage."

We select this stanza from the Quaker poet. The first and fourth lines, iambic tetrameter, the third and fourth, iambic dimeter, with a redundant syllable.

> Shĕ săt bĕnēath thĕ brōad-ărmed ēlms
> Thăt skīrt thĕ mōwĭng-mēadŏw,
> Ănd wātched thĕ gēntlĕ wĕst-wĭnd wēave
> Thĕ grāss wĭth shine ănd shădŏw.
> > *Whittier*—"Among the Hills."

> Ŏlāf, thĕ Kīng, ŏne sūmmĕr mōrn,
> Blĕw ā blăst ōn hĭs būglĕ-hōrn.
> > *Longfellow*—"The Saga of King Olaf."

> Sōngfŭl, sōulfŭl, sōrrŏwfŭl Īrelănd!
> > *Lanier*—"Ireland."

ASSONANTAL.

Assonantal rhyme is the correspondence of the vowels at the end of two lines. Such rhymes are not very frequent in our modern English verse. Rhyme by what is termed similar sound, or allowable rhymes are considered intolerable at the present time. In assonance, while the vowels of the last accented syllable and in all subsequent syllables are the same, the consonants must all be different. Formerly it was allowable to rhyme heels with fields, town with round, ask with blast, but such usage is no longer indulged in by finished writers.

There may be found an occasional perfect assonantal rhyme, as:

> Ĭ in thĕse flōwerȳ mĕads woŭld bē,
> Thĕse crȳstăl strēams shoŭld sōlăce mē;
> Tŏ whōse hărmōnioŭs būbblĭng nōise
> Ĭ, wĭth mȳ ānglĕ, woŭld rĕjoīce,
> Sĭt hēre, ănd seē thĕ tūrtlĕ-dŏve
> Cŏurt hĭs chăste māte tŏ ăcts ŏf lŏve.
> > *Izaak Walton*—"The Angler's Wish."

The first two lines of this poem of true nature furnish us a fine specimen of the perfect assonantal rhyme in the words "be" and "me." The final vowel "e" being the same, and the consonants "b" and "m" being different.

CONSONANTAL.

The last two lines of the above poem furnish us with a specimen of another kind of rhyme, by far the most common in English poetry. It is the consonantal rhyme, and is the correspondence of the vowel and the final consonant or consonants in the rhyming syllables. It will be seen that the consonants "d" and "l" in the rhyming words "dove" and "love" are different, while there is a perfect correspondence in the vowels and consonants "ove." The following stanza furnishes us with a fine example of the consonantal :

> Flŏw gēntlў, sweĕt Āftŏn, ămōng thў greĕn brāes,
> Flŏw gēntlў, sweĕt rīvĕr, thĕ thēme ŏf mў lāys;
> Mў Mārў's ăsleēp bў thў mūrmŭrĭng strēam,
> Flŏw gēntlў, sweĕt Āftŏn, dĭstūrb nŏt hĕr drēam.
> *Burns*—"Afton Water."

MASCULINE AND FEMININE.

Masculine rhymes are single rhymes, like "braes" and "lays;" "stream" and "dream" in the last stanza. They constitute one accented syllable. They are to be distinguished from those rhymes that have an accented syllable followed by an unaccented one, the last two syllables of the line rhyming with the last two of its mate. Longfellow's "Hiawatha" is a good specimen of what is described :

> Āt thĕ feēt ŏf Lāughĭng Wātĕr
> Hĭăwāthă lāid hĭs būrdĕn,
> Thrēw thĕ rĕd deĕr frōm hĭs shōuldĕrs;

And thĕ māidĕn loōked ŭp āt hĭm,
Loōked ŭp frōm hĕr māt ŏf rūshĕs,
Saīd wĭth gēntlĕ loōk ănd āccĕnt,
"Yōu ăre wĕlcŏme Hĭăwāthă!"

The above selection from Longfellow is trochaic rhythm, tetrameter measure, with the feminine or double ending. The principal rhyming syllables are usually long. Double rhyme adds one short syllable. Triple rhyme, of which we shall next speak, two. Such syllables in iambic and anapestic verses are redundant; in lines of any other kind they are usually included in the measure.

TRIPLE.

Triple rhymes have three corresponding syllables; as,

Căre, măd tŏ seē ă măn săe happȳ,
E'ĕn drōwned hĭmsēlf ămăng thĕ nāppȳ!
Ăs beēs fleē hāme wĭ' lādes ŏ' treāsŭre,
Thĕ mĭnutĕs wĭnged thĕir wăy wĭ' pleāsŭre;
Kĭngs măy bĕ blēst, bŭt Tām wăs glō-rĭ-oŭs,
O'ĕr ā' thĕ cāres ŏ' life vĭc-tō-rĭ-oŭs.
Burns—"Tam O'Shanter."

This is an iambic tetrameter. All the lines are redundant, the fifth and sixth furnishing a fine example of triple rhyme.

MIDDLE.

Middle rhymes are a correspondence of sounds at the middle and the close of a verse. It occurs at the natural pause or suspension of the voice in the line, and serves to mark the two sections of the verse.

We give an example, an iambic tetrameter, the second and third lines redundant:

OF RHYME.

> Thĕ splēndŏr fălls ŏn căstlĕ wălls
> Ănd snōwў sūmmĭts ōld ĭn stōrў:
> Thĕ lōng līght shākes ăcrōss thĕ lākes,
> Ănd thĕ wīld cătărăct lēaps ĭn glōrў.
> *Tennyson*—"The Princess."

It was said that Burns was the poet of the many, while Coleridge was the poet of the few. Coleridge was one of the most tasteful of writers and used the middle rhyme with pleasing effect in one of his finest poems—a poem written to help pay the expenses of a trip he and Wordsworth were taking together. He realized twenty-five dollars from its sale. Wordsworth suggested largely for it, and wrote some of its stanzas. We select three stanzas:

> Ănd throūgh thĕ drĭfts thĕ snōwў clĭfts
> Dĭd sĕnd ă dĭsmăl sheĕn :
> Nŏr shāpes ŏf mĕn nŏr bēasts wĕ kĕn—
> Thĕ īce wăs āll bĕtweĕn.

> Thĕ īce wăs hēre, thĕ īce wăs thēre,
> Thĕ īce wăs āll ărōund :
> Ĭt crăcked ănd grōwled, ănd rōared ănd hōwled,
> Lĭke nōisĕs ĭn ă swōund !

> Ăt lēngth dĭd crōss ăn Ālbătrŏss:
> Throūgh thĕ fōg ĭt cāme ;
> Ăs ĭf ĭt hăd beĕn ă Chrĭstĭan sōul,
> Wĕ hāiled ĭt ĭn Gŏd's nāme.
> *Coleridge*—"The Rhyme of the Ancient Mariner."

Middle Rhyme in the hands of the skillful poet adds a charm and lends music to the rhythm. In the hands of those not skilled it is likely to be overdrawn.

SECTIONAL.

Sectional rhyme is akin to middle rhyme. It occurs in the line and exists between syllables of the same section; as,

Lĭghtlў ănd brĭghtlў brĕaks ăwāy
Thĕ mōrnĭng frŏm hĕr māntlĕ grāy.
Byron—" Siege of Corinth."

Thĕy rūshed ănd pūshed, ănd blūide ŏutgūshed.
Burns—" Sheriff Muir."

But thĕn tŏ seē hŏw yē're nĕglĕckĭt,
Hŏw hūffed ăn' cūffed, ăn' dĭsrĕpĕckĭt!
Burns—" Twa Dogs."

Sŏ might, nŏt rīght, dĭd thrūst mĕ tŏ thĕ crōwn.
Shakespeare—" Measure for Measure."

Ăll thĭs dĕrĭsiŏn
Shăll seēm ă drēam ănd frūitlĕss vĭsiŏn.
Shakespeare—" Midsummer Night's Dream."

Thĕn yĕ māy tĕll, hŏw pēll ănd mĕll,
Bў rĕd clăymōres, ănd mūskĕts' knĕll,
Wĭ' dўĭng yĕll, thĕ tōrĭes fĕll.
Burns—" Sheriff Muir."

Whŏ cărĕth nŏr spărĕth tĭll spĕnt hĕ hăth āll,
Ŏf hōbbĭng, nŏt rōbbĭng, bĕ fēarfŭl hĕ shăll.
Thomas Tusser.

Nŏt fēarĭng nŏr cārĭng fŏr hĕll nŏr fŏr hēavĕn.
Thomas Tusser.

Rŏcks, cāves, lăkes, fĕns, bŏgs, dēns ănd shādes ŏf dēath.
Milton—" Paradise Lost."

OF RHYME. 49

Sŏ mănў ăs lŏve mĕ, ănd ūse mĕ ăright,
Wĭth trēasūre ănd plēasūre Ĭ richlў rĕquite.
Thomas Tusser.

INVERSE.

Inverse rhyme occurs between the last accented syllable before the cesura and the first accented syllable after the cesural pause. We have fine examples in the following :

Ăs Tămmĭe glŏw'rĕd, ămāzed ănd cūrĭoŭs,
Thĕ mirth ănd fūn grĕw fāst ănd fūrĭoŭs ;
Thĕ pipĕr *loud* ănd *loudĕr* blĕw ;
Thĕ dăncĕrs *quick* ănd *quickĕr* flĕw.
Burns—"Tam O'Shanter."

Sŏme, lūckў, find ă flōwĕrў spōt,
Fŏr which thĕy nĕvĕr toiled ŏr swāt ;
Thĕy drink thĕ sweĕt ănd ēat thĕ făt.
Burns—"To James Smith."

Whĕre with ĭntēntiŏn Ĭ hăve ērred,
Nŏ ŏthĕr plēa Ĭ hăve,
Bŭt, Thŏu ărt goŏd ; ănd goŏdnĕss still
Dĕlightĕth tō fŏrgive.
Burns—"A Prayer."

Ŏ Hĕndĕrsŏn, thĕ mān—thĕ brŏthĕr !
Ănd ārt thŏu gōne, ănd gōne fŏrēvĕr ?
Burns—"Elegy on M. Henderson."

Lĕt Prūdĕnce blĕss Ĕnjōymĕnt's cūp,
Thĕn rāptūred sip, ănd sip ĭt ūp.
Burns—Written in Friar's Carse Hermitage.

Yoŭr beaūtȳ's ă flōwer, ĭn thĕ mōrnĭng thăt blōws,
And wĭthĕrs thĕ fāstĕr thĕ fāstĕr ĭt grōws.
                    Burns—"Hey for a Lass."

Ŏh hăppȳ lŏve! whĕre lŏve lĭke thīs ĭs fŏund!
                    Burns—"Cotter's Saturday Night."

Cŏme ĕase ŏr cŏme trăvaĭl, cŏme plĕasŭre ŏr pāin,
Mȳ wărst wŏrd ĭs: "Wĕlcŏme ănd wĕlcŏme ăgāin!"
                    Burns—"Contented Wi' Little."

TASK, OR ODD.

Under this head are some peculiar combinations of poetry which we shall give, known as task poetry, word-matching and curious lines of word accents. Task poetry is illustrated by a stanza of George Herbert's. The task is dropping the first letter of the last two words of the second and third lines of the triplet:

    Ĭnclōse mĕ stĭll, fŏr fĕar Ĭ stărt,
    Bĕ tō mĕ rāthĕr shărp ănd tārt,
    Thăn lĕt mĕ wănt thȳ hănd ănd ārt.

    Sŭch shărpnĕss shōws thĕ sweētĕst frĭend,
    Sŭch cūttĭngs rāthĕr hĕal thăn rĕnd,
    And sŭch bĕgĭnnĭngs tŏuch thĕir ĕnd.

The following curious distich is formed of three lines of the fragments of words, so that the middle ones read with either of the other two:

```
        curs   f—    w—       d—    dis— and  p—
    A    —ed  iend—rought    —eath  —ease    —ain.
        bless— fr—    b—      br—   and      ag—
```

A cūrsĕd fiĕnd wrŏught dēath, dĭsēase ănd pāin ;
A blēssĕd friĕnd brŏught brēath ănd ēase ăgāin.

Dr. Holmes has given us an example in an "Ode for a Social Meeting ; With Slight Alterations by a Teetotaler."

Cŏme ! fĭll ă frĕsh būmpĕr,— fŏr whȳ shoŭld wĕ gō
    lōgwoŏd
Whĭle thĕ ~~nĕctăr~~ stĭll rēddĕns ŏur cūps ăs thĕy flōw ?
       dĕcōctiŏn
Pŏur ōut thĕ ~~rĭch jūicĕs,~~ stĭll brĭght wĭth thĕ sūn,
        dȳe-stŭff
Tĭll ō'er thĕ brĭmmed crȳstăl thĕ ~~rūbĭĕs~~ shăll rūn
  hălf-rĭpĕned āpplĕs
Thĕ ~~pŭrplĕ glŏbed clŭstĕrs~~ thĕir life-dĕws hăve blĕd ;
     tāste   sūgăr ŏf lēad
Hŏw sweēt ĭs thĕ ~~brēath~~ ŏf thĕ ~~frăgrănce thĕy shĕd !~~
    rănk pōisŏns   wīnes !!!
Fŏr sūmmĕr's ~~lăst rōsĕs~~ līe hĭd ĭn thĕ ~~wīnes~~
          stāblĕ-bŏys smōkĭng lŏng-nīnes
Thăt wĕre gārnĕred bȳ ~~māidĕns whŏ lāughed thrŏŭgh thĕ vīnes~~
   scōwl   hōwl   scŏff   sneēr
Thĕn ă ~~smīle,~~ ănd ă ~~glăss,~~ ănd ă ~~tōast,~~ ănd ă ~~cheēr,~~
  strȳchnīne ănd whĭskĕy, ănd rătsbăne ănd beēr
Fŏr āll ~~thĕ goŏd wīne, ănd wĕ've sŏme ŏf ĭt hĕre !~~
Ĭn cēllăr, ĭn pāntrȳ, ĭn ăttĭc, ĭn hāll,
Dŏwn, dōwn wĭth thĕ tȳrănt thăt māstĕrs ŭs āll !
~~Lŏng live thĕ găy sĕrvănt thăt lāughs fŏr ŭs āll !~~

Word matching is still another kind of odd rhyme.

Thĕn ūp wĭth yoŭr cūp tĭll yoŭ stăggĕr ĭn speēch,
And mātch mĕ thĭs cātch, thŏugh yoŭ swăggĕr ănd screēch.
                                  Scott.

Another odd rhyme in iambic rhythm written anonymously, is entitled:

SONG OF THE DECANTER.

There was an old decanter,
and its mouth was gaping wide;
the rosy wine had ebbed
away and left its
crystal side;
and the
wind
went
humming,
humming; up
and down
the sides
it flew, and
through the
reed-like, hollow
neck the
wildest notes
it blew. I placed
it in the window, where
the blast was blowing free, and
fancied that its pale mouth sang the
queerest strains to me. "They tell me
—puny conquerors!—the Plague has slain
his ten, and War his hundred-thousands of the
very best of men; but I "—'twas thus the bottle
spoke—" but I have conquered more than all your
famous conquerors, so feared and famed of yore.
Then come, ye youths and maidens, come drink
from out my cup, the beverage that dulls the
brain and burns the spirit up; that puts to
shame the conquerors that slay their scores
below; for this has deluged millions with
the lava tide of woe. Though, in the
path of battle, darkest waves of blood
may roll; yet while I killed the
body, I have damned the very
soul. The cholera, the sword,
such ruin never wrought, as
I, in mirth or malice, on the inno-
cent have brought. And still I breathe
upon them, and they shrink before my
breath; and year by year my thousands
tread the fearful road to death.

OF RHYME. 53

In the couplet below every word of the line is answered by another of the same measure and rhyme :

"Shĕ drōve hĕr flōck ŏ'er mōuntăins,
Bў grōve, ŏr rōck, ŏr fōuntăins."

Another example is :

" Nōw, Ŏ nōw, Ĭ neĕds mŭst pārt,
Pārtĭng thōugh Ĭ ābsĕnt mōurn ;
Ābsĕnce cān nŏ jōy ĭmpārt,
Jōy ŏnce flēd căn nē'er rĕtŭrn."

The Alphabetic is still another odd rhyme :

"Ŏn gōĭng fōrth lăst nĭght ă friĕnd tŏ seē,
Ĭ mēt ă mān bў trāde ă s-n-ō-b.
Reēlĭng ălōng hĕ hēld hĭs tĭpsў wāy.
'Hō ! Hō !' quŏth Ĭ, 'hĕ's d-r-ū-n-k.'
Thĕn thūs tŏ hĭm : ' Wĕre ĭt nŏt bĕttĕr făr
Yŏu wēre ă lĭttlĕ s-ō-b-e-r ?
'Twĕre hăppiĕr fŏr yŏur fămĭlў, Ĭ guĕss,
Thăn plāyĭng ŏff sŭch rūm r-ĭ-g-s.
Bĕsīdes, ăll drŭnkărds, whēn pŏlīcemĕn seē 'ĕm,
Āre tākĕn ūp ăt ōnce bў t-h-e-m.' "

A truth is frequently impressed by means of another form of odd rhyme—the Paradox. A first-class example is here given :

Thŏugh wĕ bōast ŏf mōdĕrn prōgrĕss ās ălŏft wĕ prōudlў sōar,
Ăbōve ŭntūtŏred cănnĭbāls whŏse hăbĭts wĕ dĕplōre,
Yĕt in ŏur dāilў pāpĕrs ānў dāy yŏu chănce tŏ loōk
Yŏu māy fĭnd this ădvĕrtĭsemēnt : " Wāntĕd—Ă gĭrl tŏ coōk."
Ida Goldsmith Morris—" A Paradox." In "Magazine of Poetry."

Odd rhymes are frequently employed to aid memory. Few persons understand the use of "Shall" and "Will." The following stanza memorized will be of use to every one :

> "In the first person simply Shall foretells;
> In Will a threat or else a promise dwells;
> Shall in the second or the third doth threat
> Will simply then foretells the future feat."

This quatrain is also useful to enable one to remember the formation of Latin verbs :

> "From O are formed am and em ;
> From I, ram, rim, ro, se, and sem.
> U, us, and rus are formed from um ;
> All other parts from Re do come."

Another quaint stanza enables us to remember the days of the month :

> "Thirty days hath September,
> April, June and November ;
> All the rest have thirty-one,
> Save February alone,
> Which has but twenty-eight in fine
> Till leap year gives it twenty-nine."

CENTO VERSES.

Still another curious form of poetry is denominated "Cento Verses or Patch Work."

MY LOVE.

I only knew she came and went	*Powell.*
Like troutlets in a pool ;	*Hood.*
She was a phantom of delight,	*Wordsworth.*
And I was like a fool.	*Eastman.*

OF RHYME.

"One kiss, dear maid," I said and sighed,   *Coleridge.*
Out of those lips unshorn;   *Longfellow.*
She shook her ringlets round her head,   *Stoddard.*
And laughed in merry scorn.   *Tennyson.*

Ring out, wild bells, to the wild sky,   *Tennyson.*
You heard them, O my heart;   *Alice Carey.*
'Tis twelve at night by the castle clock,   *Coleridge.*
"Belovèd, we must part."   *Alice Carey.*

"Come back, come back!" he cried in grief,   *Campbell.*
"My eyes are dim with tears,—   *Bayard Taylor.*
How shall I live through all these days?   *Osgood.*
All through a hundred years?"   *T. S. Perry.*

'Twas in the prime of summer time   *Hood.*
She blessed me with her hand;   *Hoyt.*
We strayed together, deeply blessed,   *Edwards.*
Into the dreaming land.   *Cornwall.*

The laughing bridal roses blow,   *Palmore.*
To dress her dark-brown hair;   *Bayard Taylor.*
My heart is breaking with my woe,   *Tennyson.*
Most beautiful! Most rare!   *Read.*

I clasped it on her sweet, cold hand,   *Browning.*
The precious golden link!   *Smith.*
I calmed her fears, and she was calm,   *Coleridge.*
"Drink, pretty creature, drink."   *Wordsworth.*

And so I won my Genevieve,   *Coleridge.*
And walked in Paradise: *Hervey.*
The fairest thing that ever grew   *Wordsworth.*
Atween me and the skies.   *Osgood.*

    Anonymous.

ACROSTIC.

The acrostic is a form of odd rhyme. Below we give one, written by the Lady Frances Manners, daughter of the Earl of Rutland, and wife of Henry, Lord Bergavenny. She was the author of "Precious Pearls of Perfect Godliness" and "The Monument of Matrons," written in 1582, at the end of which is this acrostic of her own name :

Frŏm sīnfŭlnĕss prĕsērve mĕ, Lōrd,
Rĕnĕw mў spīrĭt ĭn mў hărt ;
And lēt mў tōngue thĕrewīth ăccōrd,
Uttĕring ăll goōdnĕss fōr hĭs pārt.
Nŏ thōught lĕt thĕre ărīse ĭn mē
Cŏntrāirĭe tō thў prēcĕpts tĕn ;
Evĕr lĕt mē mŏst mīndfŭl bē
Stĭll fōr tŏ prāise thў nāme. Āmēn.
As ōf mў sōul, sŏ ōf mў bōdiĕ,
Bĕ thŏu mў guīdĕr, Ō mў Gōd !
Untō theĕ ōnlў dō Ĭ crīe,
Rĕmōve frŏm mē thў fūriŏŭs rōd.
Grăunt thăt mў hĕad măy still dĕvīse
All thīngs thăt plĕasĭng bē tŏ theē.
Untō mĭne ēars, ănd tō mĭne eīes,
Evĕr lĕt thĕre ă wătch sĕt beē.
Nŏne ill thăt thĕy măy hĕar ănd seē ;—
Nŏ wĭckĕd deĕde lĕt mў hănd dō,
Yn thў goŏd păths lĕt mў feĕt gō.

POUNDS, SHILLINGS AND PENCE.

	£	s.	d.
Thĭs wōrld's ă scēne ăs dārk ăs Stȳx,			
Whĕre hōpe ĭs scārce wŏrth		2	6
Ŏur jōys ăre bōrne sŏ fleētĭng hĕnce			
Thăt thĕy ăre dĕar ăt			18
Ănd yĕt tŏ stāy hĕre mōst ăre wīllĭng,			
Ălthōugh thĕy māy nŏt hāve	1		

Willis Gaylord—"Lines Written in an Album."

Ăh mē!
Ăm Ĭ thĕ swāin,
Thăt, lāte frŏm sōrrŏw freē,
Dĭd ăll thĕ cāres ŏn ēarth dĭsdāin?
Ănd still ŭntoūched, ăs āt sŏme sāfĕr gāmes
Plăyed with thĕ būrnĭng cōals ŏf lŏve ănd beaūtў's flāmes?
Wăs't Ĭ coŭld drīve ănd sōund ĕach pāssiŏn's sĕcrĕt dēpth ăt wĭll,
Ănd frŏm thŏse hūge ŏ'erwhĕlmĭngs rīse bў hēlp ŏf rĕasŏn stĭll?
Ănd ām Ĭ nōw, Ŏ hēavĕns! fŏr trўĭng thīs ĭn vāin,
Sŏ sūnk thăt Ĭ shăll nēvĕr rīse ăgāin?
Thĕn lĕt dĕspāir sēt sōrrŏw's strīng
Fŏr strāins thăt dōlefŭl bē,
Ănd Ĭ wĭll sīng
Ăh mē!

Wither—"Rhombic Measures."

CHAPTER VIII.

Nĕvĕr thĕ vērse ăpprōve ŏr hōld ăs goŏd,
Tĭll mãny ă dāy ănd mãny ă blōt hăs wrōught
Thĕ pōlĭshed wŏrk, ănd chāstĕned ēvery̆ thōught
By̆ tēnfŏld lābŏr tō pĕrfēctiŏn brōught.
Horace.

SELECTION OF WORDS.

The beauty of the poem consists in the perfection of its rhythm, and the aptness of the words selected which constitutes the rhyme.

Perfect rhythm and rhyme make a perfect poem where reason and sound sense are at the bottom of the theme. The resources of our language are such that we are entitled to receive from the poet the most rigid work of perfection. Imperfect or what are termed allowable rhymes should no longer be tolerated.

Rhyme is merely the dress with which our thoughts are clothed in rhythmic verse. Rhyme without reason and good sense is insufferable. Formerly many rhymes were allowable that at the present time would not be endured.

Thŭs Pēgăsūs, ă nĕarĕr wāy tŏ tāke,
Măy bōldly̆ dēviăte frōm thĕ cōmmŏn trăck.
Pope.

Here "take" and "track" are made to rhyme by one of the most fastidious of all poets. Pegasus is here permitted to deviate from the common track.

SELECTION OF WORDS. 59

The same author we quote from again :

Sŏme hāunt Părnāssŭs bŭt tŏ plēase thĕir ēar,
Nŏt mēnd thĕir mĭnds ; ăs sōme tŏ chŭrch rĕpāir,
Nŏt fōr thĕ dōctrĭne, bŭt thĕ mūsĭc thēre.

"Ear," "repair," "there," are here used as allowable rhymes.

We quote still another couplet from Pope, in this connection :

Thĕ vŭlgăr thŭs bў ĭmĭtātĭon ĕrr,
Ăs ōft thĕ leārned bў bēĭng sĭngŭlār.

"Err" and "singular" are imperfect rhymes. Speaking of what are termed allowable rhymes, let us quote from Pope once more :

Thĕ wĭngĕd cōursĕr, lĭke ă gēnerŏŭs hōrse,
Shŏws mōst trŭe mĕtăl whĕn yoŭ chĕck hĭs cōurse.

"Horse" and "course" are not perfect rhymes.

Hĭs fāithfŭl wĭfe fŏrēvĕr doōmed tŏ mōurn,
Fŏr him, ălās ! whŏ nēvĕr shāll rĕtūrn.
Falconer.

"Mourn" and "return" are imperfect rhymes.

Sŏ drāw hĭm hōme tŏ thōse thăt mōurn
Ĭn vāin ; ă făvoŭrāblĕ speēd,
Rŭfflĕ thў mĭrrŏwed māst, ănd lēad
Throŭgh prŏsperoŭs floōds hĭs hōlў ūrn.
Tennyson.

"Mourn" and "return"' and "mourn" and "urn" were, however, at one time perfect rhymes, but the style of pronunciation is now obsolete. The fact that pronunciation of words is constantly changing accounts also for many supposed imperfect rhymes.

FOREIGN WORDS AND EXPRESSIONS.

We believe it was Bryant who said he never looked for a foreign word to use in writing a poem but that he found one better in our own language. How true the assertion. Our own language is filled with choice words, and one has little difficulty in finding good English to express ideas and thoughts. The employment of foreign words and expressions, however, is unobjectionable, where the person using them is master of the language used, and where the selection is apt.

In fact, frequently there is a mirth and charm lent to a poem by the use of some word or expression taken from some other language than the mother tongue. A fine example can be found in one of John G. Saxe's poems, entitled :

THE PUZZLED CENSUS TAKER.

"Gŏt ănў bŏys?" thĕ Mārshăl sāid
 Tŏ ă lādў frŏm ōvĕr thĕ Rhīne ;
Ănd thĕ lādў shoōk hĕr flāxĕn hĕad,
 Ănd civĭllў ānswĕred, "*Nein!*"*

"Gŏt ănў gīrls?" thĕ Mārshăl sāid
 Tŏ thĕ lādў frŏm ōvĕr thĕ Rhīne ;
Ănd ăgāin thĕ lādў shoōk hĕr hĕad,
 Ănd civĭllў ānswĕred, "*Nein!*"

---

* ' Nein,'' German for ''no.''

SELECTION OF WORDS.

"But sŏme ăre dēad?" thĕ Mārshăl sāid
To thĕ lādў frŏm ōvĕr thĕ Rhīne;
And ăgāin thĕ lādў shoōk hĕr hēad,
And cīvĭllў ānswĕred, "*Nein!*"

"Hūsbănd, ŏf cōurse?" thĕ Mārshăl sāid
To thĕ lādў frŏm ōvĕr thĕ Rhīne;
And ăgāin shĕ shoōk hĕr flāxĕn hēad,
And cīvĭllў ānswĕred, "*Nein!*"

"Thĕ dēvĭl yoŭ hāve!" thĕ Mārshăl sāid
To thĕ lādў frŏm ōvĕr thĕ Rhīne;
And ăgāin shĕ shoōk hĕr flāxĕn hēad,
And cīvĭllў ānswĕred, "*Nein!*"

"Nŏw whāt dŏ yoŭ mēan bў shākĭng yoŭr hēad
And ālwăys ānswĕrĭng, '*Nein*'?"
'Ich kānn nĭcht Ēnglĭsch!" cīvĭllў sāid
Thĕ lādў frŏm ōvĕr thĕ Rhīne.

Charles Durbin is the author of an excellent poem, "Nongtongpaw," the first two stanzas of which we give below:

Jŏhn Būll fŏr pāstĭme toōk ă prānce,
Sŏme tīme ăgō tŏ peēp ăt Frānce;
To tālk ŏf scĭĕncĕs ănd ārts,
And knōwlĕdge gāined ĭn fōreĭgn pārts.
Mŏnsieūr, ŏbsēquioŭs, hēard hĭm spĕak,
And ānswĕred Jŏhn ĭn hēathĕn Greēk;
To āll hĕ āsked, 'bŏut āll hĕ sāw,
'T wăs "Mŏnsieŭr, jĕ voŭs n'ēntĕnds pās."

Jŏhn tŏ thĕ Pālăis Rōyăl cōme,
Its splēndŏr ālmŏst strŭck hĭm dūmb.
"I sāy, whŏse hŏuse ĭs thăt thĕre hēre?"
"Hŏuse! Jĕ voŭs n'ēntĕnds pās, Mŏnsieūr."*

---
* "I do not understand you, Mister."

"Whăt! Nŏngtŏngpāw ăgāin!" crīes Jōhn;
"Thĭs fēllŏw is sŏme mightў Dōn,
Nŏ doubt hĕ's plēntў fōr thĕ māw,
Ĭ'll breākfăst wĭth thĭs Nŏngtŏngpāw."

Mr. Field has written an excellent poem about the German Zug:

Thĕ Gĕrmăns sāy thăt "schnēll" mĕans făst, ănd "schnēllĕst" făstĕst yēt,—
Ĭn āll mў life nŏ grĭmmĕr bĭt ŏf hūmŏr hāve Ĭ mĕt!
Whў, thirteĕn'miles ăn hōur's thĕ greātĕst speēd thĕy ĕvĕr gō,
While ōn thĕ ēngĭne pīstŏn rŏds dŏ mŏss ănd lichĕns grōw,
Ănd yēt thĕ āverăge Teūtŏn will prĕsūmptŭouslў măintāin
Thăt ōne *căn't* knōw whăt swĭftnĕss is tĭll hĕ's tried thĕ sçhnēllĕst trāin!

Eugene Field— "The Schnellest Zug."

The use of a foreign word, however, merely for the sake of rhyme, is entirely out of place and not to be indulged.

The beauty of rhyme is perfectness; therefore, use such rhymes only as are perfect to the ear when correctly pronounced,—to the eye when seen.

CHAPTER IX.

THE CONSTRUCTION OF THE STANZA.

THE manner or mode of constructing the stanza should be closely observed by the writer of poetry. Form is essential to beauty, and form in all its details is looked after by the master. (1) Verse which rhymes in alternate lines is always indented. (2) Verse in couplets is never indented, but the lines are all even. (3) Where the stanza is constructed with four lines rhyming alternately and a couplet, the alternate lines are indented and the couplet is usually even or flush with the first and third lines of the stanza. (4) Where the stanza is constructed with first a couplet, then a half-line or bob-wheel, followed by another couplet, and that couplet followed by another half line rhyming with the first half line, the couplets are both even lines while the half lines are indented. No matter whether the stanza is constructed of four, six, eight, or any number of lines these rules hold good. Symmetry always renders the stanza more perfect, and a little observation will soon enable one to imitate a perfect stanza. (5) When a stanza consists of a triplet and a line or half line not rhyming, the latter is always indented. (6) Where the stanza is constructed of a line that is followed by a shorter, or half line, followed by a line rhyming with the first line, followed by the same line used similarly as a second and fourth line, followed by a triplet and an eighth line, similar to the second and fourth line, these similar lines should be indented. More might be easily added, but enough has been said to suggest the principle or art upon which verse is constructed, and usually printed. As a further illustration of what is intended, we give below an outline or skeleton of the stanzas above mentioned, written in the sign of the various measures:

1.

⏑ — ⏑ — ⏑ — ⏑ —   Gŏd grănt thăt whĕn ŏur hēads ăre grāy,
⏑ — ⏑ — ⏑ —   Whĕn twĭlĭght blŭrs thĕ pāge,
⏑ — ⏑ — ⏑ — ⏑ —   Thĕ mūsĭc ŏf ŏur dāwnĭng dāy
⏑ — ⏑ — ⏑ —   Măy chārm ŏur lōnelў āge.
        Burton W. Lockhart—"The Retrospect."

2.

— ⏑ — ⏑ — ⏑ —   Thōugh Ĭ mōve wĭth lēadĕn feēt,
— ⏑ — ⏑ — ⏑ —   Lĭght ĭtsĕlf ĭs nŏt sŏ fleēt ;
— ⏑ — ⏑ — ⏑ —   Ānd bĕfŏre yoŭ knōw mĕ gōne
⏑ — ⏑ — ⏑ — ⏑ —   Ĕtērnĭtў ănd Ĭ ăre ōne.
        William Dean Howells—"Time."

3.

⏑ — — ⏑ — ⏑ — ⏑ —   Trūe lōve nŏt heēdĕth bōlt nŏr bār,
⏑ — ⏑ — ⏑ —   Bŭt sād 't ĭs ēvĕr sō ;
⏑ — ⏑ — ⏑ — ⏑ —   Trūe lōve ănd fāte dŏ cōnstănt wār,
⏑ — ⏑ — ⏑ —   Ānd nĕ'er tŏgĕthĕr gŏ ;
⏑ — ⏑ — ⏑ — ⏑ —   Whăt littlĕ mōmĕnts lōvĕrs smile
⏑ — ⏑ — ⏑ — ⏑ —   Tŏ thē lŏng dāys bĕtweēn thĕ while.
        Isaac R. Baxley—"The Ballad of Sir Raymond."

4.

⏑ — ⏑ — ⏑ —   Thĕ mōssў mārblĕs rēst
— ⏑ — ⏑ — ⏑ —   Ŏn thĕ lĭps thăt hĕ hăs prĕst·
— ⏑ —   Ĭn theĭr bloōm ;
— ⏑ — ⏑ — ⏑ —   Ānd thĕ nāmes hĕ lōved tŏ hēar
— ⏑ — ⏑ — ⏑⏑ —   Hăve beĕn cārved fŏr mănў ă yēar
— ⏑ —   Ŏn thĕ tōmb.
        Oliver Wendell Holmes—"The Last Leaf."

THE CONSTRUCTION OF THE STANZA.

5.

—◡◡—◡—◡—　Nĕvĕr ă hēart tŭrns fălse ŏr cōld ;
—◡◡—◡—◡—　Nĕvĕr ă fāce grŏws grāy ŏr ōld ;
—◡◡—◡—◡—　Nĕvĕr ă lōve wĕ māy nŏt hōld,
—◡—◡◡—◡—◡　 Ĭn thĕ beaūtĭfŭl lănd ŏf făncў.
　　　　　Libbie C. Baer—" In the Land of Fancy."

6.

—◡—◡—◡—◡　Drāw thĕ lines ă lĭttlĕ tīghtĕr,
—◡—　　　　　　Spĭrĭt mīne !
—◡—◡—◡—◡　Māke thĕ life ă lĭttlĕ brīghtĕr,
—◡—　　　　　　Spĭrĭt mīne !
—◡—◡—◡—◡　Fŏr thĕ trūth's săke bē ă fīghtĕr,
—◡—◡—◡—◡　Shōw thĕ wŏrld lĭfe māy bĕ whītĕr,
—◡—◡—◡—◡　Pūrĕr, strōngĕr, dēarĕr, lĭghtĕr,
—◡—　　　　　　Mōre dĭvine !
　　　　　　　　John O. Coit—" Upward."

RHYTHMIC COMBINATIONS.

TROCHEES AND DACTYLS.	IAMBI AND ANAPESTS.
1. —◡—	17. ◡—◡—
2. —◡—◡	18. ◡—◡—◡
3. —◡—◡—	19. ◡—◡—◡—
4. —◡—◡—◡	20. ◡—◡—◡—◡—◡
5. —◡◡—	21. ◡—◡◡—
6. —◡◡—◡	22. ◡—◡◡—◡
7. —◡◡—◡—	23. ◡—◡◡—◡—
8. —◡◡—◡—◡	24. ◡—◡◡—◡—◡
9. —◡◡—◡◡—	25. ◡—◡◡—◡—
10. —◡—◡◡—◡	26. ◡—◡—◡◡—◡
11. —◡—◡—◡—	27. ◡—◡—◡—◡—
12. —◡—◡—◡—◡	28. ◡—◡—◡—◡—◡
13. —◡◡—◡◡—	29. ◡—◡—◡—◡—
14. —◡◡—◡◡—◡	30. ◡—◡◡—◡◡—◡
15. —◡◡—◡◡—◡—	31. ◡—◡◡—◡◡—◡—
16. —◡◡—◡◡—◡—◡	32. ◡—◡◡—◡◡—◡—◡

ANAPESTS AND IAMBI.

33. ⏑ ⏑ — ⏑ —
34. ⏑ ⏑ — ⏑ — ⏑
35. ⏑ ⏑ — ⏑ — ⏑ —
36. ⏑ ⏑ — ⏑ — ⏑ ⏑
37. ⏑ ⏑ — ⏑ ⏑ —
38. ⏑ ⏑ — ⏑ ⏑ — ⏑
39. ⏑ ⏑ — ⏑ ⏑ — ⏑ —
40. ⏑ ⏑ — ⏑ ⏑ — ⏑ ⏑
41. ⏑ ⏑ — ⏑ — ⏑ ⏑ —
42. ⏑ ⏑ — — ⏑ — ⏑ ⏑ — ⏑
43. ⏑ ⏑ — ⏑ — ⏑ ⏑ — ⏑ —
44. ⏑ ⏑ — ⏑ — ⏑ ⏑ — ⏑ ⏑
45. ⏑ ⏑ — ⏑ ⏑ — ⏑ ⏑ —
46. ⏑ ⏑ — ⏑ ⏑ — ⏑ ⏑ — ⏑
47. ⏑ ⏑ — ⏑ ⏑ — ⏑ ⏑ — ⏑ —
48. ⏑ ⏑ — ⏑ ⏑ — ⏑ ⏑ — ⏑ ⏑

These groups of rhythmic feet, or word accents, are capable of many combinations. We have forty-eight groups. To combine them is not difficult. By combining them we shall be enabled to write trochaic, dactylic, iambic, and anapestic rhythms.

To illustrate:

21 : 38.

"How dear to my heart are the scenes of my childhood."

Examine the rhythmic combinations:

⏑ — ⏑ ⏑ — ⏑ ⏑ — ⏑ ⏑ — ⏑

We find we have a combination of 21 : 38, being anapestic tetrameter.

21 : 37.

"Mid pleasures and palaces though we may roam."

⏑ — ⏑ ⏑ — ⏑ ⏑ — ⏑ ⏑ —

We have as a combination 21 : 37, an anapestic tetrameter.

1 : 18.

"I am dying, Egypt, dying."

— ⏑ — ⏑ — ⏑ —

This combines group 1 with 18 and gives a trochaic tetrameter.

1 : 18

"When the humid shadows hover."

It will be seen the first line of the beautiful poem, "Rain on the Roof," is the same combination, 1 : 18— trochaic tetrameter.

James Whitcomb Riley has very recently written a dialect poem entitled, "The Green Grass av Owld Ireland;" from which we select the fourth stanza. The first, third and fifth lines being combinations of groups 18 : 11 — the lines being iambic tetrameter; while group 19, being an iambic trimeter, forms lines two, four and six, the seventh line being a mixed iambic and anapestic tetrameter formed of 18 : 22.

> Gŏd blēss yĕz, freē Ămērĭkȳ!
> Ĭ lōve yĕz, dōck ănd shōre!
> Ĭ kēm tŏ yēz ĭn pōvĕrtȳ
> Thăt's wŏrstĭn' mē nŏ mōre.
> Bŭt mōst Ĭ'm lŏvĭn' Ērĭn yĕt,
> Wĭd āll hĕr grāves, d' yĕ seē,
> Bȳ rēasŏn āv thĕ greĕn grăss ăv ŏwld Īrelănd.

The following lines are by Elsa D'Esterre Keeling. The first, second and third lines combine groups 17 : 19— iambic tetrameter; and the fourth line, group 17, and is iambic dimeter. We select the fourth stanza:

> Lăst, Wĭntĕr cōmes; fŏr Ēld hăs brōught ĭts snōw,
> Ănd sāys, "Sĭt quĭĕt, shēltĕred frŏm thĕ stōrm."
> Ănd Ĭ sĭt ĭn mȳ ēasȳ chāir, ănd Ō,
> Thĕ heārth hŏw wārm!

8 : 6

"Cōme tŏ mĕ, dĕarĕst, Ĭ'm lōnelȳ wĭthōut theĕ."

A combination of group 8 : 6—dactylic tetrameter.

We might add example after example, but enough has been given to illustrate these rhythmic combinations.

The vertical bar is used to separate poetic feet. It is placed between each accented foot. If the measure is dissyllabic the vertical bar distinguishes it, thus:

1 : 18 : 1   18.

Once up | on a | midnight | dreary, | while I | pondered | weak
  and | weary.

Poe.—"The Raven."

The trisyllabic measure is marked as follows :·

Pause not to | dream of the | future be | fore us :
Pause not to | weep the wild | cares that come | o'er us :
Hark, how cre | ation's deep, | musical | chorus,
  Uninter | mitting, goes | up into | Heaven!
Never the | ocean-wave | falters in | flowing;
Never the | little seed | stops in its | growing;
More and more | richly the | rose-heart keeps | glowing,
  Till from its | nourishing | stem it is | riven.

Frances S. Osgood.—"Labor."

The vertical bar is sometimes used by authors of versification to represent or denote accent, as follows :

Once | upon | a mid | night drear | y, while | I pon | dered weak | and wear | y.

The macron — and the breve ⌣ are far preferable, as well as the acute accent, marked thus : ′

Ōnce up | ŏn a | mĭdnight | drēary, | whĭle I | pōndered | wēak
  and | wēary.

The scansion of verse becomes a pleasure when we understand rhythmic combinations and the use of accentuation marks.

THE FIVE LINE STANZA.

A pleasing form of our poetry is the stanza of five lines. It is composed of the single line, the couplet, the triplet, and quatrain. The combinations thus made are many and elegant. We can devise no better method of studying the art of composing this stanza, than that of giving examples from our best authors. Then, by a close analysis of each example given, we can tell the meter, rhythm and form. A study of each example will soon familiarize the student with this form of the stanza. From a poem by Sir Philip Sidney, we take the following, an iambic pentameter :

> Mỹ trūe-lŏve hāth mỹ heārt, ănd Ī hăve hīs,
> Bỹ jŭst ĕxchānge ŏne tō thĕ ōthĕr gīven :
> Ī hōld hĭs dēar, ănd mīne hĕ cānnŏt mīss,
> Thĕre nĕvĕr wās ă bĕttĕr bārgăin drīven :
> Mỹ trūe-lŏve hāth mỹ hēart, ănd Ī hăve hĭs.
> "My True-Love Hath My Heart."

Another fine example of the effect of a repetition of the subject of the poem, the same constituting the fifth line of the stanza, is found in the following iambic pentameter lines, entitled,

> Lĭngĕr nŏt lōng ! Hōme ĭs nŏt hōme wĭthōut theĕ ;
> Ĭts dēarĕst tōkĕns ōnlỹ māke mĕ mōurn ;
> Ŏh ! Lĕt ĭts mēmŏry, lĭke ă chāin ăbōut theĕ,
> Gēntlỹ cŏmpēl ănd hāstĕn thỹ rĕtūrn.
> Lĭngĕr nŏt lŏng.
> *Anonymous*—"Linger Not Long."

John G. Saxe is the author of the following. It is trochaic tetrameter, except the fourth line, which is a trochaic dimeter. We give the first stanza :

> Kĭss mĕ sŏftlў ănd spēak tŏ mĕ lōw,—
> Mālĭce hăs ēvĕr ă vĭgĭlănt ēar ;
> Whăt ĭf Mālĭce wĕre lūrkĭng nēar?
> Kĭss mĕ, dēar !
> Kĭss mĕ sŏftlў ănd spēak tŏ mĕ lōw.
> "Kiss Me Softly."

The little poem by Sir John Suckling furnishes a fine example of a stanza in trochaic rhythm :

> Whȳ sŏ pāle ănd wăn, fŏnd lŏvĕr?
> Prȳtheĕ, whȳ sŏ pāle?
> Wĭll, whĕn loōkĭng wēll căn't mōve hĕr,
> Loōkĭng ĭll prĕvāil?
> Prȳtheĕ, whȳ sŏ pāle?
> "Why So Pale and Wan, Fond Lover."

One of the finest poems, written by Percy Bysshe Shelley, is entitled, "To a Skylark." It is a trochaic rhythm, the first four lines are trochaic trimeter, the fifth trochaic hexameter. We give the first stanza :

> Hāil tŏ theē, blĭthe spĭrĭt !
> Bĭrd thŏu nĕvĕr wĕrt,
> Thăt frŏm hĕavĕn ŏr nēar ĭt,
> Pōurĕst thȳ fŭll hēart
> Ĭn prŏfūse străins ŏf ŭnprēmĕdĭtătĕd ārt.
> "To a Skylark."

Charlotte Smith is the author of a bright poem. It is iambic tetrameter, the first and third and fourth lines rhyming, and the second and fifth, the third and fourth being a couplet. We give the third stanza:

> Cŏme, sŭmmĕr vīsĭtānt, ăttāch
> Tŏ mȳ reĕd-roōf yoŭr nĕst ŏf clāy;
> Ănd lĕt mȳ ēar yoŭr mūsĭc cātch,
> Lŏw twĭttĕrĭng ūndĕrnēath thĕ thātch,
> Ăt thĕ grăy dāwn ŏf dāy.
> "The Swallow."

We give an example from a poem of nature by Mary Bolles Branch. It is iambic tetrameter. The first, fourth and fifth lines rhyme, and the second and third. The second and third, and fourth and fifth lines are couplets. We select the third stanza, describing the rock in the brook. How delicate and true the description:

> Thĕ rŏck ĭs rōugh ănd brōkĕn ŏn ĭts ēdge
> Wĭth jūttĭng cōrnĕrs, būt thĕre cōme ălwāy
> Thĕ mĕrrȳ rīpplĕs wĭth thĕir tĭnȳ sprāy,
> Tŏ prĕss ĭt ēre thĕy flōw ŏn bȳ thĕ sĕdge,
> Thĕy nēvĕr fāil thĕ ōld rŏck's brōkĕn ēdge.
> "My Little Brook."

Tennyson furnishes an excellent iambic pentameter stanza in blank verse. We give the first stanza of the poem.

> Tĕars, īdlĕ tēars, Ĭ knōw nŏt whăt thĕy mēan,
> Tĕars frŏm thĕ dĕpths ŏf sōme dĭvīne dĕspāir
> Rīse ĭn thĕ heārt, ănd gāthĕr tō thĕ ēyes,
> Ĭn loŏkĭng ŏn thĕ hăppȳ Āutŭmn-fiĕlds,
> Ănd thĭnkĭng ŏf thĕ dāys thăt āre nŏ mōre.
> "Tears, Idle Tears."

Thomas Moore, the author of so many touching and

pathetic lines, has written few better than "The Lake of the Dismal Swamp." It is iambic rhythm. We give the first stanza :

> They māde hĕr ă grāve, toŏ cōld ănd dămp
> Fŏr ă heārt sŏ wārm ănd trūe;
> And shĕ's gōne tŏ thĕ Lāke ŏf thĕ Dīsmăl Swâmp
> Whĕre, āll nĭght lōng, bў ă fīre-flў lămp,
> Shĕ pāddlĕs hĕr whīte cănoê !
> "The Lake of the Dismal Swamp."

Another form of this stanza is given in the following, in iambic measure :

> Ĕntĕrs tŏdāy
>   Ănōthĕr bōdў ĭn chūrch yărd sōd,
>   Ănōthĕr soul ŏn thĕ life ĭn Gōd.
> Hĭs Chrīst wăs būriĕd—ănd lĭves ălwāy :
> Trŭst Hĭm, ănd gō yoŭr wāy.
>   *Dinah Maria Mulock*—"Buried Today."

We give the third stanza of a touching poem in iambic rhythm :

> Ănd Ō, sĭnce thăt bābў slĕpt,
> Sŏ hūshed, hŏw thĕ mōthĕr hăs kĕpt,
>   Wĭth ă tēarfŭl plĕasŭre,
>   Thăt lĭttlĕ dĕar trĕasŭre,
> Ănd ō'er thĕm thōught ănd wĕpt !
>   *William Cox Bennett*—"Baby's Shoes."

Whittier describes a visit to Hampton Beach. The rhythm is iambic. We give the twelfth stanza :

> Whăt heēd Ĭ ŏf thĕ dūstў lănd
>   Ănd noīsў tōwn ?
> Ĭ seē thĕ mīghtў deēp ĕxpānd
> Frŏm its whĭte līne ŏf glīmmerĭng sănd
> Tŏ where thĕ blūe ŏf hĕaven ŏn blūĕr wāves shŭts dōwn !
>   "Hampton Beach."

A poem by Samuel Taylor Coleridge, contains this excellent stanza in iambic rhythm. It is the second one of the poem:

> Fŏr shāme, mў friĕnd! rĕnōunce thĭs īdlĕ strāin!
> Whăt woūldst thŏu hāve ă goōd greăt măn ŏbtāin?
> Wĕalth, tītlĕ, dĭgnĭtў, ă gōldĕn chāin,
> Ŏr heāp ŏf cōrsĕs which hĭs swōrd hăth slāin?
> Goōdnĕss ănd greātnĕss āre nŏt meāns, bŭt ēnds.
>   "The Good Great Man."

Edmund Clarence Stedman, one of our best writers, furnishes a dashing poem. It is in trochaic rhythm. We give a stanza:

> Hārk! thĕ jĭnglĕ
> Ŏf thĕ slēigh-bĕlls' sōng!
> Ēarth ănd āir ĭn snōwў sheĕn cŏmmĭnglĕ;
> Swĭftlў, thrōng
> Nōrselănd făncĭes, ās wĕ sāil ălōng.
>   "The Sleigh-Ride."

Who is there that has not read of the fabled youth—

> "Ă yoūth, whŏ bōre, 'mĭd snōw ănd īce,
> Ă bānnĕr with thĕ strānge dĕvīce—
> Ĕxcēlsĭōr!"

a youth that pressed on, harkening not the voices that gave him warning, until overtaken by death. The poem is by Longfellow. It is an iambic tetrameter, except the last line of the stanza, which is iambic dimeter. We have selected the fifth stanza:

> "Ŏh stāy," thĕ māidĕn sāid, "ănd rēst
> Thў weārў heād ŭpōn thĭs breāst!"
> Ă teār stoŏd in hĭs brīght blŭe eўe
> Bŭt still hĕ ānswĕred, with ă sīgh,
> Ĕxcēlsĭōr.
>   "Excelsior."

Edmund Waller is the author of a pretty poem in iambic rhythm. The third stanza is given.

> Smăll ĭs thĕ wŏrth
> Ŏf beaūtў frŏm thĕ līght rĕtīred;
> Bĭd hĕr cŏme fŏrth,
> Sŭffĕr hĕrsēlf tŏ bē dĕsīred,
> Ănd nŏt blŭsh sō tŏ bē ădmīred.
> —"Go Lovely Rose."

Henry Kirke White added to the poem, this stanza:

> Yĕt, thōugh thoŭ fāde,
> Frŏm thў dĕad lēaves lĕt frāgrănce rĭse;
> Ănd tēach thĕ māid,
> Thăt gōodnĕss Tīme's rŭde hănd dĕfīes,
> Thăt vĭrtŭe lĭves whĕn beaūtў dīes.

Longfellow ever teems in good thoughts. This one in iambic rhythm is worth remembering. We give the eighth stanza of the poem:

> Ănd hē whŏ hăs nŏt leārned tŏ knōw
> Hŏw fālse ĭts spārklĭng bŭbblĕs shŏw,
> Hŏw bĭttĕr āre thĕ drŏps ŏf wōe,
> Wĭth whīch ĭts brĭm măy ōvĕrflōw,
> Hĕ hăs nŏt leārned tŏ līve.
> —"The Goblet of Life."

Another charming poem by Longfellow, is entitled "Christmas Bells." It is iambic rhythm. We give the seventh stanza:

> Thĕn pēaled thĕ bĕlls mōre loūd ănd dēep:
> "Gŏd ĭs nŏt dēad; nŏr dŏth hĕ slēep!
> Thĕ Wrŏng shăll fāil,
> Thĕ Rĭght prĕvāil,
> Wĭth pēace ŏn ēarth, gŏod-wĭll tŏ mĕn!"
> "Christmas Bells."

THE CONSTRUCTION OF THE STANZA.

"A Woman's Question," is the title of a poem written by Adelaide Anne Proctor in iambic rhythm, furnishing us an example of the middle or line rhyme in the fifth line, as well as another form. We give the first stanza:

> Before I trust my fate to thee,
> Or place my hand in thine,
> Before I let thy future give
> Color and form to mine,
> Before I peril all for thee, question thy soul to-night for me.
> —"A Woman's Question."

THE SIX LINE STANZA.

Endless are the varieties of our English stanza. The art of the poet is susceptible of a high degree of cultivation. Our best authors have from time to time found new and beautiful combinations. The six line stanza is one capable of producing the very best of results. We have selected many forms of the six line stanzas with a view of illustrating their combinations and formations. Our first selection is in anapestic rhythm,—anapestic tetrameter. We give the first stanza:

> There's a little low hut by the river's side,
> Within the sound of its rippling tide;
> Its walls are grey with the mosses of years,
> And its roof all crumbled and old appears:
> But fairer to me than castle's pride
> Is the little low hut by the river's side!
> P. B. *Shillaber*—"My Childhood Home."

A stanza by Tennyson, in anapestic rhythm is given. The first, second, third, fourth and sixth lines trimeter, the fifth, tetrameter.

Cŏme īntŏ thĕ gârdĕn, Māud,
For thĕ blāck băt, night, hăs flōwn!
Cŏme īntŏ thĕ gārdĕn, Māud,
Ĭ ăm hēre ăt thĕ gāte, ălōne;
Ănd thĕ wōodbĭne spīcĕs ăre wāftĕd ăbrōad,
Ănd thĕ mûsk ŏf thĕ rōsĕs blōwn.
—"Come Into the Garden, Maud."

Another form of this stanza, in iambic tetrameter, the lines rhyming alternately, is given. The first stanza is selected:

Shĕ wālks ĭn beaūtў, like thĕ nīght
Ŏf cloūdlĕss clīmes ănd stărrў skīes,
Ănd āll thăt's bēst ŏf dārk ănd brīght
Mĕet īn hĕr āspĕct ānd hĕr ēyes,
Thŭs mēllŏwed tō thăt tēndĕr light
Whĭch hēaven tŏ gaūdў dāy dĕnīes.
Byron—"She Walks in Beauty."

Here is another six line stanza rhyming in alternate lines. It is a poem of exquisite finish and delicacy of touch, tender and pathetic, by Edgar Allen Poe, entitled "Annabel Lee." The poem was composed by Poe in memory of his child-wife, who was his cousin and to whom he was devotedly attached; whom he loved "with a love that the winged seraphs of heaven coveted her and me." It is anapestic rhythm:

Ĭt wăs mānў ănd mānў ă yēar ăgō,
Ĭn ă kīngdŏm bў thĕ sēa,
Thăt ă māidĕn līved whŏm yoū mǎy knōw
Bў thĕ nāme ŏf Ānnăbĕl Lēe;
Ănd thĭs māidĕn shĕ līved wĭth nŏ ŏthĕr thōught
Thăn tŏ lōve, ănd bĕ lōved bў mĕ.
—"Annabel Lee."

Sorrow and adversity are depicted in these lines by one of England's best writers. It is iambic rhythm and a fine form of the stanza,—dimeter and tetrameter lines :

        Spring it is cheery,
        Winter is dreary,
Green leaves hang, but the brown must fly;
        When he's forsaken,
        Withered and shaken,
What can an old man do but die?
      Hood—"What Can an Old Man do but Die?"

Another form of this stanza, in iambic rhythm, is composed of a quatrain, rhyming in alternate lines, and a couplet :

I love, and have some cause to love, the earth,—
  She is my Maker's creature, therefore good;
She is my mother, for she gave me birth;
  She is my tender nurse, she gives me food;
But what's a creature, Lord, compared with thee?
Or what's my mother or my nurse to me?
      Francis Quarles—"Delight in God."

Robert Herrick is the author of the following in iambic rhythm :

Fair pledges of a fruitful tree,
  Why do ye fall so fast?
  Your date is not so past
But you may stay yet here awhile
To blush and gently smile,
  And go at last.
      "To Blossoms."

A fine trochaic stanza is to be found in "Twelfth Night,"

Act II, scene 3. The third and sixth lines rhyme, the other lines rhyming in couplets:

> Whăt ĭs lōve? 'Tĭs nŏt hĕreāftĕr;
> Prĕsĕnt mīrth hăth prĕsĕnt lāughtĕr;
> Whāt's tŏ cōme ĭs stĭll ŭnsūre:
> Ĭn dĕlāy thĕre līes nŏ plēntў,—
> Thĕn cŏme kĭss mĕ, Swēet-ănd-twēntў,
> Youth's ă stŭff wĭll nŏt ĕndūre.
>
> *Shakespeare*—"O Mistress Mine."

An ardent love stanza composed by John Moultrie, is to be found in the following in iambic rhythm, rhyming in couplets:

> "Fŏrgĕt thĕe?"—Ĭf tŏ drēam bў nīght, ănd mūse ŏn thĕe bў dāy,
> Ĭf āll thĕ wŏrshĭp, dēep ănd wĭld, ă pŏĕt's hĕart căn pāy,
> Ĭf prāyĕrs ĭn ābsĕnce brēathed fŏr thĕe tŏ Hēavĕn's prŏtēctĭng pōwer,
> Ĭf wĭngĕd thŏughts thăt flĭt tŏ thĕe—ă thōusănd ĭn ăn hŏur,
> Ĭf būsў Fāncў blēndĭng thĕe wĭth āll mў fūtŭre lŏt,—
> Ĭf thĭs thŏu cāll'st "fŏrgĕttĭng," thŏu ĭndēed shălt bĕ fŏrgŏt!
>
> "Forget Thee?"

Ralph Hoyt is the author of a poem depicting old age. It is touching and pathetic and portrays true to life some of the sad events of this existence. The poem is written in trochaic rhythm. The first, second, third, fourth and sixth lines being trochaic pentameter, and the fifth trochaic dimeter. We have selected the seventh stanza:

> "Āngĕl," sāid hĕ sădlў, "Ī ăm ōld;
> Ēarthlў hōpe nŏ lōngĕr hăth ă mŏrrŏw;
> Yĕt, whў Ī sĭt hĕre thŏu shălt bĕ tōld."
> Thĕn hĭs ēye bĕtrāyed ă pĕarl ŏf sŏrrŏw,
> Dōwn ĭt rōlled!
> "Āngĕl," sāid hĕ sădlў, "Ī ăm ōld."
>
> "Old."

Another form of the six line stanza is the quatrain rhyming in alternate lines, with the couplet. The following is iambic rhythm and the first stanza of the poem :

>Friĕnd ăftĕr friĕnd dĕpărts ;
> Whŏ hāth nŏt lōst ă friĕnd ?
>Thĕre īs nŏ ūniŏn hēre ŏf heărts
> Thăt fĭnds nŏt hēre ăn ēnd !
>Wĕre thīs frăil wōrld ŏur fĭnăl rēst,
>Līvĭng ŏr dȳĭng nōne wĕre blĕst.
>   *James Montgomery*—"Parted Friends."

A dainty poem, exquisite in its form, is by Sarah Roberts. It is trochaic rhythm. We give the first stanza :

>Hēre Ĭ cŏme crēepĭng, crēepĭng ēverȳwhēre ;
> Bȳ thĕ dūstȳ rōadsĭde,
> Ŏn thĕ sūnnȳ hĭllsĭde,
> Clōse bȳ thĕ noisȳ brōok,
> Ĭn ēverȳ shādȳ nōok,
>Ĭ cŏme crēepĭng, crēepĭng ēverȳwhēre.
>   "The Voice of the Grass."

Burns is not the first who used the form of the stanza following. He, however, used it frequently in his writings and it is known as the stanza of Burns. It is iambic rhythm:

>Stĭll thōu ărt blĕssed, cŏmpāred wĭ' mē !
>Thĕ prĕsĕnt ōnlȳ toŭchĕth thēe :
>Bŭt, ōch ! Ĭ băckwărd căst mȳ ē'e
> Ŏn prōspĕcts drēar ;
>Ăn' fōrwărd, thŏugh Ĭ cānnă' sēe,
> Ĭ guĕss ăn' fēar.
>   "To a Mouse."

"The Little Beach Bird" is the theme of a poem by Richard Henry Dana. It is also in iambic rhythm. We give the first stanza:

> Thŏŭ lĭttlĕ bĭrd, thŏŭ dwēllĕr bȳ thĕ sēa,
> Whȳ tākĕst thŏu ĭts mĕlănchŏlȳ voīce?
> Whȳ wĭth thăt bōdĭng crȳ
> Ō'er thĕ wāves dŏst thŏŭ flȳ?
> Ŏ, rāthĕr, bĭrd, wĭth mē
> Throŭgh thĕ făir lānd rĕjoīce!
>
> "The Little Beach Bird."

An interesting stanza may be formed in alternate lines, the first, second and fourth trimeter, the third tetrameter, and the fifth and sixth a tetrameter couplet, as follows:

> Tĕll mē Ĭ hāte thĕ bōwl,—
> Hăte īs ă feĕblĕ wŏrd;
> Ĭ lōathe, ăbhŏr,—mȳ vērȳ sōul
> Bȳ strōng dĭsgŭst ĭs stĭrred
> Whĕn'ĕr Ĭ seē, ŏr hēar, ŏr tĕll
> Ŏf thĕ dărk bĕvĕrăge ŏf hĕll!
>
> *Anonymous*—"Go Feel What I Have Felt."

In trochaic rhythm we give—

> Sō, goŏd nĭght!
> Slūmbĕr ōn tĭll mōrnĭng lĭght;
> Slūmbĕr tĭll ănōthĕr mŏrrŏw
> Brīngs ĭts stōres ŏf jōy ănd sōrrŏw;
> Feārlĕss, ĭn thĕ Fāthĕr's sĭght!
> Slūmbĕr ōn. Goŏd nĭght!
>
> *Körner*—"Good Night."

William Cullen Bryant is the author of this patriotic stanza, in iambic rhythm:

Ŏ MŌTHĔR ŏf ă mīghty̆ rāce,
Yĕt lōvely̆ īn thy̆ yoūthfŭl grāce !
Thĕ ēldĕr dāmes, thy̆ hāughty̆ peērs,
Ădmīre ănd hāte thy̆ bloōmĭng yēars ;
  Wĭth wōrds ŏf shāme
Ănd tāunts ŏf scōrn thĕy jōin thy̆ nāme.
"America."

Charles Kingsley is the author of a poem in iambic rhythm, from which we give the second stanza :

Thĕ creēpĭng tide căme ūp ălōng thĕ sānd,
Ănd ō'er ănd ō'er thĕ sānd,
Ănd rōund ănd rōund thĕ sānd,
  Ăs fār ăs eȳe coŭld seē ;
Thĕ blīndĭng mīst cămed dōwn ănd hīd thĕ lānd:
Ănd nēvĕr hōme cămed shē.
"The Sands of Dee."

In trochaic rhythm Longfellow has written a poem entitled "Sea Weed." It is a neat form of the six-line stanza. The first, third, fourth and sixth lines are tetrameter, the second and fifth dimeter. We give the fifth stanza

Sō whĕn stōrms ŏf wĭld ĕmōtiŏn
  Strīke thĕ ōceăn
Ŏf thĕ pōĕt's sōul, ĕre lōng,
Frōm ĕach cāve ănd rōcky̆ fāstnĕss
  Ĭn ĭts vāstnĕss
Flōats sŏme frāgmĕnt ŏf ă sōng.
"Sea Weed."

Maria Gowan Brooks is the author of these exquisite lines

in trochaic rhythm. The quatrain is tetrameter, the couplet dimeter. We give the second stanza:

> Thŏu, tŏ whŏm Ĭ lōve tŏ heārkĕn;
> Cōme, ĕre nīght ărōund mĕ dărkĕn;
> Thōugh thў sōftnĕss bût dĕcēive mĕ,
> Sāy thŏu'rt trūe, ănd Ĭ'll bĕliēve theĕ;
>   Vēil, ĭf ĭll thў sōul's ĭntĕnt,
>   Lĕt mĕ thĭnk ĭt ĭnnŏcĕnt!
>   "Day, in Melting Purple Dying."

THE SEVEN LINE STANZA.

> Ŏf āll thŏse ārts ĭn whĭch thĕ wīse ĕxcēl,
> Nātūre's chĭĕf māstĕrpiĕce ĭs wrītĭng wēll;
> Nŏ wrītĭng lĭfts ĕxāltĕd mān sŏ hīgh
> Ăs sācrĕd ănd sŏul-mōvĭng pŏĕsў.
>   *Buckingham.*

This stanza may not be so generally used as the ones of four, five and six lines, still many beautiful and exquisitely finished poems are to its credit. It is also capable of many nicely formed combinations. The various forms that may be selected from our best poems, examined and analyzed, will soon make us familiar with the stanza of seven lines. The first selection is a sweet, spicy, little love poem by Charles Sibley, entitled "The Plaidie." How true to nature are these little word accents in iambic rhythm. An analysis of the first line of the stanza shows a line composed of three iambic feet, with a redundant syllable; the second line is composed of a trochee, and two iambuses; the third line is composed of an anapest and two iambuses, with a redundant syllable; the fourth line is composed of an anapest and two iambuses; the fifth line is composed of one iambus and a redundant syllable ; the sixth line is like the third ; the seventh is composed of three iambuses. The fifth line is a monometer, the others trimeter :

THE PLAIDIE.

Ŭpŏn ăne stōrmў Sūndăy,
  Cōmĭng ădoōn thĕ lāne,
Wĕre ă scōre ŏf bōnnĭe lāssĭes—
  Ănd thĕ sweētĕst Ĭ măintāin
    Wăs Cāddĭe,
Thăt Ĭ toŏk ŭnnēath mў plāidĭe,
  Tŏ shiĕld hĕr frōm thĕ rāin.

Shĕ sāid thăt thĕ dāisiĕs blūshed
  Fŏr thĕ kīss thăt Ĭ hăd tā'en ;
Ĭ wădnă hăe thoŭght thĕ lāssĭe
  Wăd sāe ŏf ă kīss cŏmplāin :
    " Nŏw, lāddĭe !
Ĭ wīnnă stăy ūndĕr yoŭr plāidĭe,
  Ĭf Ĭ găng hāme ĭn thĕ rāin !"

Bŭt ōn ăn āfter Sūndăy,
  Whĕn clōud thĕre wăs nŏt āne,
Thĭs sēlfsăme wīnsŏme lāssĭe
  (Wĕ chānce tŏ meēt ĭn thĕ lāne)
    Săid, "Lāddĭe,
Whў dĭnnă yĕ weār yoŭr plāidĭe ?
  Whă kēns bŭt ĭt măy rāin ?"

"How Many Times," a poem in iambic rhythm, by Charles Lovell Beddoes, gives expression of great love. We have selected the second stanza :

How mănȳ tĭmes dŏ Ī lōve, ăgāin?
Tĕll mē hŏw mănȳ bēads thĕre āre
Ĭn ă sīlvĕr chāin
Ŏf thĕ ēvenĭng rāin,
Ŭnrāvĕled frōm thĕ tŭmblĭng māin,
Ănd thrēadĭng thĕ eȳe ŏf ă yĕllŏw stār:
Sŏ mănȳ tĭmes dŏ Ī lōve, ăgāin.
"How Many Times."

Elizabeth Barrett Browning has written a delicately finished and pathetic poem entitled, "My Heart and I." We give the seventh and last stanza. It is iambic rhythm:

Yĕt, whō cŏmplāins? Mȳ heărt ănd Ī?
Ĭn thīs ăbūndănt eărth nŏ dōubt
Ĭs lĭttlĕ roōm fŏr thĭngs wŏrn ōut;
Dīsdāin thĕm, breāk thĕm, thrōw thĕm bȳ;
Ănd īf bĕfōre thĕ dāys grĕw rōugh,
Wĕ ōnce wĕre lōved, thĕn—wĕll ĕnōugh
Ī thĭnk wĕ've fāred, mȳ heărt ănd Ī.
"My Heart and I."

From an old manuscript in the time of Henry VIII, written anonymously, the following stanza in iambic rhythm is taken:

Ăh, mȳ sweĕt sweētĭng;
Mȳ lĭttlĕ prĕttȳ sweētĭng,
Mȳ sweētĭng wīll Ī lōve whĕrēvĕr Ĭ gō;
Shĕ īs sŏ prōpĕr ănd pūre,
Trŭe, stĕadfăst, stāblĕ ānd dĕmūre,
Thĕre īs nŏne sŭch, yoŭ māy bĕ sūre,
Ăs mȳ sweĕt sweētĭng.
"My Sweet Sweeting."

THE CONSTRUCTION OF THE STANZA. 85

Tennyson's "Song of the Milkmaid," from "Queen Mary," is a fine specimen of the seven line stanza. It is trochaic measure :

        Shāme ŭpōn yoŭ, Rōbĭn,
        Shāme ŭpōn yoŭ nōw !
        Kĭss mĕ woŭld yoŭ? with mў hānds
        Mĭlkĭng thĕ cōw ?
        Dāĭsĭes grōw ăgāin,
        Kĭng cŭps blōw ăgāin,
        Ănd yoŭ cāme ănd kĭssed mĕ mĭlkĭng thĕ cōw.

Jean Ingelow is the author of "Songs of Seven," which contains a love song in anapestic rhythm :

    Ĭ lēaned ŏut ŏf wĭndŏw, Ĭ smēlt thĕ whīte clōvĕr,
    Dărk, dārk wăs thĕ gārdĕn, Ĭ sāw nŏt thĕ gāte ;
    "Nŏw, ĭf thĕre bĕ foŏtstĕps, hĕ cōmes, mў ŏwn lŏvĕr,—
    Hŭsh, nīghtĭngăle, hŭsh ! Ŏ sweĕt nīghtĭngăle, wāit
        Tĭll Ĭ lĭstĕn ănd hēar
        Ĭf ă stĕp drăwĕth nēar,
        Fŏr mў lŏve hĕ ĭs lāte !
                "Seven Times Three, Love."

A poem greatly admired is by Rev. Charles Kingsley. It is an anapestic rhythm. The stanza which we have selected is an anapestic tetrameter, and analyzed is as follows: The first line is composed of two anapestic and two iambic feet ; the second line is like the first ; the third is composed of four iambic feet ; the fourth is composed of one iambic and three anapestic feet ; the fifth is composed of one anapestic and three iambic feet ; the sixth is like the third ; and the seventh line is like the fifth, the anapestic foot prevailing denotes the rhythm of the stanza. The third stanza is as follows :

>Thrĕĕ cōrpsĕs lăy ōut ŏn thĕ shīnĭng sānds
>In thĕ mōrnĭng glēam ăs thĕ tide wĕnt dōwn,
>And thĕ wŏmĕn ăre weēpĭng ănd wrīngĭng thĕir hānds
>Fŏr thōse whŏ wĭll nĕvĕr cŏme bāck tŏ thĕ tōwn,
>Fŏr mĕn mŭst wŏrk, ănd wŏmĕn mŭst weēp ;
>And thĕ soōnĕr ĭts ōvĕr, thĕ soōnĕr tŏ sleēp ;
>And goŏd-bȳe tŏ thĕ bār ănd ĭts moānĭng.
>"The Three Fishers."

"My Love is Dead," is a poem by Thomas Chatterton, in trochaic measure composed of nine stanzas, from which we have selected the second. The measure is mixed, the trochaic foot prevailing. The stanza is tetrameter, except the fifth and sixth lines, they being dimeter. The first and third, the second and fourth lines rhyme. The fifth and sixth being a rhyming couplet :

>Blāck hĭs hāir ăs thĕ sūmmĕr nīght,
>Whīte hĭs nĕck ăs thĕ wīntĕr snōw,
>Rŭddȳ hĭs fāce ăs thĕ mōrnĭng līght ;
>Cōld hĕ lies ĭn thĕ grāve bĕlōw.
>Mȳ lōve ĭs dĕad
>Gōne tŏ hĭs dĕath-bĕd,
>All ūndĕr thĕ wīllŏw treē.
>"My Love is Dead."

Henry N. Cobb is the author of the following lines in iambic rhythm. The first four lines being pentameter, the fifth and sixth dimeter, and the seventh a monometer. We give the first stanza of the poem :

THE CONSTRUCTION OF THE STANZA. 87

> Thĕ wāy ĭs dārk, mў Fāthĕr! Clōud ŏn clōud
> Ĭs gāthĕrĭng thĭcklў ō'er mў hēad, ănd lōud
> Thĕ thūndĕrs rōar ăbōve mĕ. Sēe, Ĭ stănd
> Lĭke ōne bĕwīldĕred! Fāthĕr, tăke mў hănd,
>   Ănd thrōugh thĕ glōom
>   Lĕad sāfelў hōme
>   Thў chīld!
>   " Father, Take my Hand."

In a fine descriptive poem Francis Bret Harte thus narrates the cause of the fear of the inhabitants of a seaport town, in iambic rhythm. We give the second stanza :

> Gŏod cāuse fŏr fēar! Ĭn thĕ thĭck mĭddāy
> Thĕ hūlk thăt lāy bў thĕ rŏttĭng piēr,
> Fīlled wĭth chīldrĕn ĭn hăppў plāy,
> Pārtĕd thĕ mōorĭngs ănd drīftĕd clēar,—
> Drīftĕd clĕar bĕyōnd thĕ rēach ŏr cāll,—
> Thĭrtĕen chīldrĕn thĕy wēre ĭn āll,—
> Āll ădrĭft ĭn thĕ lōwĕr bāy!
>   "A Greyport Legend."

A ride made famous in iambic tetrameter is that of Sheridan's from Winchestertown. We give the first stanza :

> Ŭp frōm thĕ Soūth ăt breāk ŏf dāy
> Brīngĭng tŏ Wĭnchĕstĕr frĕsh dĭsmāy,
> Thĕ ăffrĭghtĕd āir wĭth ă shŭddĕr bōre,
> Lĭke ă hĕrăld ĭn hāste, tŏ thĕ chiēftaĭn's dōor,
> Thĕ tĕrrĭblĕ grūmblĕ, ănd rūmblĕ, ănd rōar,
> Tĕllĭng thĕ băttlĕ wăs ōn ŏnce mōre,
> Ănd Shĕrĭdăn twĕntў mīles ăwāy.
>   *Thomas Buchanan Read*—"Sheridan's Ride."

Another little poem depicting rural sport, is by Thomas Tod Stoddart, in trochaic rhythm. It is very cleverly written and the stanza worth reading to a lover of the sport. We give the first stanza:

> Sing, sweet thrushes, forth and sing!
> Meet the morn upon the lea;
> Are the emeralds of the spring
> On the angler's trysting-tree?
> Tell, sweet thrushes, tell to me!
> Are there buds on our willow-tree?
> Buds and birds on our trysting-tree?
> "The Angler's Trysting-Tree."

What a fine sentiment is contained in this stanza, the last one of a poem by Mrs. Craik. It is iambic rhythm:

> O soul, forget the weight that drags thee down,
> Deathfully, deathfully:
> Know thyself. As this glory wraps thee round,
> Let it melt off the chains that long have bound
> Thy strength. Stand free before thy God and cry—
> "My Father, here am I:
> Give to me as thou wilt—first cross, then crown."
> "The Aurora on the Clyde."

And by the same author we find a fine iambic stanza taken from a poem entitled "Sitting on the Shore":

> O life, O silent shore,
> Where we sit patient: O great sea beyond
> To which we turn with solemn hope and fond,
> But sorrowful no more:
> A little while, and then we too shall soar
> Like white-winged sea-birds into the Infinite Deep;
> Till then, Thou, Father—wilt our spirits keep.
> "Sitting on the Shore."

Let us give still another from the same author. It is from a poem in anapestic rhythm entitled, "Sleep on Till Day":

> Yĕt lĭfe's bŭt ă vīsĭŏn toŏ lōvelў tŏ stāy:
> Mŏrn pāssĕs, noŏn hāstĕns, ănd pleāsŭres dĕcāy;
> Ănd ēvenĭng ăppróachĕs ănd clōsĕs thĕ dāy:
> Thĕn lāid wĭth prāisĕs
> Ŭndĕr thĕ dāisĭes:
> Smĭlĭng wĕ'll creēp tŏ ŏur pĭllŏw ŏf clāy,
> Ănd sleēp ŏn tĭll Dāy, mў lŏve, sleēp ŏn tĭll Dāy.

For one desirous of selecting a wife, the following stanza may be of some practical help. The poem is an iambic tetrameter. Here is the third stanza:

> Ĭf Ĭ coŭld fīnd ă lāssĭe—mĭld,
> Wōmăn ĭn wĭt, ĭn heārt ă chīld:
>   Blĭthe—jŭst tŏ sweētĕn sŏrrŏw;
> Sĕdāte ĕnoŭgh tŏ tēmpĕr mĭrth—
> Meĕk-heārtĕd, rĭch ĭn hōusehŏld wŏrth—
> Nŏt quĭte thĕ ūglĭĕst gīrl ŏn ēarth,—
>   Ĭ'd mārrў hĕr tŏmōrrŏw.
>   *Craik*—"The Six Sisters."

A "Dream in the Woods," written by Thomas Hood, in iambic rhythm, is a poem of excellent merit—contemplative in character. We give the sixty-seventh stanza:

> Bŭt hāughtў peēr ănd mīghtў kīng
> Ŏne doōm shăll ōvĕrwhēlm!
>   Thĕ ōakĕn cēll
>   Shăll lōdge hĭm wēll
> Whŏse scēptrĕ rūled ă rēalm—
> Whĭle hē whŏ nĕvĕr knēw ă hōme
> Shăll fĭnd ĭt ĭn thĕ ēlm!
>   "The Elm Tree."

Henry Carey is the author of "God Save the King," written in dactylic rhythm. We give a stanza :

> Gŏd săve ŏur grācioŭs kĭng,
> Lŏng līve ŏur nōblĕ kĭng,
> Gŏd săve thĕ kīng !
> Sĕnd hĭm vĭctōrĭoŭs
> Hāppȳ ănd glōrĭoŭs,
> Lŏng tŏ rĕign ōvĕr ŭs,
> Gŏd săve thĕ kĭng !

A patriotic poem by Francis Bret Harte furnishes this excellent stanza in trochaic rhythm. The second one of the poem is selected :

> " Lĕt mĕ ŏf mȳ heărt tăke cōunsĕl :
> Wăr ĭs nŏt ŏf līfe thĕ sūm ;
> Whō shăll stāy ănd rēap thĕ hărvĕst
> Whĕn thĕ aūtŭmn dāys shăll cōme ? "
> Bŭt thĕ drūm
> Ĕchŏed, "Cōme !
> Dēath shăll rēap thĕ brăvĕr hărvĕst," săid thĕ
> sōlĕmn sōundĭng drūm.
> "The Reveille."

Lord Tennyson is the author of a soul-stirring poem in dactylic rhythm. The second stanza is given :

> Bē nŏt dēaf tŏ thĕ soūnd thăt wărns !
> Bĕ nŏt gŭlled bȳ ă dĕspŏt's plēa !
> Āre fĭgs ŏf thĭstlĕs, ŏr grāpes ŏf thōrns ?
> Hōw shoŭld ă dĕspŏt sĕt mĕn freē ?
> Fōrm ! fōrm, Rĭflĕmĕn, fōrm !
> Rĕadȳ, bĕ rēadȳ tŏ meēt thĕ stŏrm !
> Rĭflĕmĕn, rĭflĕmĕn, rĭflĕmĕn, fōrm !
> "The War."

THE CONSTRUCTION OF THE STANZA.

Phœbe Carey has written many tender and charming poems. The art of the poet was one she thoroughly understood. This stanza, the last one of the poem, is in trochaic rhythm :

> Āh wīse mōthĕr ! ĭf yoŭ prōved
> Lōvĕr nēvĕr crōssed hĕr wāy,
> Ĭ woŭld thĭnk thĕ sēlf-sămĕ wāy.
> Ĕvĕr sīnce thĕ wōrld hăs mōved,
> Bābes seĕm wŏmĕn īn ă dāy ;
> Ānd, ălās ! ănd wēll ă dāy !
> Mĕn hăve woōed ănd māidĕns lōved !
>   *Phœbe Cary*—" Gracie."

Matthew Arnold has written a fine poem, which he entitles "A Question." It is trochaic rhythm. We give the first and second stanzas :

> Jōy cŏmes ănd gōes, hōpe ĕbbs ănd flōws
> Līke thĕ wāve ;
> Chānge dŏth ŭnknīt thĕ trānquĭl strēngth ŏf mēn.
> Lōve lĕnds līfe ă līttlĕ grāce,
> Ă fēw săd smīles ănd thēn
> Bōth ăre lāid ĭn ōne cŏld plāce, —
> Ĭn thĕ grāve.

> Drēams dăwn ănd flȳ, frĭends smīle ănd dīe
> Līke sprĭng flōwers;
> Ŏur vāuntĕd līfe ĭs ōne lŏng fūnĕrāl.
> Mĕn dĭg grāves wĭth bĭttĕr tēars
> Fŏr theĭr dēad hŏpes ; ănd āll,
> Māzed wĭth dōubts ănd sīck wĭth fēars,
> Cōunt thĕ hōurs.
>   "A Question."

What is known as the Rhyme-Royal, a stanza invented by Chaucer, is still another form of the seven line stanza. The first four lines being an ordinary quatrain, with alternate lines rhyming, the fifth line repeating the rhyme of the fourth, and the last two rhymes forming a rhyming couplet. We give a stanza illustrating :

> And thou, sweet Music, dancing's only life,
> The ear's sole happiness, the air's best speech,
> Loadstone of fellowship, charming-rod of strife,
> The soft mind's paradise, the sick man's leech,
> With thine own tongue thou trees and stones can'st teach,
> That, when the air doth dance her finest measure,
> Then art thou born, the gods' and men's sweet pleasure.
> Sir John Davies—"The Dancing of the Air."

THE EIGHT LINE STANZA.

This stanza is used extensively in writing poetry. No form, unless it should be the quatrain, is in such general use. It is capable of great variety. The stanza may be composed of four couplets, or a six line stanza and a couplet, or a seven line stanza with an odd rhyming line.

As our object is not only the familiarizing ourselves with the various forms of the stanza, but also to learn perfectly the art of scansion, become perfectly acquainted with the rhythm and meter of verse, we shall endeavor to select from the best authors the various forms of the eight line stanza, assuring the reader that he cannot be too familiar with the formation of the stanzas, if he has a desire to become perfectly acquainted with the art of versification.

The selections given, while but a single stanza of some excellent poem, will certainly be a help to the reader who will undoubtedly follow up the poem and give to it a thor-

THE CONSTRUCTION OF THE STANZA. 93

ough reading. First, we have selected the fourth stanza of Thomas Hood's "The Song of the Shirt." It is iambic rhythm. The stanza is as follows :

>Ŏh ! mēn wĭth sīstĕrs dēar !
> Ŏh ! mēn wĭth mōthĕrs ănd wīves !
> ĭt ĭs nŏt līnĕn yoŭ're weārĭng ōut,
> Bŭt hūmăn crēatŭres' līves !
> Stītch—stĭtch—stītch !
> Ĭn pōvĕrtȳ, hūngĕr ănd dīrt,
> Sēwĭng ăt ŏnce, wĭth ă dōublĕ thrēad,
> Ă SHRŌUD ăs wēll ăs ă shīrt !

What can be more beautiful than the poem of Edward Coate Pinkney entitled, "A Health?" It is also in iambic rhythm. The poem is composed of five stanzas. We have selected the last, as follows :

> Ĭ fīll thĭs cūp tŏ ōne mădĕ ūp
>   Ŏf lōvelĭnĕss ălōne,
> Ă wōmăn, ŏf hĕr gēntlĕ sēx
>   Thĕ seēmĭng părăgōn.
> Hĕr hēalth ! ănd woūld ŏn ēarth thĕre stoōd
>   Sŏme mōre ŏf sŭch ă frāme,
> Thăt līfe mĭght bē ăll pōĕtrȳ,
>   Ănd wēarĭnĕss ă nāme.

Philip Pendleton Cooke gives us a fine example of an eight line stanza in a little poem entitled, "Florence Vane." It is iambic rhythm. We select the third stanza :

> Thōu wăst lōvelĭĕr thăn thĕ rōsĕs
>   Ĭn thĕir prīme ;
> Thȳ vōice ĕxcēlled thĕ clōsĕs
>   Ŏf sweētĕst rhȳme ;
> Thȳ heārt wăs ă rĭvĕr
>   Wĭthōut ă māin.
> Woŭld Ĭ hăd lōved theĕ nĕvĕr,
>   Flōrĕnce Vāne.

Samuel Daniel has written a neat little poem entitled, "Love is a Sickness." We give the last stanza:

> Lŏve ĭs ă tŏrmĕnt ōf thĕ mīnd,
>   Ă tēmpĕst ēvĕrlāstĭng;
> Ănd Jōve hăth māde ĭt ōf ă kīnd,
>   Nŏt wĕll, nŏr fūll, nŏr făstĭng.
>   Whȳ sō?
> Mŏre wē ĕnjōy ĭt, mōre ĭt dĭes;
> Ĭf nŏt ĕnjōyed, ĭt sīghĭng crĭes
>   Hĕigh-hō.

James Shirley is the author of a fine poem in iambic rhythm entitled, "Death the Leveler." The last stanza is selected:

> Thĕ gārlănds wĭthĕr ōn yoŭr brōw,
>   Thĕn bōast nŏ mōre yoŭr mīghtȳ deĕds;
> Ŭpŏn dĕath's pŭrplĕ āltăr nōw
>   Seĕ whĕre thĕ vĭctŏr-vīctĭm bleĕds;
>   Yoŭr heăds mŭst cōme
>   Tŏ thĕ cōld tômb;
> Ōnlȳ thĕ āctiŏns ōf thĕ jŭst
> Smĕll sweĕt, ănd blŏssŏm īn theĭr dŭst.

Alexander Rogers gives us a beautiful stanza, in a love poem entitled, "Behave Yourself Before Folk." We select the fifth stanza, which is iambic rhythm:

> Yĕ tĕll mĕ thăt mȳ lĭps ăre sweĕt:
> Sĭc tāles, Ĭ doŭbt ăre ā' dĕceĭt;—
> Ăt ōnȳ rāte, ĭt's hărdlȳ meĕt
>   Tŏ prĭe theĭr sweĕts bĕfōre fŏlk.
>   Bĕhāve yoŭrsĕl' bĕfōre fŏlk,—
>   Bĕhāve yoŭrsĕl' bĕfōre fŏlk,—
> Gĭn thăt's thĕ cāse, thĕre's tĭme ănd plăce,
>   Bŭt sŭrelȳ nō bĕfōre fŏlk!

John G. Saxe, the author of so many excellent poems, who delighted the reading public throughout his life, tells us he is growing old in these finished lines entitled, "I'm Growing Old." We give the fourth stanza. It is iambic tetrameter :

> Ĭ feēl ĭt in mў chānğĭng tāste ;
> Ĭ seē ĭt in mў chānğĭng hāir ;
> Ĭ seē ĭt in mў grōwĭng wāist ;
> Ĭ seē ĭt in mў grōwĭng hēir ;
> Ă thōusănd sīgns prŏclāim thĕ trūth,
> Ăs plāin ăs trūth wăs ēvĕr tōld,
> Thăt, ēvĕn in mў vāuntĕd yoūth,
> Ĭ'm grōwĭng ōld ! "

An anonymous poem entitled, "The Grave of Bonaparte " is a beautiful eight line stanza in anapestic rhythm. We have selected the first stanza :

> Ŏn ă lōne-bărrĕn īsle, whĕre thĕ wĭld-roărĭng bĭllŏws
> Ăssāil thĕ stĕrn rōck, ănd thĕ lōud-tĕmpĕsts rāve,
> Thĕ hĕrŏ lĭes stĭll, whĭle thĕ dĕw-drŏppĭng wĭllŏws,
> Lĭke fŏnd-weĕpĭng moŭrnĕrs lĕan ŏvĕr thĕ grāve.
> Thĕ lĭghtnĭngs măy flāsh, ănd thĕ lōud-thŭndĕrs rāttlĕ ;
> Hĕ heĕds nŏt, hĕ hĕars nŏt, hĕ's freē frŏm ăll pāin ;—
> Hĕ sleēps hĭs lăst sleĕp—hĕ hăs foŭght hĭs lăst băttlĕ !
> Nŏ sōund căn ăwāke hĭm tŏ glōrў ăgāin !

"A Doubting Heart," by Adelaide Anne Proctor, is a pathetic poem in iambic rhythm, expressive of sorrow and adversity. We give the third stanza :

> Thĕ sūn hăs hĭd ĭts rāys
> Thĕse mănў dāys ;
> Wĭll drēarў hoŭrs nĕvĕr lĕave thĕ ēarth ?
> Ŏ dōubtĭng hĕart !
> Thĕ stōrmў clōuds ŏn hīgh
> Vēil thĕ săme sŭnnў skў
> Thăt soōn, fŏr sprĭng ĭs nīgh,
> Shăll wāke thĕ sŭmmĕr īntŏ gōldĕn mĭrth.

We present below a stanza of eight lines, the second, fourth, sixth and eighth lines rhyming. It is taken from one of the finest poems in the English language, "Man was Made to Mourn," by Robert Burns. It is iambic rhythm. We give the eleventh stanza :

   Ŏ Dēath ! thĕ poōr măn's dēarĕst friĕnd,
    Thĕ kīndĕst ānd thĕ bēst !
   Wĕlcŏme thĕ hōur mў āgĕd līmbs
    Ăre lāid wĭth theē ăt rēst !
   Thĕ greāt, thĕ wēalthў, fēar thў blōw,
    Frŏm pōmp ănd plēasŭre tŏrn ;
   Bŭt Ō, ă blĕst rĕliĕf tŏ thōse
    Thăt wēarў-lādĕn mōurn !

The "Cavalry Song" by Edmund Clarence Stedman taken from "Alice of Monmouth," is a poem showy and animated, a very neat form of the eight line stanza. It is also iambic rhythm. We give the second stanza :

   Dăsh ōn bĕneāth thĕ smōkĭng dōme :
    Throŭgh lēvĕl lightnĭngs gāllŏp neārĕr !
   Ŏne loōk tŏ Hēavĕn ! Nŏ thōughts ŏf hōme ;
    Thĕ guīdŏns thăt wĕ beār ăre dēarĕr.
     CHĀRGE !
   Clīng ! Clāng ! fŏrwărd āll !
   Hĕaven hĕlp thōse whŏse hōrsĕs fāll ;
    Cŭt lĕft ănd right !

Caroline E. Norton is known the world over by "Bingen on the Rhine." The poem is highly descriptive, tender and sympathetic, touching a keynote that reverberates and swells as the reader cons each line. It is in iambic measure —an iambic heptameter :

His trĕmblĭng vōice grĕw fāint ănd hōarse—hĭs gāsp wăs chĭldĭsh wēak,—
His eȳes pŭt ōn ă dȳĭng loŏk,—hĕ sīghed ănd cēased tŏ spēak ;
Hĭs cōmrăde bĕnt tŏ lĭft hĭm, bŭt thĕ spărk ŏf lĭfe hăd flēd !
Thĕ sōldiĕr ōf thĕ Lĕgiŏn, īn ă fōrĕign lānd—ĭs dēad !
Ănd thĕ sŏft moŏn rōse ŭp slōwlȳ, ănd cālmlȳ shē loŏked dōwn
Ŏn thĕ rēd sănd ŏf thĕ băttlĕ-fiēld wĭth bloŏdȳ cōrsĕs strēwn ;
Yĕs, cālmlȳ ōn thăt drēadfŭl scēne hĕr pāle lĭght seēmed tŏ shīne,
Ăs ĭt shōne ŏn dĭstănt Bīngĕn—făir Bīngĕn ōn thĕ Rhīne !

John G. Saxe is the author of "American Aristocracy," from which we have selected the first stanza. It is iambic rhythm :

Ŏf āll thĕ nōtăblĕ thĭngs ŏn ēarth,
Thĕ queērĕst ōne ĭs prīde ŏf bīrth
Ămōng ŏur "fiĕrce dĕmōcrăcȳ !"
Ă brĭdge ăcrōss ă hŭndrĕd yēars,
Wĭthoŭt ă prŏp tŏ sāve ĭt frŏm snēers,
Nŏt ēvĕn ă coŭplĕ ŏf rōttĕn peērs,—
Ă thĭng ŏf lāughtĕr, fleērs ănd jeērs,
Ĭs Ămĕrĭcăn ărĭstōcrăcȳ !

How true to nature is this poem by Joanna Baillie, entitled "The Heath-Cock." It is iambic rhythm. We select the first stanza :

Goŏd mōrrŏw tō thȳ sāblĕ bēak
Ănd glōssȳ plūmăge dārk ănd sleĕk,
Thȳ crĭmsŏn moōn ănd āzŭre eȳe,
Cŏck ŏf thĕ hēath, sŏ wĭldlȳ shȳ ;
Ĭ seē theĕ slȳlȳ cōwerĭng throŭgh
Thăt wīrȳ wĕb ŏf sĭlvĕrȳ dĕw',
Thăt twĭnklĕs ĭn thĕ mōrnĭng āir,
Līke cāsemĕnts ŏf mȳ lādȳ fāir.

The Italian Heroic meter in which Tasso and Ariosto wrote, known as the "Ottava Rima," is a stanza of eight iambic pentameter lines. The stanza consists of six lines rhyming alternately, and the seventh and eighth a rhyming couplet. Lord Byron wrote "Don Juan" in this stanza, a selection from the first canto, is here given:

> 'Tĭs sweēt tŏ hēar thĕ wātch-dŏg's hōnĕst bārk
> Băy deēp-mŏuthed wēlcŏme ās wĕ drāw nĕar hōme ;
> 'Tĭs sweēt tŏ knōw thĕre īs ăn eȳe wĭll mārk
> Ŏur cōmĭng, ānd loŏk brīghtĕr whēn wĕ cōme ;
> 'Tĭs sweēt tŏ bē ăwākĕned bȳ thĕ lārk,
> Ŏr lūlled bȳ fāllĭng wātĕrs ; sweēt thĕ hūm
> Ŏf beēs, thĕ vōice ŏf gīrls, thĕ sōng ŏf bīrds,
> Thĕ līsp ŏf chīldrĕn, ānd thĕir ēarliĕst wōrds.

THE NINE LINE STANZA.

The nine line stanza gives fine effect to English poetry, and hence may be termed a favorite among writers. It is capable of many combinations. One form, however, of the nine line stanza is fixed, and it is this form that is so justly praised and highly noted. It is the Spenserian, so named from Edmund Spenser, the author of "The Fairy Queen," who composed that beautiful poem in that stanza. While Spenser is generally accredited as being the inventor of the form of the stanza that now bears his name, and is so widely used, he borrowed it from Italian poetry.

Many of the highest types of poetical composition, we find in this stanza—Byron's "Childe Harold," Burns' "Cotter's Saturday Night," Beattie's "Minstrel," Thomson's "Castle of Indolence." The Spenserian stanza consists of nine lines, the first eight being iambic pentameter, the ninth an iambic hexameter. The stanza is composed of

THE CONSTRUCTION OF THE STANZA. 99

two quatrains rhyming in alternate lines. The last line of the first quatrain rhymes with the first line of the second quatrain ; the ninth line rhyming with the eighth.

<blockquote>
Ah ! whō căn tĕll hŏw hārd ĭt ĭs tŏ clīmb
Thĕ steēp whĕre Fāme's prŏud tĕmplĕ shīnes ăfār !
Ah ! whō căn tĕll hŏw mănỹ ă sōul sŭblīme
Hăs fĕlt thĕ inflŭĕnce ōf mălīgnănt stār,
And wāged wĭth Fōrtŭne ān ĕtērnăl wār ;
Chēcked bỹ thĕ scōff ŏf Prīde, bỹ Ĕnvỹ's frōwn,
And Pōvĕrtỹ's ŭncōnquĕrāblĕ bār;
In life's lŏw vāle rĕmōte hăs pīned ălōne,
Thĕn drōpped ĭntō thĕ grāve, ŭnpītiĕd ănd ŭnknōwn !
Beattie—"The Minstrel."
</blockquote>

We have also selected a stanza from a beautiful poem, "Philip, My King," an illustration of childhood. It is by Dinah Maria Mulock Craik. It is iambic rhythm. We select the first stanza :

<blockquote>
Loŏk āt mĕ wĭth thỹ lārge brŏwn eȳes,
   Phīlĭp, mỹ kīng !
Rŏund whōm thĕ ĕnshādŏwĭng pūrplĕ lies
Ŏf bābỹhoŏd's rōyăl dīgnĭtīes.
Lăy ōn mỹ nēck thỹ tīnỹ hānd
   Wĭth Lōve's ĭnvīncĭblĕ scēptĕr lādĕn ;
Ĭ ām thĭne Ĕsthĕr, tō cŏmmānd
   Tĭll thōu shălt fĭnd ă queēn-hăndmāidĕn,
Phīlĭp, mỹ kīng !
</blockquote>

Another fine nine line stanza is from the pen of Sir Charles Sedley, entitled, "Phillis is My Only Joy." It is trochaic rhythm. We give the first stanza ·

Phīllĭs ĭs mў ōnlў jōy,
　　Fāithlĕss ās thĕ wind ŏr sēas;
　Sōmetĭmes cōmĭng, sōmetĭmes cōy,
　　Yĕt shĕ nĕvĕr fāils tŏ plēase.
　　　Ĭf wĭth ă frŏwn
　　　Ĭ ām cāst dōwn,
　　　Phīllĭs, smilĭng
　　　Ănd bĕguilĭng,
　Mākes mĕ hāppĭĕr thān bĕfōre.

Robert Burns touched the hearts of all Scotland, as well as the reading world, when he gave to the public, "The Cotter's Saturday Night." It is a poem that portrays vividly the life of the Scottish peasant, and is so true and accurate as to bring home to all, the scenes it so faithfully depicts. The rhythm is iambic. We select the third stanza:

　　Ăt lēngth hĭs lōnelў cōt ăppēars ĭn view,
　　　Bĕnēath thĕ shēltĕr ŏf ăn āgĕd tree;
　　Thĕ ĕxpēctănt weē thĭngs tōddlĭn', stāchĕr thrōugh
　　　Tŏ meēt thĕir dād, wĭ' flichtĕrĭn' nŏise ăn' gleē.
　　Hĭs weē bĭt īnglĕ blĭnkĭng bōnnĭlў,
　　　Hĭs clēan heārthstōne, hĭs thrīftĭe wifīe's smile,
　　Thĕ līspĭng īnfănt prāttlĭng ōn hĭs kneē,
　　　Dŏes ā' hĭs wēarў cārkĭng cāres bĕguile,
　　Ănd mākes hĭm quite fŏrgēt hĭs lābŏr ănd hĭs tōil.

William Cullen Bryant is the author of this stanza, selected from one of his poems entitled, "June." The measure is iambic. We give the third stanza:

　　　Thĕre throūgh thĕ lōng, lōng sūmmĕr hōurs
　　　　Thĕ gōldĕn light shoŭld līe,
　　　Ănd thĭck yŏung hĕrbs ănd groūps ŏf flōwers
　　　　Stănd ĭn thĕir beautў bў.

> The oriole should build and tell
> His love-tale close beside my cell;
> The idle butterfly
> Should rest him there, and there be heard
> The housewife bee and humming-bird.

Another beautiful poem is selected from the same author. Who hasn't read William Cullen Bryant's "Robert of Lincoln," and admired the charming rhythm? The measure is mixed, the trochaic prevailing. We select the fifth stanza:

> Six white eggs on a bed of hay,
>   Flecked with purple, a pretty sight!
> There as the mother sits all day,
>   Robert is singing with all his might;
>   Bob-o'-link, bob-o'-link,
>   Spink, spank, spink;
> Nice good wife, that never goes out,
> Keeping house while I frolic about.
>   Chee, chee, chee.

From Byron's "Childe Harold," Canto III, we select the following stanza from his description of "Waterloo." No grander poem of its kind was ever written. It is written in Spenserian stanza, which is always iambic rhythm. The first eight lines are iambic pentameter, the ninth line being an hexameter·

> Ah! then and there was hurrying to and fro,
> And gathering tears, and tremblings of distress,
> And cheeks all pale which but an hour ago
> Blushed at the praise of their own loveliness;
> And there were sudden partings, such as press
> The life from out young hearts, and choking sighs
> Which ne'er might be repeated; who would guess
> If evermore should meet those mutual eyes
> Since upon night so sweet such awful morn could rise!

How beautiful are the "Lines" by Thomas Campbell, "On leaving a Scene in Bavaria." We select the seventh stanza. It is iambic rhythm :

> Yĕs ! Ĭ hăve lōved thў wīld ăbŏde,
>   Ŭnknōwn, ŭnplōughed, ŭntrŏddĕn shōre ;
> Whĕre scārce thĕ woōdmăn fĭnds ă rōad,
>   Ănd scārce thĕ fĭshĕr plĭes ăn ōar ;
>   Fŏr măn's nĕglĕct Ĭ lŏve theĕ mōre ;
> Thăt ārt nŏr ăvărĭce Ĭntrŭde
>   Tŏ tāme thў tōrrĕnt's thūndĕr-shŏck,
>   Ŏr prūne thў vīntăge ŏf thĕ rŏck
> Măgnĭfĭcĕntlў rŭde.

A fine variation of the Spenserian stanza is found in the following from Percy Bysshe Shelley's lines entitled, "The Sun is Warm, the Sky is Clear." It is iambic rhythm. We select the third stanza :

> Ălās ! Ĭ hăve nŏr hōpe nŏr hēalth,
> Nŏr pēace wĭthĭn, nŏr cālm ărōund,
> Nŏr thăt Cŏntĕnt sŭrpăssĭng wēalth
> Thĕ sāge ĭn mĕdĭtātĭŏn fōund,
> Ănd wālked wĭth inwărd glōrў crōwned,—
> Nŏr fāme, nŏr pōwĕr, nŏr lŏve, nŏr lēisŭre,
> Ŏthĕrs Ĭ seĕ whŏm thĕse sŭrrōund ;
> Smīlĭng thĕy līve, ănd cāll lĭfe plĕasŭre ;
> Tŏ mē thăt cŭp hăs beĕn dĕalt ĭn ănŏthĕr mēasŭre.

THE TEN LINE STANZA.

This form of the stanza is widely used. It may be employed in many combinations. Five couplets make a beautiful ten line stanza. Three triplets and a single line may be used. The quatrain doubled and the couplet combined form the stanza. It can be formed of two five line stanzas ;

of a six line and a quatrain ; of a seven line and a triplet. We select a stanza from Shakespeare, entitled, "Blow, Blow, Thou Winter Wind," from "As You Like It," act ii, scene 7. It is iambic rhythm. We select the first stanza :

> Blŏw, blŏw, thŏu wīntĕr wind,
> Thŏu ārt nŏt sŏ ŭnkind
> Ăs măn's ĭngrătĭtūde ;
> Thў tooth ĭs nōt sŏ keēn,
> Bĕcāuse thŏu ārt nŏt seēn,
> Ălthōugh thў brēath bĕ rūde.
> Hĕigh-hō! sĭng hĕigh-hō! ŭntō thĕ greēn hŏllў ;
> Mŏst friĕndshĭp ĭs fēignĭng, mŏst lŏvĭng mĕre fŏllў;
> Thĕn hĕigh-hō, thĕ hŏllў !
> Thĭs life ĭs mŏst jŏllў !

Our next selection is a poem from John Keats. It is one of the best of that celebrated writer's productions. It is entitled, "Ode to a Nightingale." We select the seventh stanza :

> Thŏu wāst nŏt bōrn fŏr dēath, ĭmmōrtăl Bird!
> Nŏ hŭngrў gĕnĕrātĭŏns trēad theĕ dōwn ;
> Thĕ vōice Ĭ hĕar thĭs pāssĭng night wăs hēard
> Ĭn āncĭĕnt dāys bў ēmpĕrŏr ănd clōwn ;
> Pĕrhăps thĕ sĕlf-săme sōng thăt fōund ă pāth
> Thrŏugh thĕ săd heārt ŏf Rūth, whĕn sĭck fŏr hōme,
> Shĕ stoōd ĭn tēars ămĭd thĕ ālĭĕn cōrn ;
> Thĕ săme thăt ŏft-tĭmes hăth
> Chărmed măgĭc câsemĕnts ōpenĭng ōn thĕ fōam
> Ŏf pĕrĭlŏus sēas, ĭn fāerў lănds fŏrlōrn.

Charles Mackay has written an excellent poem which has been oft quoted, entitled, "Tell Me, Ye Winged Winds." It is iambic measure. We select the first stanza :

Tell me, ye winged winds,
　That round my pathway roar,
Do ye not know some spot
　Where mortals weep no more?
Some lone and pleasant dell,
　Some valley in the west,
Where free from toil and pain,
　The weary soul may rest?
The loud wind dwindled to a whisper low,
And sighed for pity as it answered, "No."

Milton's "May Morning" is another charming ten line stanza. It is also iambic rhythm, as follows:

Now the bright morning star, day's harbinger,
Comes dancing from the east, and leads with her
The flowery May, who from her green lap throws
The yellow cowslip and the pale primrose.
Hail, bounteous May! that doth inspire
Mirth and youth and warm desire;
Woods and groves are of thy dressing,
Hill and dale doth boast thy blessing,
Thus we salute thee with our early song,
And welcome thee, and wish thee long.

"The Owl," a poem by Bryan W. Proctor, furnishes another excellent ten line stanza, in a mixed anapestic and iambic rhythm, the iambic prevailing. We select the first stanza:

In the hollow tree, in the old gray tower,
　The spectral owl doth dwell;
Dull, hated, despised, in the sunshine hour,
　But at dusk he's abroad and well!
Not a bird of the forest e'er mates with him;
　All mock him outright by day;
But at night, when the woods grow still and dim,
　The boldest will shrink away!
O, when the night falls, and roosts the fowl,
Then, then, is the reign of the horned owl!

A rare old poem is "The Ivy Green," and its author is no less a personage than Charles Dickens. It is mixed anapestic and iambic rhythm, the iambic foot prevailing :

> Ŏ, ă dāintў plānt ĭs thĕ ĭvў greēn,
> Thăt creēpĕth ŏ'er rūĭns ōld !
> Ŏf right chŏice foōd ăre hĭs meāls, Ĭ weēn,
> Ĭn hĭs cēll sŏ lōne ănd cōld.
> Thĕ wālls mŭst bĕ crūmblĕd, thĕ stōnes dĕcāyed,
> Tŏ pleāsŭre hĭs dāintў whĭm ;
> Ănd thĕ mōuldĕrĭng dūst thăt yēars hăve māde,
> Ĭs ă mĕrrў meāl fŏr hīm.
> Creēpĭng whēre nŏ līfe ĭs seēn,
> Ă rāre ŏld plānt ĭs thĕ ĭvў greēn.

No less loved by everyone is Mrs. S. J. Hale. All school boys have read " It Snows," written by her. The poem is but a glimpse of the actual reality of the delight of the youth at a sight of snow and the rare pleasure of the winter sports. It is anapestic rhythm. We give the first stanza :

> "Ĭt snōws !" crĭes thĕ Schoōl-bŏy, "Hŭrrāh !" ănd hĭs shōut
> Ĭs rĭngĭng throŭgh pārlŏr ănd hāll,
> Whĭle swift ăs thĕ wĭng ŏf ă swāllŏw, hĕ's ōut,
> Ănd hĭs plāymătes hăve ānswĕred hĭs cāll ;
> Ĭt mākes thĕ heărt leāp bŭt tŏ wĭtnĕss thĕir jōy ;
> Prŏud weālth hăs nŏ pleāsŭre, Ĭ trōw,
> Līke thĕ rāptŭre thăt thrŏbs ĭn thĕ pūlse ŏf thĕ bōy,
> Ăs hĕ gāthĕrs hĭs treāsŭres ŏf snōw;
> Thĕn lāy nŏt thĕ trăppĭngs ŏf gŏld ŏn thĭne hĕirs,
> Whĭle heālth, ănd thĕ rĭchĕs ŏf nātŭre, ăre thĕirs.

Harrison Weir is the author of "Christmas in the Woods." It is a six line stanza and a quatrain combined. It is anapestic rhythm. We select the first stanza :

From ūndĕr thĕ bōughs ĭn thĕ snów-clăd woōd
Thĕ mērle ănd thĕ māvĭs ăre peēpĭng,
Ălīke sĕcūre frŏm thĕ wind ănd thĕ floōd,
Yĕt ă sīlĕnt Chrĭstmăs keēpĭng.
Stĭll hăppȳ ăre thĕy,
Ănd thĕir loōks ăre gāy,
Ănd thĕy frĭsk ĭt frŏm bōugh tŏ bōugh ;
Sĭnce bĕrrĭes brĭght rēd
Hăng ōvĕr thĕir hēad,
Ă rĭght goōdlȳ fēast, Ĭ trōw.

"Pack Clouds Away," a poem by Thomas Heywood, in iambic rhythm, is a neat, pretty, dainty poem of love. We select the second stanza:

Wāke frŏm thȳ nĕst, rōbĭn-rĕdbrēast !
Sĭng, bĭrds, ĭn ēverȳ fūrrŏw ;
Ănd frŏm ĕach bĭll lĕt mūsĭc shrĭll
Gĭve mȳ fāir lŏve goŏd-mŏrrŏw !
Blăckbĭrd ănd thrŭsh, ĭn ēverȳ būsh,
Stăre, lĭnnĕt, ānd cŏck-spārrŏw,
Yoŭ prĕttȳ ēlves, ămŏng yoŭrsĕlves,
Sĭng mȳ fāir lŏve goŏd-mōrrŏw.
Tŏ gīve mȳ lŏve goŏd-mōrrŏw,
Sĭng, bĭrds, ĭn ēverȳ fūrrŏw.

Another fine ten line poem is by Thomas Gray. It is entitled, "Ode on a Distant Prospect of Eaton College." It is iambic rhythm. We give the last stanza :

Tŏ ĕach hĭs sŭffĕrĭngs : ạll ăre mĕn,
Cŏndĕmned ălĭke tŏ grōan ;
Thĕ tĕndĕr fŏr ănōthĕr's pāin,
Thĕ ŭnfeēlĭng fŏr hĭs ōwn.
Yĕt, ăh ! whȳ shoŭld thĕy knŏw thĕir făte,
Sĭnce sŏrrŏw nĕvĕr cōmes toŏ lāte,
Ănd hăppĭnĕss toŏ swĭftlȳ flīes?
Thŏught woŭld dĕstrōy thĕir părădīse.
Nŏ mōre ; whĕre ĭgnŏrănce ĭs blĭss,
'Tĭs fŏllȳ tō bĕ wīse.

THE SONNET.

One of the finest forms of the stanza in our English poetry is the Sonnet. Borrowed by the Italians from the early Provencial poets, it was assiduously cultivated by them, and brought to a high state of perfection. Many beautiful sonnets are found in the writings of Petrarch, Ariosto, Guido, and Dante. The Sonnet is a poetical piece containing fourteen iambic pentameter lines. It is generally lyrical in its nature. In fact it is the primordial form of modern English lyric poetry. It deals with *one* idea of a grave nature, presented under various aspects. The sonnet was introduced into English poetry in the early part of the sixteenth century by the Earl of Surrey and Sir Thomas Wyatt. The Italian sonnet then introduced is termed the correct and strict form. After the introduction of the sonnet into the English from the Italians, another form of the fourteen line stanza was used by English poets, in which the succession of rhymes was different in order from that authorized by the Italian form. To distinguish the two forms, the Italian was termed the regular, while all the others were called irregular, and are governed by separate and distinct rules or laws to be used in the formation of the different kinds of sonnets.

The sonnet in its structure is more elaborate than any form of the stanza. The Italian is always a positive and fixed form in some respects. It consists of two divisions. A major and a minor portion. The major portion consists of eight lines, called the octave ; the minor portion consists of six lines, called the sestette. The octave is composed of two quatrains. The quatrains are similar in form and construction. The first and fourth lines of each quatrain rhyme with each other, and the second and third lines rhyme. The octave, however, has but two rhymes, for the first and fourth lines of the first quatrain rhyme with the first and fourth lines of the second quatrain ; the same is true of the second and third lines of both quatrains. The octave is joined to the sestette by a close grammatical structure. The octave is a fixed form.

In the construction of the sestette of the Italian form of the sonnet, the first and fourth, the second and fifth, the third and sixth lines rhyme ; or, the first, third and fifth rhyme with the second, fourth and sixth of the sestette. All other forms of the sonnet are not termed pure. Our best poets have used the sonnet to pour forth their most sublime thoughts expressive of love, friendship, praise, adoration, grief and sorrow. It seems peculiarly adopted as a form to express the most intense feelings of the human mind, and to enable the writer to give vent to the finer feelings and thoughts.

A beautiful sonnet by Richard Watson Gilder expresses in admirable language the sonnet :

WHAT IS A SONNET?

MAJOR PORTION—FIRST QUATRAIN.

Whăt is ă sŏnnĕt ? 'Tis ă pĕarlў shĕll
 Thăt mūrmŭrs ōf thĕ făr-ŏff mūrmŭrĭng sĕa ;
 Ă prēciŏŭs jĕwĕl cārved mŏst cūrĭŏŭslў ;
 Ĭt is ă lĭttlĕ pīctŭre pāintĕd wĕll.

MAJOR PORTION—SECOND QUATRAIN.

Whăt is ă sŏnnĕt ? 'Tis thĕ tĕar thăt fĕll
 Frŏm ā greăt pŏĕt's hĭddĕn ēctăsў ;
 Ă twō-ĕdged swŏrd, ă stār, ă sŏng—ăh mē !
 Sŏmetĭmes ă hĕavў-tŏllĭng fūnerăl bĕll.

THE CONSTRUCTION OF THE STANZA. 109

MINOR PORTION.

This wās thĕ flāme thăt shoŏk wĭth Dāntĕ's brēath,
Thĕ sōlĕmn ōrgăn whĕreōn Mīltŏn plāyed,
And thē clĕar glāss whĕre Shākespĕare's shādŏw fălls ;
A sēa thĭs ĭs—bĕwāre, whŏ vĕntŭrēth !
Fŏr līke ă fiôrd thĕ nārrŏw floōr ĭs lāid
Deĕp ās mĭd-ōceăn tō sheĕr mōuntăin wălls.

John Milton thus describes his own blindness in a sonnet of the regular model :

ON HIS BLINDNESS.

To Cyriack Skinner.

OCTAVE.

Whĕn I cŏnsīdĕr hōw mў līght ĭs spĕnt
Ĕre hālf mў dāys, ĭn thĭs dărk wōrld ănd wīde,
And thāt ŏne tălĕnt, whĭch ĭs dēath tŏ hīde,
Lŏdged wĭth mĕ ūselĕss, thōugh mў sōul mŏre bĕnt

Tŏ sērve thĕrewĭth mў Mākĕr, ānd prĕsĕnt
Mў trūe ăccōunt, lĕst Hē, rĕtūrnĭng, chīde ;
"Dŏth Gŏd ĕxāct dăy-lābŏr, līght dĕnīed ?"
I fōndlў āsk. Bŭt Pātiĕnce, tō prĕvĕnt

SESTETTE.

Thăt mūrmŭr soŏn rĕplīes, "Gŏd dōth nŏt neēd
Ĕithĕr măn's wŏrk, ŏr hĭs ŏwn gĭfts ; whŏ bĕst
Bĕar hĭs mĭld yŏke, thĕy sērve hĭm bĕst. Hĭs stāte
Ĭs kĭnglў ; thōusănds ăt hĭs bĭddĭng speĕd,
And pōst ŏ'er lănd ănd ōceăn wĭthōut rĕst ;
Thĕy ālsŏ sērve whŏ ōnlў stānd ănd wāit !"

Longfellow has written many exquisitely charming sonnets. None better than, "A Summer Day by the Sea:"

> Thĕ sūn ĭs sēt; ănd ĭn hĭs lātĕst bēams
> Yŏn lĭttlĕ clōud ŏf āshĕn grāy ănd gōld,
> Slōwlȳ ŭpŏn thĕ āmbĕr āir ŭnrōlled,
> Thĕ fāllĭng māntlĕ ŏf thĕ Prŏphĕt seēms.
> Frŏm thē dĭm hēadlănds mānȳ ă līghthōuse glēams,
> Thĕ streēt-lămps ŏf thĕ ōceăn; ănd bĕhōld,
> Ŏ'erhēad thĕ bănnĕrs ŏf thĕ night ŭnfōld;
> Thĕ dāy hăth pāssed ĭntō thĕ lānd ŏf drēams.
> Ŏ sūmmĕr dāy, bĕsīde thĕ jōyŏŭs sēa!
> Ŏ sūmmĕr dāy, sŏ wŏndĕrfūl ănd whīte,
> Sŏ fūll ŏf glādnĕss ānd sŏ fūll ŏf pāin!
> Fŏrēvĕr ānd fŏrēvĕr shălt thŏu bē
> Tŏ sōme thĕ grăvestŏne ŏf ă dĕad dĕlight,
> Tŏ sōme thĕ lāndmărk ŏf ă nēw dŏmāin.

The following by Ella Wheeler Wilcox is a good example of the sonnet:

> Mĕthĭnks ōfttĭmes mȳ heărt ĭs līke sŏme beē,
> Thăt gōes fŏrth throŭgh thĕ sūmmĕr dăy ănd sīngs,
> Ănd găthĕrs hōnĕy frŏm ăll grōwĭng thĭngs
> Ĭn gārdĕn plŏt, ŏr ōn thĕ clōvĕr lēaf.
> Whĕn thĕ lŏng āftĕrnoōn grōws lāte, ănd shē
> Woŭld seēk hĕr hīve, shĕ cānnŏt lĭft hĕr wĭngs,
> Sŏ hĕavĭlȳ thĕ toō sweĕt bŭrdĕn clĭngs,
> Frŏm whĭch shĕ would nŏt, ănd yĕt would, flȳ freē.
> Sŏ with mȳ fūll fŏnd heărt; fŏr whĕn ĭt trīes
> Tŏ lĭft ĭtsĕlf tŏ peāce-crŏwned hĕights ăbōve
> Thĕ cŏmmŏn wāy whĕre cŏuntlĕss feĕt hăve trŏd,
> Lŏ! thĕn, thĭs bŭrdĕn ŏf dĕar hūmăn tīes,
> Thĭs grōwĭng wēight ŏf prĕciŏus ēarthlȳ lōve,
> Bĭnds dōwn thĕ spĭrĭt thăt would sōar tŏ Gŏd.

The regular model is varied in the sestette. Below we give forms of these variations. "Echo and Silence," is an excellent sonnet:

> In eddying course, when leaves began to fly,
> And Autumn in her lap the store to strew,
> As 'mid wild scenes I chanced the Muse to woo,
> Through glens untrod, and woods that frowned on high,
> Two sleeping nymphs with wondering mute I spy!
> And, lo, she's gone—in robe of dark-green hue,
> 'Twas Echo from her sister Silence flew,
> For quick the hunter's horn resounded to the sky!
> In shade affrighted Silence melts away.
> Not so her sister. Hark! for onward still,
> With far-heard step, she takes her listening way,
> Bounding from rock to rock, and hill to hill.
> Ah, mark the merry maid in mockful play
> With thousand mimic tones the laughing forest fill!
> Samuel Egerton Brydges.

Another elegant sonnet is:

ON THE GRASSHOPPER AND CRICKET.

> The poetry of earth is never dead:
> When all the birds are faint with the hot sun,
> And hide in cooling trees, a voice will run
> From hedge to hedge about the new-mown mead,
> That is the grasshopper's—he takes the lead
> In summer luxury,—he has never done
> With his delights; for, when tired out with fun,
> He rests at ease beneath some pleasant weed.
> The poetry of earth is ceasing never:
> On a lone winter evening when the frost
> Has wrought a silence, from the stove there shrills
> The cricket's song, in warmth increasing ever,
> And seems, to one in drowsiness half lost,
> The grasshopper's among some grassy hills.
> John Keats.

William Shakespeare deigned to trangress the laws of the Italian model and mold one of his own. Can it not be said what was fit for Shakespeare's use is all sufficient for any person? These sonnets, one hundred fifty-four in number, are wonderful in composition and merit. They are devoted to friendship and love. Their form consists of three quatrains and a couplet. Many of the best poets have written sonnets on the Shakesperian model:

THE APPROACH OF AGE.

When I do count the clock that tells the time,
   And see the brave day sunk in hideous night;
When I behold the violet past prime,
   And sable curls all silvered o'er with white;
When lofty trees I see barren of leaves,
   Which erst from heat did canopy the herd,
And summer's green all girded up in sheaves,
   Borne on the bier with white and bristly beard;
Then of thy beauty do I question make,
   That thou among the wastes of time must go,
Since sweets and beauties do themselves forsake,
   And die as fast as they see others grow;
And nothing 'gainst Time's scythe can make defence,
Save breed, to brave him when he takes thee hence.
William Shakespeare.

Mr. Frederick Locker-Lampson, an English poet, has written a sonnet fashioned after the Shakesperian model. It is entitled, "Love, Time and Death:"

Ah me, dread friends of mine—Love, Time and Death!
   Sweet Love, who came to me on sheeny wing,
And gave her to my arms—her lips, her breath,
   And all her golden ringlets clustering;
And Time, who gathers in the flying years,
   He gave me all—but where is all he gave?
He took my Love and left me barren tears;
   Weary and lone, I follow to the grave.

THE CONSTRUCTION OF THE STANZA. 113

Thĕre Dēath wĭll ēnd thĭs vīsiŏn hālf dĭvine,
Wăn Dēath, whŏ wāits ĭn shădŏw ēvĕrmōre,
Ănd sĭlĕnt ēre hĕ gāve thĕ sūddĕn sign ;
Ŏh, gĕntly̆ lēad mĕ throūgh thy̆ nārrŏw doōr,
Thŏu gĕntlĕ Dēath, thŏu trūstĭĕst friĕnd ŏf mīne.
Ăh mē, fŏr Lōve wĭll Dēath my̆ Lōve rĕstōre?

A fine sonnet after the same model is by Thomas Hood:

FALSE POETS AND TRUE.

Loŏk hōw thĕ lārk sŏars ūpwărd ānd ĭs gōne,
Tūrnĭng ă spĭrĭt ās hĕ nēars thĕ sky̆!
Hĭs vōice ĭs hēard, bŭt bōdy̆ thēre ĭs nōne
Tŏ fĭx thĕ vāgue ĕxcūrsiŏns ŏf thĕ eȳe.
Sŏ pōĕts' sōngs ăre wĭth ŭs, thŏugh thĕy dīe
Ŏbscūred ănd hĭd by̆ dēath's ŏblĭviŏŭs shrōud,
Ănd ēarth ĭnhērĭts thē rĭch mĕlŏdy̆,
Līke rāinĭng mūsĭc frōm thĕ mōrnĭng clōud.
Yĕt, fēw thĕre bē whŏ pīpe sŏ sweēt ănd loūd,
Thĕir vōicĕs rēach ŭs throūgh thĕ lāpse ŏf spāce ;
Thĕ nōisy̆ dāy ĭs dēafĕned by̆ ă crōwd
Ŏf ūndĭstinguĭshed bīrds, ă twĭttering rāce ;
Bŭt ōnly̆ lārk ănd nīghtĭngāle fŏrlōrn
Fĭll ūp thĕ sĭlĕncēs ŏf nīght ănd mōrn.

A granddaughter of the famous orator, Richard Brinsley Sheridan, herself famous as a poetess of extraordinary merit, pays this compliment to her loved treasures, in a sonnet:

TO MY BOOKS.

Sĭlĕnt cŏmpāniŏns ŏf thĕ lōnely̆ hōur,
Friĕnds whŏ căn nĕvĕr āltĕr ōr fŏrsāke.
Whŏ fŏr ĭncōnstănt rōvĭng hăve nŏ pōwer,
Ănd āll nĕglēct, pĕrfōrce, mŭst cālmly̆ tāke,—
Lĕt mē rĕtūrn tŏ yoū ; thĭs tūrmŏil ēndĭng
Whĭch wōrldly̆ cāres hăve īn my̆ spĭrĭt wrōught.
Ănd, ō'er yoŭr ōld fămĭliăr pāgĕs bēndĭng,
Rĕfrēsh my̆ mīnd wĭth māny ă trānquĭll thōught,

Till happy meeting there, from time to time,
　Fancies, the audible echo of my own,
'T will be like hearing in a foreign clime
　My native language spoke in friendly tone,
And with a sort of welcome I shall dwell
On these, my unripe musings, told so well.

Caroline Elizabeth Norton.

William Lisle Bowles furnishes a fine sonnet on the river Rhine. Mr. Bowles had great ability as a sonneteer:

THE RIVER RHINE.

'Twas morn, and beauteous on the mountain's brow
　[Hung with the beamy clusters of the vine]
　Streamed the blue light, when on the sparkling Rhine
We bounded, and the white waves round the prow
In murmurs parted. Varying as we go,
　Lo, the woods open, and the rocks retire,
　Some convent's ancient walls or glistening spire
'Mid the bright landscape's track unfolding slow.
Here dark, with furrowed aspect, like despair,
　Frowns the bleak cliff; there on the woodland's side
　The shadowy sunshine pours its streaming tide;
While Hope, enchanted with the scene so fair,
　Would wish to linger many a summer's day,
　Nor heed how fast the prospect winds away.

Matthew Arnold's sonnet of "Quiet Work" is a lesson in itself. It is not strictly a sonnet of the regular type, the difference, however, is very slight. The second and third lines of the first and second quatrains do not rhyme together, making more than two rhymes in the octave. Arnold's sonnets, twenty-three in number, are all first-class, but none of them strictly pure:

QUIET WORK.

Ŏne lĕssŏn, Nātūre, lĕt mĕ lēarn ŏf theē,
　Ŏne lĕssŏn whīch ĭn ēverў̆ wīnd ĭs blōwn,
　Ŏne lĕssŏn ŏf twŏ dūtĭes kĕpt ăt ōne
Thrŏŭgh thē lŏud wŏrld prŏclāim theĭr ēnmĭtў̆,
Ŏf tōil ŭnsĕvĕred frŏm trănquīlĭtў̆ ;
　Ŏf lăbŏr thăt ĭn lāstĭng frūit ŏutgrōws
　Făr nōisĭĕr schēmes, ăccōmplĭshed ĭn rĕpōse,
Toŏ greāt fŏr hāstĕ, toŏ hīgh fŏr rĭvălrў̆.
Yĕs, whīle ŏn ēarth ă̆ thōusănd dīscŏrds ring,
　Măn's sēnselĕss ūprŏar mīnglĭng wĭth hĭs tōil,
　Stĭll dŏ thў̆ quīĕt mīnĭstĕrs mŏve ōn,
Theĭr glōrĭoŭs tāsks ĭn sīlĕnce pĕrfĕctĭng ;
　Stīll wŏrkĭng, blāmĭng stĭll ŏur vāin tŭrmōil,
　Lābŏrĕrs thăt shāll nŏt fāil, whĕn măn ĭs gōne.

One of the finest sonnets in our language is entitled :

NIGHT.

Mў̆stērĭoŭs Night ! whĕn ōur fĭrst pārĕnt knēw
　Theĕ frŏm rĕpōrt dĭvīne, ănd heārd thў̆ nāme,
　Dĭd hē nŏt trĕmblĕ fŏr thĭs lŏvelў̆ frāme,—
Thĭs glōrĭoŭs cānŏpў̆ ŏf light ănd blūe ?
Yĕt 'neath ă̆ cūrtăin ŏf trănslūcĕnt dĕw,
　Băthed ĭn thĕ rāys ŏf thē greăt sĕttĭng flāme,
　Hĕspĕrŭs, wĭth thĕ hōst ŏf heāvĕn cāme,
Ănd lō ! crĕātĭon wīdĕned ĭn măn's vīew.
Whŏ coūld hăve thought sŭch dārknĕss lăy cŏncēaled
　Wĭthĭn thў̆ bēams, Ŏ Sūn ! ŏr whō coŭld fīnd,
Whĭlst flў̆ ănd lĕaf ănd īnsĕct stoōd rĕvēaled,
　Thăt tŏ sŭch coūntlĕss ōrbs thŏu mād'st ŭs blīnd !
Whў̆ dŏ wĕ thĕn shŭn dĕath wĭth ănxioŭs strīfe !
Ĭf light căn thŭs dĕcēive, whĕrefŏre nŏt līfe ?

Joseph Blanco White.

THE BALLADE.

The French ballade is radically different from the English ballad. Of late years it has come into general use, and it is now fairly well known to lovers of the poetic art. The ballade was attempted in England as early as the sonnet, more than three-hundred years ago, but it did not succeed. The ballade consists of three stanzas and a half stanza, clept an envoy, addressed to some prince or power, title or theme. The arrangement of the first stanza is repeated in the others; and the burden or refrain concludes all three stanzas, as well as the envoy. Eight line stanzas using three rhymes are generally used; but ten line stanzas using four rhymes are of frequent occurrence, and permissible. There is also a variety of the ballade known as the double ballade. It is simply a ballade of six stanzas of either eight or ten lines, repeating the arrangement of the first stanza, and the ballade may conclude with or without an envoy, as the writer may desire.

Then we have still another form of the ballade. It is a ballade with a double refrain. The stanzas are always of but eight lines; and the fourth and eighth lines of the first stanza are repeated in the fourth and eighth lines of the other stanzas, while the envoy consists of two couplets, the first refrain occurring in the second line, and the second refrain occurring in the fourth line of the envoy.

BALLADE OF BLUE CHINA.

Thĕre's ă jōy wĭthŏut cănkĕr ŏr cărk,
Thĕre's ă plĕasŭre ĕtĕrnăllў nĕw,
'Tĭs tŏ glōte ŏn thĕ glāze ănd thĕ mārk
Ŏf chĭnă thăt's āncĭĕnt ănd blūe;

Ŭnchĭpped ăll thĕ cēntŭrĭes throūgh
   Ĭt hăs pāssed, sīnce thĕ chīme ŏf ĭt rāng,
Ănd thĕy făshiŏned ĭt, fīgŭre ănd hūe,
   Ĭn thĕ rēign ŏf thĕ Ĕmpĕrŏr Hwāng.

Thĕse drāgŏns (thĕir tāils, yoŭ rĕmārk,
   Ĭntŏ būnchĕs ŏf gīllўflŏwers grēw)—
Whĕn Nōăh cămme ōut ŏf thĕ ārk,
   Dĭd thēse līe ĭn wāit fŏr hĭs crēw?
Thĕy snōrtĕd, thĕy snăpped, ănd thĕy slēw,
   Thĕy wĕre mīghtў ŏf fīn ănd ŏf fāng,
Ănd thĕir pōrtrăits Cĕlēstĭăls drēw
   Ĭn thĕ rēign ŏf thĕ Ĕmpĕrŏr Hwāng.

Hĕre's ă pōt wĭth ă cōt ĭn ă pārk,
   Ĭn ă pārk whĕre thĕ pēach-blŏssŏms blēw,
Whĕre thĕ lōvĕrs ĕlōped ĭn thĕ dārk,
   Lĭved, dīed, ănd wĕre chānged ĭntŏ twō
Brĭght bīrds thăt ĕtĕrnăllў flēw
   Throŭgh thĕ bōughs ŏf thĕ Māy, ăs thĕy sāng ;
'Tĭs ă tāle wăs ŭndōubtĕdlў trūe
   Ĭn thĕ rēign ŏf thĕ Ĕmpĕrŏr Hwāng.

ENVOY.

Cŏme, snārl ăt mў ēcstăsĭes, dō,
   Kĭnd crĭtĭc, yoŭr "tŏngue hăs ă tāng "
Bŭt—ă sāge nĕvĕr heēdĕd ă shrēw
   Ĭn thĕ rēign ŏf thĕ Ĕmpĕrŏr Hwāng.
                                Andrew Lang.

THE BALLADE OF PROSE AND RHYME.

(BALLADE A DOUBLE REFRAIN).

Whĕn thĕ wāys ăre hĕavў wĭth mīre ănd rūt,
   Ĭn Nŏvĕmbĕr fōgs, ĭn Dĕcĕmbĕr snōws,
Whĕn thĕ Nōrth Wĭnd hōwls ănd thĕ doōrs ăre shŭt
   Thĕre ĭs plăce ănd ĕnoŭgh fŏr thĕ pāins ŏf prōse;

But whenever a scent from the whitethorn blows,
  And the jasmine-stars at the casement climb,
And a Rosalind-face at the lattice shows,
    Then hey!—for the ripple of laughing rhyme!

When the brain gets dry as an empty nut,
  When the reason stands on its squarest toes,
When the mind (like a beard) has a "formal cut,"—
    There is place and enough for the pains of prose;
But whenever the May-blood stirs and glows,
  And the young year draws to the "golden prime,"
And Sir Romeo sticks in his ear a rose,—
    Then hey!—for the ripple of laughing rhyme!

In a theme where the thoughts have a pedant strut,
  In a changing quarrel of "Ayes" and "Noes,"
In a starched procession of "If" and "But,"—
    There is place and enough for the pains of prose;
But whenever a soft glance softer grows
  And the light hours dance to the trysting-time,
And the secret is told that "no one knows,"—
    Then hey! for the ripple of laughing rhyme!

ENVOY.

In the work-a-day world,—for its needs and woes,
    There is place and enough for the pains of prose;
But whenever the May-bells clash and chime,
    Then hey! for the ripple of laughing rhyme!
                                    Austin Dobson.

THE CHANT ROYAL.

Another variation of the ballade is known as the Chant Royal. It is a ballade of five stanzas of eleven lines, with an envoy of five lines. It is not, however, a practical form of verse and is difficult of construction. We give below a very excellent Chant Royal by Mr. Austin Dobson:

THE CONSTRUCTION OF THE STANZA.

THE DANCE OF DEATH.
(CHANT ROYAL, AFTER HOLBEIN).

*"Contra vim Mortis
Non est Medicamen in hortis."*

Hĕ is thĕ dēspŏts' Dēspŏt. Āll mŭst bīde,
　Lātĕr ŏr soōn, thĕ mēssăge ŏf hĭs might ;
Prīncĕs ănd pōtĕntātes thĕir hēads mŭst hīde,
　Tŏuched bў thĕ āwfŭl sĭgĭl ŏf hĭs rīght ;
Bĕsīde thĕ Kaisĕr hĕ ăt ēve dŏth wāit
Ănd pōurs ă pōtiŏn ĭn hĭs cūp ŏf stāte ;
Thĕ stātelў Queēn hĭs bĭddĭng mūst ŏbēy,
Nŏ keēn-eўed Cārdĭnāl shăll hĭm ăffrāy ;
　Ănd tō thĕ Dāme thăt wāntŏneth hĕ sāith—
"Lĕt bē, Sweĕtheārt, tŏ jŭnkĕt ānd tŏ plāy."
　Thĕre īs nŏ king mŏre tĕrrĭblē thăn Dēath.

Thĕ lūstў Lōrd, rĕjōicĭng īn hĭs prīde,
　Hĕ drāwĕth dōwn ; bĕfōre thĕ ārmĕd Knīght
Wĭth jīnglĭng brīdăl-rēin hĕ stĭll dŏth rīde ;
　Hĕ crōssĕth thĕ strōng Cāptăin īn thĕ fīght ;
Hĕ bēckŏns thĕ grāve Ēldĕr frōm dĕbāte ;
Hĕ hāils thĕ Ābbŏt bў hĭs shāvĕn pāte,
Nŏr fōr thĕ Ābbĕss' wāilĭng wĭll dĕlāy ;
Nŏ brāwlĭng Mĕndĭcănt shăll sāy hĭm nāy ;
　Ĕ'en tō thĕ pўx thĕ Priĕst hĕ fŏllŏwĕth,
Nŏr căn thĕ Leĕch hĭs chīllĭng fīngĕr stāy.
　Thĕre īs nŏ king mŏre tĕrrĭblē thăn Dēath.

Āll things mŭst bōw tŏ hĭm. Ănd wōe bĕtīde
　Thĕ Wīne-bĭbbĕr—thĕ Rōystĕrĕr bў nīght ;
Hĭm thĕ fĕast-măstĕr mānў bōuts dĕfīed,
　Hĭm 'twīxt thĕ plĕdgĭng ănd thĕ cūp shăll smīte ;
Wŏe tō thĕ Lĕndĕr āt ŭsūriŏŭs rāte,
Thĕ hārd Rĭch Măn, thĕ hīrelĭng Ādvŏcāte ;
Wŏe tō thĕ Jŭdge thăt sĕllĕth right fŏr pāy ;
Wŏe tō thĕ thief thăt līke ă beăst ŏf prēy
　Wĭth creēpĭng trĕad thĕ trăvĕlĕr hărrўeth :—
Thĕse, īn thĕir sīn, thĕ sŭddĕn swōrd shăll slāy.
　Thĕre īs nŏ king mŏre tĕrrĭblē thăn Dēath.

He hath no pity,—nor will be denied,
   When the low hearth is garnished and bright,
Grimly he flingeth the dim portal wide,
   And steals the Infant in the Mother's sight ;
He hath no pity for the scorned of fate :—
He spares not Lazarus lying at the gate,
Nay, nor the Blind that stumbleth as he may ;
Nay, the tired Ploughman,—at the sinking ray,
   In the last furrow,—feels an icy breath,
And knows a hand hath turned the team astray
   There is no king more terrible than Death.

He hath no pity. For the new-made Bride,
   Blithe with the promise of her life's delight,
That wanders gladly by her Husband's side,
   He with the clatter of his drum doth fright ;
He scares the Virgin at the Convent grate ;
The maid half-won, the Lover passionate ;
He hath no grace for weakness and decay :
The tender Wife, the Widow bent and gray,
   The feeble Sire whose footstep faltereth,—
All these he leadeth by the lonely way—
   There is no king more terrible than Death.

ENVOY.

Youth for whose ear and monishing, of late
I sang of Prodigals and lost estate,
Have thou thy joy of living and be gay ;
But know not less that there must come a day,—
   Aye, and perchance e'en now it hasteneth,—
When thine own heart shall speak to thee and say,—
   There is no king more terrible than Death.

THE RONDEAU.

The rondeau is a form of verse introduced from the French by the English. Its form dates back to the fourteenth century. The rondeau is composed of thirteen verses or lines, of which eight have one rhyme and five another. These lines are divided in three unequal strophes; the four first words of the first line serve as the refrain, and occur after the eighth and thirteenth lines. It is a delicate form of poetry and capable of the highest degree of excellence and finish. Many delight to use it for that reason, and have succeeded in producing poems of rare beauty. The practice of new meters and the study of new forms aids the poet and enables him to rise higher in his art. Form and precision are necessary to a high degree of excellence. The rondeau in its true type, has a fixed exotic form, susceptible of a highly English polish. Lope de Vega and Hurtado de Mendoza wrote sonnets on sonnet making; Voiture imitated them as regards the rondeau. Here is a paraphrase of Voiture:

You bĭd mĕ trȳ, Blūe Eȳes, tŏ wrīte
A rōndeaŭ. Whāt!—fŏrthwīth?—tŏnīght?
  Rĕflēct. Sŏme skĭll Ĭ hăve, 'tĭs trūe;—
  Bŭt thĭrteēn līnes!—ănd rhȳmed ŏn twō!
"Rĕfrāin," ăs wēll. Ăh, hāplĕss plīght!
Stĭll, thĕre ăre fīve līnes,—rānged ărĭght.
Thĕse Gāllĭc bōnds, Ĭ fĕared, woŭld frĭght
  Mȳ ēasȳ Mūse. Thĕy dĭd, tĭll yoū—
    Yoŭ bĭd mĕ trȳ!

Thăt mākes thĕm ēight. Thĕ pōrt's ĭn sīght;—
'T ĭs āll bĕcāuse yoŭr eȳes ăre brĭght!
  Nŏw jŭst ă pāir tŏ ēnd ĭn "oō,"—
  Whĕn māids cŏmmānd, whăt căn't wĕ dō!
Bĕhōld!—thĕ rōndeaŭ, tāstefŭl, līght,
    Yoŭ bĭd mĕ trȳ!

TO A JUNE ROSE.

O royal Rose! the Roman dressed
His feast with thee; thy petals pressed
  Augustan brows; thine odor fine,
  Mixed with the three-times mingled wine,
Lent the long Thracian draught its zest.
What marvel then, if host and guest,
By Song, by Joy, by Thee caressed,
  Half-trembled on the half-divine,
    O royal Rose!

And yet—and yet—I love thee best
In our old gardens of the West,
  Whether about my thatch thou twine,
  Or Hers, that brown-eyed maid of mine,
Who lulls thee on her lawny breast,
    O royal Rose!
        Austin Dobson.

FOR MY DEAR LOVE.
(AN OPAL.)

For my dear love I long to bring
Some rare and dainty offering.
  I'll steal a rainbow from the sky
  To paint my joy when she is nigh;
The fairness of her form to sing,
I'll mount me on a poet's wing;
Through winter frost, each flower of spring
  Shall speak and tell her how I sigh
    For my dear love.

Nay, nay, this is but loitering;
See, here, a tiny, rounded thing,
  Where all sweet shades imprisoned lie,
  Her blush, the flowers, the rainbow sky;
Now, I will set this in a ring,
    For my dear love.
  Margaret B. Logan—"The Magazine of Poetry."

THE RONDEL.

The rondel is a poem, in two rhymes, containing fourteen lines. The refrain of the rondel is but a repetition of the first and second lines as the seventh and eighth, and again as the thirteenth and fourteenth. It is the original form of the rondeau.

THE WANDERER.

Love comes back to his vacant dwelling,—
    The old, old Love that we knew of yore!
    We see him stand by the open door,
With his great eyes sad, and his bosom swelling.

He makes as though in our arms repelling,
    He fain would lie as he lay before;—
Love comes back to his vacant dwelling,—
    The old, old Love that we knew of yore!

Ah, who shall help us from over-telling
    That sweet forgotten, forbidden lore!
    E'en as we doubt in our heart once more,
With a rush of tears to our eyelids welling,
Love comes back to his vacant dwelling.
                             Austin Dobson.

RONDEL.

These many years since we began to be,
What have the gods done with us? what with me?
What with my love? They have shown me fates and fears,
Harsh springs, and fountains bitterer than the sea,
Grief a fixed star, and joy a vane that veers,
      These many years.

With her, my love, with her have they done well?
But who shall answer for her? who shall tell
Sweet things or sad, such things as no man hears?
May no tears fall; if no tears ever fell,
From eyes more dear to me than starriest spheres
      These many years

But if tears ever touched, for any grief,
Those eyelids folded like a white-rose leaf,
Deep double shells where through the eye-flower peers,
Let them weep once more only, sweet and brief,
Brief tears and bright, for one who gave her tears
    These many years.
                      A. C. Swinburne.

THE ROUNDEL.

Another variation of the rondeau is the Roundel. It is formed of three stanzas of three lines each, containing only two rhymes. A refrain composed of the first four or five words or syllables of the first line constituting the refrain or burden, which is at the end of both the first and third stanzas:

THE ROUNDEL.

A Roundel is wrought as a ring or a star-bright sphere,
  With craft of delight and with cunning of sound unsought,
That the heart of the hearer may smile if to pleasure his ear
      A roundel is wrought.

Its jewel of music is carven of all or of aught—
  Love, laughter or mourning—remembrance of rapture or fear—
That fancy may fashion to hang in the ear of thought.

As a bird's quick song runs round, and the hearts in us hear—
  Pause answers to pause, and again the same strain caught
So moves the device whence, round as a pearl or tear,
      A roundel is wrought.
                      A. C. Swinburne.

THE VILLANELLE.

The villanelle is still another form of French poetry introduced and adopted by our English writers. It is a poem of but two rhymes written in tercets. The first and third lines of the first stanza alternating as the third line in each successive stanza, and at the close forming a couplet.

VILLANELLE.

(TO M. JOSEPH BOULMIER, AUTHOR OF "LES VILLANELLES.")

Villanelle, why art thou mute?
  Hath the singer ceased to sing?
Hath the Master lost his lute?

Many a pipe and scrannel flute
  On the breeze their discords fling;
Villanelle, why art *thou* mute?

Sound of tumult and dispute,
  Noise of war the echoes bring;
Hath the Master lost his lute?

Once he sang of bud and shoot
  In the season of the Spring;
Villanelle, why art thou mute?

Fading leaf and falling fruit
  Say, "The year is on the wing,
Hath the Master lost his lute?"

Ere the axe lie at the root,
  Ere the winter come as king,
Villanelle, why art thou mute?
Hath the Master lost his lute?
                        Andrew Lang.

FOR A COPY OF THEOCRITUS.
(VILLANELLE.)

O Singer of the field and fold,
  Theocritus! Pan's pipe was thine—
Thine was the happier Age of Gold.

For thee the scent of new-turned mould,
  The bee-hives and the murmuring pine,
O Singer of the field and fold !

Thou sang'st the simple feasts of old,—
  The beechen bowl made glad with wine—
Thine was the happier Age of Gold.

Thou bad'st the rustic loves be told,—
  Thou bad'st the tuneful reeds combine,
O Singer of the field and fold !

And round thee, ever-laughing, rolled
  The blithe and blue Sicilian brine—
Thine was the happier Age of Gold.

Alas for us ! Our songs are cold ;
  Our Northern suns too sadly shine :—
O Singer of the field and fold,
Thine was the happier Age of Gold !
  Austin Dobson.

THE SESTINA.

The sestina or sestine is another French form of verse, quaint and difficult. It, like many others, is from Provence, France, hence termed Provencial. It had its origin in the thirteenth century, and was invented by Arnauld Daniel, a troubadour. As its name indicates it is a stanza composed of six lines, each line or verse ending in the same six words arranged in a prescribed order, but not rhyming. The sestina concludes with an envoy of three lines, which must contain all six of the final words ; three of these words must be in the body of the verses and three at the end of the verses or lines. Mr. Swinburne varies this form by making the six final rhyme by threes. We give his poem at length :

SESTINA.

I saw my soul at rest upon a day
As a bird sleeping in the nest of night,
Among soft leaves that give the starlight way
To touch its wings but not its eyes with light;
So that it knew as one in visions may,
And knew not as men waking, of delight:

This was the measure of my soul's delight;
It has no power of joy to fly by day,
Nor part in the large lordship of the light;
But in a secret, moon-beholden way
Had all its will of dreams and pleasant night,
And all the love and life that sleepers may.

But such life's triumph as men waking may
It might not have to feed its faint delight
Between the stars by night and sun by day,
Shut up with green leaves and a little light:
Because its way was as a lost star's way,
A world's not wholly known of day or night.

All loves, and dreams, and sounds, and gleams of night
Made it all music that such minstrels may,
And all they had they gave it of delight;
But in the full face of the fire of day
What place shall be for any starry light,
What part of heaven in all the wide sun's way?

Yet the soul woke not, sleeping by the way,
Watched as a nursling of the large-eyed night,
And sought no strength nor knowledge of the day,
Nor closer touch conclusive of delight,
Nor mightier joy, nor truer than dreamers may,
Nor more of song than they, nor more of light.

For who sleeps once, and sees the secret light
  Whereby sleep shows the soul a fairer way
Between the rise and rest of day and night,
  Shall care no more to fare as all men may,
But be his place of pain or of delight,
  There shall he dwell, beholding night as day.

Song, have thy day, and take thy fill of light
  Before the night be fallen across thy way;
Sing while he may, man hath no long delight.
Algernon Charles Swinburne.

SESTINA.

Fra tutti il primo Arnaldo Daniello gran maestro d'amor.
—PETRARCH.

In fair Provence, the land of lute and rose,
Arnaut, great master of the lore of love,
First wrought sestines to win his lady's heart,
For she was deaf when simpler staves he sang,
And for her sake he broke the bonds of rhyme,
And in this subtler measure hid his woe.

"Harsh be my lines," cried Arnaut, "harsh the woe,
My lady, that enthorned and cruel rose,
Inflicts on him that made her live in rhyme!"
But through the meter spake the voice of Love,
And like a wild-wood nightingale he sang
Who thought in crabbed lays to ease his heart.

It is not told if her untoward heart
Was melted by the poet's lyric woe,
Or if in vain so amorously he sang;
Perchance through cloud of dark conceits he rose
To nobler heights of philosophic love,
And crowned his later years with sterner rhyme.

This thing alōne wĕ knōw; thĕ triplĕ rhȳme
Ŏf him whŏ bāred hĭs vāst ănd pāssiŏnăte heārt
Tŏ āll thĕ crōssĭng flāmes ŏf hāte ănd lōve,
Wĕars īn thĕ mīdst ŏf āll ĭts stōrm ŏf wōe—
Ăs sōme lŏud mōrn ŏf Mārch mă̆y beār ă rōse—
Thĕ ĭmprĕ̆ss ōf ă sōng thăt Ārnăut sāng.

"Smĭth ŏf hĭs mōthĕr-tōngue," thĕ Frĕnchmăn sāng
Ŏf Lāuncelŏt ānd ŏf Gălăhăd, thĕ rhȳme
Thăt bēat sŏ̆ blŏ̆od-lĭke āt ĭts cōre ŏf rōse,
Ĭt stīrred thĕ sweēt Frăncēscă's gĕntlĕ heārt
Tŏ tāke thăt kĭss thăt brŏught hĕr sō mŭch wōe,
Ănd sēaled ĭn fīre hĕr mārtȳdōm ŏf lōve.

Ănd Dāntĕ, fŭll ŏf hĕr ĭmmōrtăl lōve,
Stăyed hĭs dĕar sōng, ănd sōftlȳ, sweētlȳ sāng
Ăs thŏugh hĭs vōice brŏ̆ke wĭth thăt weĭght ŏf wōe;
Ănd tō thĭs dāy wĕ thĭnk ŏf Ārnăut's rhȳme
Whĕnĕvĕr pĭtȳ āt thĕ lăbŏrĭng heārt
Ŏn fāir Frăncēscă's mēmorȳ drōps thĕ rōse.

Ăh! Sōverĕign Lōve, fŏrgīve thĭs weăkĕr rhȳme!
Thĕ mĕn ŏf ōld whŏ sāng wĕre greăt ăt heārt,
Yĕt hăve wĕ toō knŏwn wōe, ănd wōrn thȳ rōse."

E. W. Gosse.

THE TRIOLET.

Another form borrowed from the French is the triolet. It is a short poem of eight lines. Its peculiarity consists in the first lines being repeated as the fourth and again as the seventh lines; while the second line is repeated as the eighth.

A KISS.

Rōse kĭssed mē tŏdāy.
 Wĭll shĕ kĭss mĕ tŏmōrrŏw?
Lĕt ĭt bē ăs ĭt māy,
 Rōse kĭssed mē tŏdāy.

But thĕ plēasŭre gĭves wāy
Tō ă sāvoŭr ŏf sōrrŏw;
Rōse kĭssed mē tŏdāy.—
Wĭll shĕ kĭss mĕ tŏmōrrŏw?
Austin Dobson.

Ălās, thĕ strōng, thĕ wīse, thĕ brāve,
Thăt bōast thĕmsĕlves thĕ sōns ŏf mēn!
Ŏnce thĕy gŏ dōwn ĭntō thĕ grāve—
Ălās, thĕ strōng, thĕ wīse, thĕ brāve,
Thĕy pĕrĭsh ānd hăve nŏne tŏ sāve,
Thĕy āre sŏwn, ānd ăre nŏt rāised ăgāin;
Ălās, thĕ strōng, thĕ wīse, thĕ brāve,
Thăt bōast thĕmsĕlves thĕ sōns ŏf mēn!
Andrew Lang.

VIRELAY.

The virelay is an ancient French song or short poem. Owing to the peculiarities of its formation it is termed the Veering Lay. The French form contained only two rhymes, one of which is made to lead at the beginning and the other at the end of the poem. The English virelay is composed of more than two rhymes, and the rhymes change place or alternate. Here is a specimen of an ancient little poem of this type.

Thŏu crŭĕl fāir, Ĭ gō,
Tŏ seēk ŏut ānў fāte bŭt theē;
Sĭnce thēre ĭs nōne căn woūnd mē sō,
Nŏr thāt hăs hālf thў crŭĕltў,
Thŏu crŭĕl fāir, Ĭ gō.

Fŏrēvĕr, thēn, fărewēll!
'Tĭs ă lŏng lēave Ĭ tāke; bŭt ōh!
Tŏ tārrў wĭth theĕ hēre ĭs hĕll,
Ănd twĕntў thōusănd hēlls tŏ gō—
Fŏrēvĕr, thēn, fărewēll.
Cotton.

Here is another specimen of one of our early virelays. It is a stanza of an old song of the fifteenth century :

> Rōbĭn săt ōn thĕ goōd greĕn hĭll,
>   Keĕpĭng ă flŏck ŏf fie,[1]
> Mĕrrў Mākўn sāid hĭm till,[2]
>   Rōbĭn, rûe ŏn mē,
> Ĭ hāve lŏved theē, ĭn speēch ănd stĭll,[3]
>   Thēse yĕars twō ŏr threē,
> Mў sēcrĕt sōrrŏw ŭnlēss thŏu dēll[4]
>   Dōubtlĕss ĭn soōth Ĭ dē.[5]
>
> Robert Henryson.

[1] Sheep. [2] Unto or to. [3] Silence. [4] Assuage. [5] Die.

THE PANTOUM.

French poets anxious for something new adopted a Malayan form, the Pantoum. It is not of much practical use, but serves to illustrate the quaint and peculiar in verse. It is best adapted to the light, airy and frivolous things of life, and used in describing comic or ludicrous affairs. Mr. Austin Dobson has exercised his ingenuity and literary skill writing a pantoum entitled "In Town." It will be perceived the pantoum consists of a series of quatrains ; the second and fourth lines of the first stanza reappear as the first and third lines of the second stanza, and the second and third lines of the second stanza reappear as the first and fourth lines of the third stanza, and so on until the end of the poem. The first and third lines of the first stanza are again used as the third and fourth lines of the last stanza. Mr. Dobson's pantoum is in dactylic rhythm and is here given :

IN TOWN

The blue fly sung in the pane.—TENNYSON.

Toiling in Town now is "horrid,"
   (There is that woman again!)—
June in the zenith is torrid,
   Thought gets dry in the brain.

There is that woman again:
   "Strawberries! fourpence a pottle!"
Thought gets dry in the brain;
   Ink gets dry in the bottle.

"Strawberries! fourpence a pottle!"
   O for the green of a lane!—
Ink gets dry in the bottle;
   "Buzz" goes a fly in the pane!

O for the green of a lane,
   Where one might lie and be lazy!
"Buzz" goes a fly in the pane;
   Bluebottles drive me crazy!

Where one might lie and be lazy,
   Careless of town and all in it!—
Bluebottles drive me crazy;
   I shall go mad in a minute!

Careless of town and all in it,
   With some one to soothe and to still you;—
I shall go mad in a minute;
   Bluebottle, then I shall kill you!

With some one to soothe and to still you;—
   As only one's feminine kin do,—
Bluebottle, then I shall kill you:
   There now! I've broken the window!

As önlў öne's fĕmĭnīne kĭn dŏ,—
Sŏme mūslĭn-clăd Măbĕl ŏr May !—
Thĕre nŏw, Ĭ've brōkĕn thĕ wĭndŏw !
Blūebŏttlĕ's ŏff ănd ăwāy !

Sŏme mūslĭn-clăd Măbĕl ŏr May,
 Tŏ dāsh ŏne wĭth eaū dĕ Cŏlōgne ;—
Blūebŏttlĕ's ŏff ănd ăwāy ;
 Ănd whў shoŭld Ĭ stāy hĕre ălōne !

Tŏ dāsh ŏne wĭth eaū dĕ Cŏlōgne,
 All ōvĕr ŏne's ēmĭnĕnt fŏrehĕad ;—
Ănd whў shoŭld Ĭ stāy hĕre ălōne !
 Tōilĭng Ĭn Tōwn nŏw Ĭs "hŏrrĭd."

BLANK VERSE.

Blank verse is without rhyme. It is, however, a favorite form of poetic art with many writers of verse. All poetry was in blank verse until rhyming was introduced by Chaucer. For a long while its devotees condemned rhyme. Rhyming was termed frivolous and its practice and use discountenanced by some of the best writers of early English poetry. It gradually gained favor, however, until today, instead of our best and sweetest thoughts finding expression in blank verse, as was formerly the case, we find them expressed in rhyme. To blank verse, however, the world of literature is greatly indebted. It was in blank verse Milton wrote "Paradise Lost" and Bryant "Thanatopsis." The first may be termed the first and greatest of English poems in blank verse. For while it was used in Greek and Latin poetry, it was in little use in English poetry, until the appearance of Milton's "Paradise Lost." It immediately came into general favor in writing epic poetry. Before this its chief use in English was its use in dramatic composition.

The second, "Thanatopsis," is justly termed one of the best and grandest of conceptions of an elegiac character. Blank verse is ten-syllabled, that is, composed of five poetic feet. It is also termed Heroic verse, and is iambic pentameter. Blank verse usually ends with an important word.

THANATOPSIS.

To him who in the love of Nature holds
Communion with her visible forms she speaks
A various language; for his gayer hours
She has a voice of gladness, and a smile
And eloquence of beauty, and she glides
Into his dark musings with a mild
And gentle sympathy that steals away
Their sharpness ere he is aware.
William Cullen Bryant.

LIFE.

Life is the transmigration of a soul
Through various bodies, various states of being:
New manners, passions, new pursuits in each;
In nothing, save in consciousness, the same.
Infancy, adolescence, manhood, age,
Are alway moving onward, alway losing
Themselves in one another, lost at length
Like undulations on the strand of death.
James Montgomery.

ADDRESS TO LIGHT.

Hail, holy Light, offspring of Heaven, first-born,
Or of the eternal, co-eternal beam,
May I express thee unblamed? since God is light,
And never but in unapproached light
Dwelt from eternity, dwelt then in thee,
Bright effluence of bright essence increate.
John Milton.

MEN.

Měn āre bŭt chĭldrĕn ōf ă lārgĕr grōwth ;
Ŏur āppĕtītes ăs āpt tŏ chānge ăs thēirs,
Ănd fūll ăs crāvĭng, toō, ănd fūll ăs vāin ;
Ănd yēt thĕ sōul shŭt ŭp ĭn hĕr dărk roōm,
Viēwĭng sŏ clēar ăbroād, ăt hōme seĕs nōthĭng ;
Bŭt like ă mōle ĭn ēarth, būsў ănd blind,
Wŏrks āll hĕr fōllў ŭp, ănd cāsts ĭt ōutwărd
Tŏ thĕ wŏrld's viēw.
John Dryden.

A COUNTRY LIFE.

Hŏw blēst thĕ mān whŏ ĭn thĕse pēacefŭl plāins,
Plŏughs hĭs pătĕrnăl fiēld ; făr frŏm thĕ nōise,
Thĕ cāre, ănd būstlĕ ŏf ă būsў wŏrld !
Ăll ĭn thĕ sācrĕd, sweēt sĕquĕstĕred vāle
Ŏf sōlĭtūde, thĕ sēcrĕt prīmrŏse-pāth
Ŏf rūrăl life, hĕ dwēlls ; ănd wĭth hĭm dwēll
Pĕace ānd Cŏntĕnt, twĭns ŏf thĕ sўlvăn shāde,
And āll thĕ grācĕs ŏf thĕ gōldĕn āge.
Michael Bruce.

CHAPTER X.

MEASURES EXEMPLIFIED.

Trochaic.

Tāstefŭl, grācefŭl, plēasĭng mēasŭre
Ānd tŏ wrīte theĕ īs ă plēasŭre.

THERE is real music about a well written poem composed in this measure. The stress or accent is laid on the odd syllables, and the even ones are unaccented or short.

Trochees are often mixed with iambuses, but that can make no difference in the scansion, as the number of feet in a verse or line must be reckoned by the number of accented syllables. Trochaic verse admits of the cutting off of the final syllable ; of the use of single rhymed endings, or in other words, single rhymed trochaic omit the final or unaccented syllable. While a foot may end in one accented syllable, a foot in no instance can be permitted to commence with simply one syllable. This is true in trochaic, iambic, or any other kind of measure. Frequently we find a line ending in one syllable in dimeter, trimeter, or tetrameter verse. Hence we have lines of three, five and seven syllables. Trochaic retrenched of the last unaccented syllable is, however, trochaic still.

Iambuses are admitted frequently in trochaic verse as we have already noticed. It is not usual, however, to introduce a trochaic line with an iambic foot, although it is permissible. Double rhymes are always less frequent than single ones; hence lines oftener terminate in trochaic measures catalectic than in full trochaic. But the accented syllable is always counted a foot. The inconvenience that naturally results from writing a line of full trochees is at once apparent. There must always be a double ending to the rhymes. This cannot always happen. It is also useless. There is no good reason why trochaic of any length should not be allowed to terminate in a single rhyme.

One or more unaccented syllables are termed hypermetrical.

When trochaic ends in a single accented syllable, constituting a foot, such accented syllable is not to be termed an "additional" syllable. The verse is simply catalectic.

No additional, unaccented syllable is ever allowed before the first foot. By permitting this you destroy all distinction between iambic and trochaic. It is well to observe also, in this connection, that iambic measure is never shorn of the unaccented syllable in the first foot. Iambic measure never commences with a single accented syllable. It must always commence with a regular foot, and so, too, must trochaic.

Measure, Monometer.
Rhythm, Trochaic.
Formula, Ab.
Sign, — ᴗ

EXAMPLE (1).

1.	2.	3.
Hĕltĕr,	Sĭngĭng,	Hŭrrў,
Skĕltĕr,	Swĭngĭng,	Skŭrrў,
Skātĕrs gō.	Thĕy gŏ bȳ.	Seĕ thĕm glīde.
Chāngĭng,	Whĭskĭng,	Rāttlĭng,
Rāngĭng,	Frĭskĭng,	Bāttlĭng,
Ĭn ă rōw.	Ās thĕy flȳ.	Skātĕr's prīde.

"The Skaters."

Measure, Dimeter.
Rhythm, Trochaic.
Formula, Ab × 2.
Sign, — ᴗ × 2.

EXAMPLE (1).

Nōne dŏ hēar
Ūse tŏ sweār :
Ōaths dŏ frāy
Fīsh ăwāy ;
Wĕ sĭt stīll,
Wătch oŭr quīll :
Fīshĕrs mŭst nŏt wrānglĕ.
Chalkhill—" The Angler."

One peculiarity of the above poem, many of its lines might be termed safely anapestic meter. The trochaic foot, however, prevails and the poem is trochaic.

A fine specimen of trochaic dimeter is furnished in the following, with single rhyme :

EXAMPLE (2).

Ĭn ă māze
Lŏst, Ĭ gāze:
Căn ŏur ēyes
Rēach thў sīze ?
Māy mў lāys
Swēll wĭth prāise
Wŏrthў theē !
Wŏrthў mē !
Mūse, ĭnspīre
Āll thў fīre !
Bārds ŏf ōld
Ŏf hĭm tōld,
Whĕn thĕy sāid
Ātlăs' hĕad
Prŏpped thĕ skīes.
Seĕ ! ănd bĕlĭĕve yoŭr ēyes !

Seĕ hĭm strīde
Vāllĕys wīde;
Ŏvĕr woŏds,
Ŏvĕr floŏds.
Whĕn hĕ trĕads,
Moūntăin hĕads,
Grŏan ănd shāke :
Ārmĭes quāke,
Lĕst hĭs spūrn
Ŏvĕrtūrn
Măn ănd steēd.
Troōps, tăke heēd ;
Lĕft ănd rĭght
Speĕd yoŭr flīght,
Lĕst ăn hōst,
Bĕnēath hĭs foŏt bĕ lŏst.

John Gay—" A Lilliputian Ode."

This poem is also attributed to Alexander Pope and it is published in his works.

Measure, Trimeter.
Rhythm, Trochaic.
Formula, Ab × 3.
Sign, — ⌣ × 3.

EXAMPLE (1).

Gō nŏt, hăppў dāy,
  Frŏm thĕ shīnĭng fiēlds,
Gō nŏt, hăppў dāy,
  Tĭll thĕ māidĕn yiēlds.
Rōsў īs thĕ Wēst,
  Rōsў īs thĕ Sōuth,
Rōsĕs āre hĕr cheēks,
  Ănd ă rōse hĕr mōuth.
Whĕn thĕ hăppў Yēs
  Făltĕrs frŏm hĕr lĭps,
Păss ănd blŭsh thĕ nēws
  Ō'er thĕ blōwĭng shĭps,
Ŏvĕr blōwĭng sēas,
  Ŏvĕr sēas ăt rēst,
Păss thĕ hăppў nēws,
  Blŭsh ĭt thrō' thĕ Wēst,
Tĭll thĕ rĕd măn dānce
  Bȳ hĭs rĕd cēdăr-treē,
Ănd thĕ rĕd măn's bābe
  Lĕap, bĕyōnd thĕ sēa.
Blŭsh frŏm Wēst tŏ Ēast,
  Blŭsh frŏm Ēast tŏ Wēst,
Tĭll thĕ Wēst ĭs Ēast,
  Blŭsh ĭt thrō' thĕ Wēst.
Rōsў īs thĕ Wēst,
  Rōsў īs thĕ Sōuth,
Rōsĕs āre hĕr cheēks,
  Ănd ă rōse hĕr mōuth.
      Alfred Tennyson—"Maud."

EXAMPLE (2).

LYRICS AND EPICS.

Ĭ woŭld bē thĕ Lȳrĭc,
  Ĕvĕr ōn thĕ līp,
Rāthĕr thān thĕ Ĕpĭc
  Mēmŏrȳ lĕts slĭp!
Ĭ woŭld bē thĕ dīamŏnd
  Āt mў lādў's ēar,
Rāthĕr thān thĕ Jūne-rŏse
  Wŏrn bŭt ōnce ă yĕar!
Thomas Bailey Aldrich—"Lyrics and Epics."

EXAMPLE (3).

Swĭngĭng ŏn ă bĭrch-treĕ
  Tŏ ă sleēpў tūne,
Hŭmmĕd bў āll thĕ breēzĕs
  Ĭn thĕ mōnth ŏf Jūne!
Lĭttlĕ lēaves ă-flūttĕr,
  Sōund lĭke dāncĭng drŏps
Ŏf ă broōk ŏn pĕbblĕs;
  Sōng thăt nēvĕr stŏps.
Lucy Larcom—"Swinging On a Birch Tree."

Measure, Tetrameter.
Rhythm, Trochaic.
Formula, Ab × 4.
Sign, — ◡ × 4.

EXAMPLE (1).

"Your Mission" is an excellent poem in trochaic tetrameter. We select the last stanza

"Do not, then, stand idly waiting
 For some greater work to do;
Fortune is a lazy goddess,
 She will never come to you.
Go and toil in any vineyard,—
 Do not fear to do and dare,
If you *want* a field of labor,
 You can find it anywhere."
                    Ellen M. H. Gates.

EXAMPLE (2).

Sound, sweet song, from some far land,
Sighing softly close at hand,
 Now of joy, and now of woe!
Stars are wont to glimmer so.
Sooner thus will good unfold;
Children young and children old
 Gladly hear thy numbers flow.
        Goethe—"Sound, Sweet Song."

Another poem that will never die illustrates this measure. In addition to its perfect versification there is something of heaven's own music, something supernal, in the poem. Its lines are so elevating and pure, with a sweet tenderness of expression unsurpassed:

"Every tinkle on the shingles
 Has an echo in the heart."

EXAMPLE (3).

The fifth of six stanzas is here given:

And another comes, to thrill me
 With her eyes' delicious blue;
And I mind not—musing on her,
 That her heart was all untrue;

> I rĕmĕmbĕr būt tŏ lŏve hèr
>   Wĭth ă pāssĭŏn kĭn tŏ pāin,
> Ānd my̆ heārt's quĭck pūlsĕs vībrāte
>   Tŏ thĕ pāttĕr ŏf thĕ rāin.
>   *Coates Kinney*—" Rain on the Roof."

Measure, Pentameter.
Rhythm, Trochaic.
Formula, Ab × 5.
Sign, — ⌣ × 5.

EXAMPLE (1).

> Tāll thĕ plūmăge ŏf thĕ rūsh-flŏwer tŏssĕs;
>   Shārp ănd sŏft ĭn māny ă cūrve ănd līne,
> Glēam ănd glŏw thĕ sēa-cŏlōred mārsh-mŏssĕs,
>   Sālt ănd splēndĭd frŏm thĕ cīrclĭng brīne;
> Strēak ŏn strēak ŏf glīmmerĭng sēa shīne crŏssĕs
>   Āll thĕ lānd sēa-sātŭrāte ăs wĭth wīne.
>   *A. C. Swinburne*—" By the North Sea."

EXAMPLE (2).

> " Mōthĕr, dĕar, whăt ĭs thĕ wātĕr sāyĭng?
>   Mōthĕr, dĕar, why̆ dōes thĕ wĭld sēa rŏar? "
> Crȳ thĕ chīldrĕn ŏn thĕ whīte sănd plāyĭng,—
>   Ŏn thĕ whīte sănd, hālf ă mīle frŏm shōre,
> " Līttlĕ ōnes, Ĭ fēar ă stōrm ĭs grōwĭng.
>   Cōme ăwāy! Ŏh, lĕt ŭs hāstĕn hōme! "
> Cālls thĕ mōthĕr; ănd thĕ wīnd ĭs blōwĭng;
>   Flāshĭng ŭp ă mīllĭon ēyes ŏf fōam.
>   *Anonymous*—" The High Tide."

The following poem is by one of our best authors, and the poem from which selection is taken one of his best lyrics. The measures are mixed and present an example of:

MEASURES EXEMPLIFIED.

1st, Dimeter ; 2nd, Trimeter ; 3rd, Pentameter ; 4th, Dimeter ; 5th, Pentameter.

EXAMPLE (3).

> Jĭnglĕ ! Jĭnglĕ !
>   Hōw thĕ fiĕlds gŏ bȳ !
> Ĕarth ănd âir ĭn snōwў sheĕn cŏmmīnglĕ,
>   Fär ănd nīgh ;
>   Ĭs thĕ grōund bĕnēath ŭs, ōr thĕ skȳ ?
>   *Edmund Clarence Stedman*—"The Sleigh Ride."

Measure, Hexameter.
Rhythm, Trochaic.
Formula, Ab × 6.
Sign, — ‿ × 6.

EXAMPLE (1).

> Nĕvĕr yĕt hăs pōĕt sūng ă pĕrfĕct sōng,
>   Būt hĭs life wăs rootĕd like ă tree's, ămōng
> Ĕarth's greăt feedĭng fōrcĕs—ĕvĕn ăs crăgs ănd mōuld,
>   Rhȳthms thăt stir thĕ fōrĕst bȳ firm fībrĕs hōld.
>   *Lucy Larcom*—"The Trees."

From the works of the same author we take another example—the first and third stanzas :

EXAMPLE (2).

> Hăppȳ fiĕlds ŏf sūmmĕr, āll yoŭr âirȳ grăssĕs
> Whĭspĕrĭng ănd bōwĭng whĕn thĕ Wĕst wĭnd păssĕs,
> Hăppȳ lärk ănd nĕstlĭng, hĭd bĕnēath thĕ mōwĭng,
> Root sweĕt mūsĭc ĭn yoŭ, tō thĕ white clōuds grōwĭng.
>
> Hăppȳ lĭttlĕ chĭldrĕn, skies ăre bright ăbōve yoŭ,
> Treēs bĕnd dōwn tŏ kĭss yoŭ, breēze ănd blŏssŏm lōve yoŭ;
> Ānd wĕ blĕss yoŭ, plāyĭng ĭn thĕ fiĕld-păths māzȳ,
> Swĭngĭng wĭth thĕ hārebĕll, dāncĭng wĭth thĕ dāisȳ !
>   *Lucy Larcom*—" Happy Fields of Summer."

Example (3).

Nŏw thĕ hāre ĭs snāred ănd dĕad bĕsīde thĕ snōw-yărd,
Ănd thĕ lārk bĕsīde thĕ drēarȳ wĭntĕr sēa,
Ănd mȳ bābȳ ĭn hĭs crādlĕ ĭn thĕ chŭrch-yărd
Wāitĕth thēre ŭntĭl thĕ bĕlls brĭng mē.
                    Charles Kingsley—"The Merry Lark."

Each couplet of the trochaic hexameter is sometimes divided into alternate lines of six and five syllables, forming the trochaic 11s of our hymns.

Measure, Heptameter.
Rhythm, Trochaic.
Formula, Ab × 7.
Sign, — ⌣ × 7.

Iambic heptameter is what is termed ballad meter, being lines of tetrameter and trimeter alternately. There can be no good reason shown why trochaics can not also be used in the same manner. One thing, however, must necessarily be observed, where it is thus divided, every other line becomes iambic   While the first and third lines will be trochaic and catalectic, the second and fourth will be iambic and hypermeter.

Trochaics of seven feet are exceedingly rare. We find few examples. It is not certainly on account of the extreme length, for trochaics octometer of late years are plentiful and can no longer be termed "prosodial anomalies," as they were formerly termed.

This is the 7s and 6s of our hymns :

"Stŏp, poŏr sĭnnĕr, stŏp ănd thĭnk,"
  Bĕfōre yoŭ fŭrthĕr gō ;
Wĭll yoŭ spōrt ŭpŏn thĕ brĭnk
  Ŏf ĕvĕrlāstĭng wŏe ? "

It will be observed the second and fourth lines are iambic. If, however, the lines were not alternated they would be trochaic.

EXAMPLE (1).

Clĕŏn seēs nŏ chărms ĭn nātŭre, ĭn ă dāisў Ī ;
Clĕŏn hēars nŏ ānthĕm rĭngĭng īn thĕ sēa ănd skȳ ;
Nātŭre sīngs tŏ mē fŏrēvĕr, eārnĕst lĭstenĕr Ī ;
Stāte fŏr stāte, wĭth āll ăttĕndănts, whō woŭld chānge ? Nŏt Ī.
Charles Mackay—"Cleon and I."

EXAMPLE (2).

Hōlȳ, hōlȳ, hōlȳ ! Thōugh thĕ dārknĕss hide Theĕ,
Thōugh thĕ ēye ŏf sīnfŭl mān Thȳ glōrȳ māy nŏt seē,
Ōnlȳ Thŏu, Ō Gōd, ărt hōlȳ ; there ĭs nōne bĕsīde Theĕ,
Pĕrfĕct Thŏu ĭn pôwer, ĭn lŏve ănd pūrĭtȳ !
Reginald Heber—"Trinity Hymn."

EXAMPLE (3).—

Hāstĕn sīnnĕr tō rĕpĕnt theĕ, tūrn tŏ Gōd ănd live,
 Seēk fŏr mĕrcȳ, bĕg fŏr pārdŏn, Gōd ălōne căn gīve ;
Lēave thĕ sīnfŭl thrōng fŏrēvĕr, sīnnĕr, whȳ dĕlāy ?
 Seēk fŏrgĭvenĕss, seēk hĭs blĕssĭng, hāste theĕ, hāste ăwāy !—

Trūst Hĭm, sīnnĕr, hĕ wĭll blĕss theĕ, ōnlȳ mĕrcȳ crāve
 Trūst thȳ lŏvĭng, lŏvĭng Sāvioŭr, Hĕ ălōne căn sāve.
Cōme tŏ Jēsŭs, tō thȳ Sāvioŭr, plĕad bĕfōre toŏ lāte,
 Cōme ĭn sōrrŏw, cōme rĕpēntănt, dŏ nŏt lōngĕr wāit.

Chrīst hăs lĕft a trūe rĕlĭgiŏn, thāt wĕ māy nŏt ērr,
 Cōme ănd shāre ĭt, choŏse ĭt, sīnnĕr, will yoŭ nŏt prĕfĕr
Ā rĕlĭgiŏn thăt căn sāve yoŭ ĭn thăt wōrld ăbōve ?
 Whĕre ĭs blĭss ănd ēndlĕss plĕasŭre—Gŏd ălōne ĭs lŏve.
"Hasten Sinner to Repent Thee."

Measure, Octometer.
Rhythm, Trochaic.
Formula, Ab × 8.
Sign, — ⌣ × 8.

EXAMPLE (1).

She wăs wālkĭng ĭn thĕ sprīng-tĭme, ĭn thĕ mōrnĭng-tīde ŏf līfe,
Lĭttlĕ rēckŏnĭng ŏf thĕ joūrnĕy, ŏf ĭts pērĭls ănd ĭts strīfe;
Fōr thĕ flōwers wĕre peēpĭng cōylў, ănd thĕ sūnshĭne glĭstĕned brīght,
Ănd thĕ dēwdrŏps lĭngĕred, quĭvĕrĭng, lĭke fāirў bĕlls ŏf līght.
Nŏt ă clōud wăs ĭn thĕ hēavĕns, nŏt ă sūrge wăs ŏn thĕ deēp,
Fŏr thĕ rīmplĕd seā lăy brēathĭng ĭn ăn ūnĭmpāssiŏned sleĕp,
Ănd thĕ frĕsh greēn lĕaves wĕre nŏddĭng, tō thĕ whĭspĕrs ŏf thĕ breēze—
"Ōh! thĕ wŏrld mŭst bĕ ă pārădīse wĭth prŏmĭsĕs līke thĕse!
Thĕre's nŏ cănkĕr ĭn thĕ blŏssŏms, ănd nŏ blīght ŭpŏn thĕ treēs."
Hunter— "The Curtain."

EXAMPLE (2).

Ĭn thĕ sprĭng ă fūllĕr crīmsŏn cōmes ŭpŏn thĕ rōbĭn's brĕast;
Ĭn thĕ sprĭng thĕ wāntŏn lāpwĭng gĕts hĭmsĕlf ănōthĕr crĕst;
Ĭn thĕ sprĭng ă līvelĭĕr īrĭs chāngĕs ŏn thĕ būrnĭshed dōve;
Ĭn thĕ sprĭng ă yoŭng măn's fāncў līghtlў tūrns tŏ thŏughts ŏf lōve.
Alfred Tennyson— "Locksley Hall."

EXAMPLE (3).

Āh, dĭstĭnctlў Ī rĕmĕmbĕr, ĭt wăs ĭn thĕ blēak Dĕcĕmbĕr,
    Ănd ĕach sēpărăte dўĭng ĕmbĕr wrŏught ĭts ghōst ŭpŏn thĕ floōr.
Ēagĕrlў Ĭ wĭshed thĕ mōrrŏw; vāinlў Ĭ hăd sōught tŏ bōrrŏw
    Frŏm mў boōks sūrcĕase ŏf sōrrŏw,—sōrrŏw fŏr thĕ lōst Lĕnōre,—
Fŏr thĕ rāre ănd rādĭănt māidĕn whŏm thĕ āngĕls nāme Lĕnōre,—
    Nāmelĕss hĕre fŏrĕvĕr mōre.
Edgar A. Poe— "The Raven"

IAMBIC.

As before observed the iambic measure is used more than all others combined. Accent in iambic verse is placed on the even syllables, and the odd ones are unaccented.

This measure must always be commenced with a regular foot of two syllables, although the first may be a trochee, and often is. However, the first foot cannot be commenced with a single syllable. By an attempt to commence the first foot of the verse with a single accented syllable, you will simply change the measure to trochaic. A single syllable not accented, frequently is added to the end of the verse. It is, however, not to be reckoned as anything but supernumerary unless we should term the ending an amphibrach.

Dactyls and anapests, where they serve to explain the meter of a line of poetry should be used, as it is far better to do so than to have recourse to extra metrical syllables.

It is sometimes difficult to tell the prevailing foot. However, only the accents are to be counted, and where a proper scansion is made the introduction of other feet causes no trouble. A dactyl may be often employed instead of a trochee, an anapest for an iambus. This usually occurs where one unaccented vowel precedes another in what we usually regard as separate syllables, and both are clearly heard, although uttered in such quick succession that both syllables occupy only half the time in utterance a long syllable would require, as:

> Fŭll *mānȳ ă* gĕm ŏf pūrĕst rāy sĕrēne.
> "Gray's Elegy."

> Thĕ *mūrmurĭng* wind, thĕ *quīverĭng* lĕaf,
> Shăll sŏftlȳ tĕll ŭs thŏu ărt nĕar!
> *Oliver Wendell Holmes*—" Hymn of Trust."

The words "murmuring" and "quivering" are pronounced naturally with more rapidity. So too "many a" in the first example.

Lines may contain ten syllables and yet be only iambic tetrameter. The last two syllables being hypermetrical, as:

> Thĕre wăs ăn āncĭĕnt sāge Phĭlōsŏphĕr
> Whŏ hād rĕad Ālĕxāndĕr Rōss ŏvĕr.
> *Butler's* "Hudibras."

Extra metrical syllables can, however, occur, and are permissible only at the end of a line, or verse. Such syllables are always unaccented.

Measure, Monometer.
Rhythm, Iambic.
Formula, bA.
Sign, ⌣ —.

Poems in this measure are very rare. The measure is often used, however, to construct a single line, in combination with other lines in forming a stanza.

EXAMPLE (1).

Thŭs Ĭ	Ăs ōne	Ĭ'm māde
Păss bȳ	Ŭnknōwn	Ă shāde,
Ănd dīe.	Ănd gōne!	Ănd lāid

	I' th' grāve;	Whĕre tĕll
	Thĕre hăve	Ĭ dwĕll.
	Mў cāve:	Fărewĕll.

Robert Herrick—"Upon His Departure Hence."

EXAMPLE (2).

Ăt mōrn,
  Ĭ hēar
Thȳ nōte,
  Sŏ cheĕr,
Sweĕt Thrŭsh.

Thĕ whīle
  Ĭ drēam,
Ĭn sōng
  Yoŭ teēm,
Blĭthe Thrŭsh.

Gŏd māde
  Thĕ ēarth
Tŏ jōy
  Ĭn mīrth
Dĕar Thrŭsh.

Ănd thȳ
  Găy trill
Ĭs būt
  Hĭs will,
Ŏ Thrŭsh!

Măy Ĭ
  Bĕ hēard,
Līke theĕ,
  Fŏnd bĭrd,
Brĭght Thrŭsh:

Tŏ sīng
  Gŏd's prāise,
Sweĕt ās
  Thȳ lāys,
Brŏwn Thrŭsh.
    "The Thrush."

EXAMPLE (3).

Ănd hē
Whŏm wē
Seĕ dĕjēctĕd,
Nĕxt dāy
Wĕ māy
Seĕ ĕrēctĕd.
    Herrick—"Anacreontic."

EXAMPLE (4).

Hărk! hĭst!
Ăroŭnd
Ă līst!
Thĕ boŭnds
Ŏf spāce
Ăll trāce,
Ĕffāce
Ŏf sōund.
    Victor Hugo—"The Djinns."

Measure, Dimeter.
Rhythm, Iambic.
Formula, bA × 2.
Sign, ⌣ — × 2.

Example (1).

Ŏnce thrŏŭgh thĕ fōrĕst
  Ălōne Ĭ wĕnt ;
Tŏ seēk fŏr nŏthĭng
  Mў thoūghts wĕre bēnt.

Ĭ sāw ĭn thĕ shădŏw
  Ă flōwer stănd thĕre ;
Ăs stārs ĭt glĭstĕned,
  Ăs ēyes 'twăs fāir.

Ĭ soūght tŏ plŭck ĭt,—
  Ĭt gĕntlў sāid :
"Shăll Ĭ bĕ găthĕred
  Ōnlў tŏ fāde?"

Wĭth āll ĭts roōts
  Ĭ dŭg ĭt wĭth cāre,
Ănd toōk ĭt hōme
  Tŏ mў gărdĕn fāir.

Ĭn sīlĕnt cōrnĕr
  Soŏn ĭt wăs sēt ;
Thĕre grōws ĭt ēvĕr—
  Thĕre bloōms ĭt yĕt.

Goethe—"Found."

Example (2).

Thŏugh cāre ănd strife
Ĕlsewhĕre bĕ rīfe,
Ŭpŏn mў wŏrd Ĭ dŏ nŏt heēd 'ĕm ;
Ĭn bĕd Ĭ līe
Wĭth boōks hărd bў,
Ănd wĭth ĭncreāsĭng zĕst Ĭ rĕad 'ĕm.

Eugene Field—"De Amicitiis."

MEASURES EXEMPLIFIED.

Measure, Trimeter.
Rhythm, Iambic.
Formula, bA × 3.
Sign, ⏑ — × 3.

EXAMPLE (1).

Ŏh yoū thĕ vĭrgĭns nīne,
Thăt dō ŏur sōuls ĭnclīne
Tŏ nōblĕ dĭscĭplīne.
Nŏd tō thĭs vōw ŏf mīne!
Cŏme thēn, ănd nōw ĭnspīre
Mў vĭŏl ānd mў lȳre
Wĭth yoūr ĕtērnăl fīre,
Ănd māke mĕ ōne ĕntīre
Cŏmpōsĕr īn yoŭr chōir.
Thĕn Ī'll yoŭr āltărs strēw
Wĭth rōsĕs sweēt ănd nēw,
Ănd ēvĕr līve ă trūe
Ăcknōwlĕdgēr ŏf yoū.
   Robert Herrick—"A Hymn to the Muses."

EXAMPLE (2).

Lōst! lōst! lōst!
Ă gēm ŏf cōuntlĕss prīce
Cŭt frōm thĕ lĭvĭng rōck,
Ănd grāved ĭn Părădīse,
Sĕt roūnd wĭth threē tĭmes ēight
Lărge dīamŏnds, clēar ănd brĭght,
Ănd ēach wĭth sĭxtў smāllĕr ōnes,
Āll chăngefŭl ās thĕ līght.
   Mrs. Lydia H. Sigourney—"A Lost Day."

Example (3).

Cŏme, āll yĕ jŏllў shēphĕrds
That whĭstlĕ thrŏūgh thĕ glēn,
I'll tĕll yŏŭ ōf ă sēcrĕt
Thăt cōurtiĕrs dīnnă kēn :
Whăt īs thĕ greātĕst blĭss
That thĕ tōngue ŏf măn căn nāme?
'Tĭs tŏ woō ă bōnnĭe lāssiĕ
Whēn thĕ kȳe cŏmes hăme !
James Hogg—" When the Kye Comes Hame."

Measure, Tetrameter.
Rhythm, Iambic.
Formula, bA × 4.
Sign, ⌣ — × 4.

Example (1).

Fŏr while thŏu lingerĕst in dĕlīght,—
Ăn īdlĕ pŏĕt, wĭth thў rhȳme,
Thĕ sūmmĕr hōurs wĭll tāke thĕir flight
Ănd lēave theĕ ĭn ă bārrĕn clĭme.
Thomas Bailey Aldrich—" Song Time."

Example (2).

Ī ōnce knĕw āll thĕ bĭrds thăt cāme
Ănd nēstĕd ĭn ŏur ōrchărd treēs ;
Fŏr ēverў flōwĕr Ĭ hăd ă nāme—
Mў friēnds wĕre woŏd-chŭcks, tōads, ănd beēs ;
Ĭ knĕw whĕre thrīved ĭn yōndĕr glēn—
Whăt plănts woŭld soŏthe ă stōne-brŭised tōe.
Ōh ! Ī wăs vērў lĕarnĕd thēn ;
Bŭt thăt wăs vērў lōng ăgō !
Eugene Field—" Long Ago."

Example (3).

Hăve yoū nŏt hēard thĕ pōĕts tĕll
　　Hŏw cāme thĕ dāintў Bābў Bĕll
　　Ĭntŏ thĭs wŏrld ŏf ōurs?
Thĕ gātes ŏf hēaven wĕre lĕft ăjār:
Wĭth fōldĕd hānds ănd drēamў ēyes,
Wănderĭng ōut ŏf Pārădīse,
Shĕ sāw thĭs plănĕt, līke ă stār,
　　Hŭng īn thĕ glĭstenĭng dĕpths ŏf ēvĕn—
Ĭts brĭdgĕs, rŭnnĭng tō ănd frō,
Ō'er whĭch thĕ whīte-wĭnged Āngĕls gō,
　　Beārĭng thĕ hōlў dēad tŏ hĕavĕn.
Shĕ toūched ă brĭdge ŏf flōwĕrs—thōse feēt
Sŏ līght thĕy dĭd nŏt bĕnd thĕ bĕlls
Ŏf thē cĕlĕstĭal āsphŏdĕls,
Thĕy fĕll līke dĕw ŭpŏn thĕ flōwĕrs;
Thĕn āll thĕ āir grĕw strāngelў sweēt!
Ănd thūs cămĕ dāintў Bābў Bĕll
　　Ĭntŏ thĭs wŏrld ŏf ōurs.
　　　　　Thomas Bailey Aldrich—" Baby Bell."

Example (4).

" Măn wānts bŭt lĭttlĕ hēre bĕlōw,
　　Nŏr wănts thăt lĭttlĕ lōng."
'Tĭs nŏt wĭth mē ĕxāctlў sō,
　　Bŭt 'tĭs sŏ īn thĕ sŏng.
Mў wănts ăre mănў, ānd ĭf tōld,
　　Woŭld mŭstĕr mănў ă scōre:
Ănd wēre ĕach wĭsh ă mĭnt ŏf gōld,
　　Ĭ stĭll shoŭld lōng fŏr mōre.
　　　　John Quincy Adams, "The Wants of Man."

Example (5).

Mў dāys ămŏng thĕ dĕad ăre pāssed;
　　Ăroŭnd mĕ Ĭ bĕhōld,
Whĕre'ēr thĕse cāsŭăl ēўes ăre cāst,
　　Thĕ mīghtў mĭnds ŏf ōld:

Mў nĕvĕr-fāilĭng frĭĕnds ăre thĕy
Wĭth whōm Ĭ cōnvĕrse nĭght ănd dāy.

Wĭth thĕm Ĭ tāke dĕlīght ĭn wēal,
  Ănd seēk rĕliĕf ĭn wōe ;
Ănd whīle Ĭ ŭndĕrstānd ănd feēl
  Hŏw mŭch tŏ thĕm Ĭ ōwe,
Mў cheēks hăve ŏftĕn beēn bĕdĕwed
Wĭth tēars ŏf thōughtfŭl grātĭtŭde.
          Robert Southey—" The Library."

EXAMPLE (6).

Thĕ Fāys thăt tō mў chrĭstenĭng cāme
  (Fŏr cōme thĕy dĭd, mў nūrsĕs tāught mĕ,)
Thĕy dĭd nŏt brĭng mĕ wēalth ŏr fāme,
  'Tĭs vĕrў lĭttlĕ thăt thĕy brōught mĕ.
Bŭt ōne, thĕ crŏssĕst ŏf thĕ crēw,
  Thĕ ŭglў ōld ŏne, ŭnĭnvītĕd,
Sāid, " Ĭ shăll bē ăvēnged ŏn *you*,
  Mў child ; yŏu shăll grŏw ŭp shŏrt-sīghtĕd ! "
Wĭth māgĭc jūicĕs dĭd shĕ lāve
  Mīne eȳes, ănd wrōught hĕr wĭckĕd plēasŭre.
Wĕll, ŏf ăll gĭfts thĕ Fāirĭes gāve,
  Hĕrs ĭs thĕ prĕsĕnt thăt Ĭ trēasŭre !

Thĕ bōre whŏm ōthĕrs feār ănd fleē,
  Ĭ dō nŏt feār, Ĭ dō nŏt fleē hĭm ;
Ĭ pāss hĭm cālm ăs cālm căn bē;
  Ĭ dō nŏt cūt—Ĭ dō nŏt seē hĭm !
Ănd wĭth mў feēblĕ eȳes ănd dĭm,
  Whĕre *you* seĕ pătchў fiēlds ănd fĕncĕs,
Fŏr mē thĕ mĭsts ŏf Tūrnĕr swĭm—
  Mў " āzŭre dĭstănce " soōn cŏmmĕncĕs !
Năy, ăs Ĭ blĭnk ăboŭt thĕ streēts
  Ŏf thĭs bĕfōggĕd ănd mĭrў cĭtў,
Whў, ālmŏst ēverў gĭrl ŏne meēts
  Seĕms prĕtĕrnătŭrāllў prĕttў !

MEASURES EXEMPLIFIED.

"Trў spēctăclēs," ŏne's friĕnds ĭntōne ;
"Yoŭ'll seē thĕ wōrld cŏrrēctlў throŭgh thĕm."
Bŭt Ī hăve vīsiŏns ōf mў ōwn,
Ănd nōt fŏr wōrlds woŭld Ī ŭndō thĕm.
Andrew Lang—"The Fairy's Gift."

EXAMPLE (7).

Ăs, bў sŏme tўrănt's stērn cŏmmānd,
Ă wrĕtch fŏrsākes hĭs nătĭve lānd,
Ĭn fŏrĕign clīmes cŏndēmned tŏ rōam
Ăn ēndlĕss ĕxĭle frŏm hĭs hōme :
Pēnsĭve hĕ trēads thĕ dēstĭned wāy,
Ănd drĕads tŏ gō, nŏr dāres tŏ stāy :
Tĭll ōn sŏme nēighbŏrĭng mŏuntăin's brōw
Hĕ stōps, ănd tŭrns hĭs eўes bĕlōw ;
Thĕre, mēltĭng āt thĕ wēll-knōwn viēw,
Drōps ă lăst tēar, ănd bĭds ădieū ;
Sŏ, Ī thŭs doōmed frŏm theē tŏ pārt,
Găy queēn ŏf fāncў ānd ŏf ārt,
Rĕlūctănt mōve, wĭth dōubtfŭl mīnd,
Ŏft stōp, ănd ōftĕn loŏk bĕhīnd.
Sir William Blackstone—"A Lawyer's Farewell to His Muse."

Measure, Pentameter.
Rhythm, Iambic.
Formula, bA × 5.
Sign, ⌣ — × 5

EXAMPLE (1).

Fāir insĕct ! thāt, wĭth thrēad-līke lĕgs sprĕad ōut,
Ănd bloōd-ĕxtrăctĭng bĭll, ănd fĭlmў wīng,
Dŏst mŭrmŭr, ās thoŭ slōwlў sāil'st ăbōut,
Ĭn pĭtĭlĕss ēars fŭll mānў ă plāintĭve thĭng ;
Ănd tēll'st hŏw lĭttlĕ ōur lărge vēins shoŭld bleēd,
Woŭld wē bŭt yiĕld thĕm freēlў ĭn thў neĕd.
Bryant—"To a Mosquito."

Example (2).

Ētērnăl Hōpe! whĕn yŏndĕr sphēres sŭblīme
Pēaled thĕir fĭrst nōtes tŏ sōund thĕ mārch ŏf Tīme,
Thў jōyoŭs youth bĕgān—bŭt nŏt tŏ fāde.
Whĕn āll thĕ sĭstĕr plănĕts hăve dĕcāyed,
Whĕn wrāpt ĭn fĭre thĕ rĕalms ŏf ĕthĕr glōw
Ănd hĕaven's lăst thŭndĕr shākes thĕ wŏrld bĕlōw,
Thŏu, ŭndĭsmāyed, shălt ō'er thĕ rūĭns smīle,
Ănd lĭght thў tŏrch ăt Nătūre's fūnerăl pīle.
          Thomas Campbell—" Pleasures of Hope."

Example (3).

Ĭn āll mў wănderĭngs roŭnd thĭs wŏrld ŏf cāre,
Ĭn āll mў grĭefs—ănd Gŏd hăs gīven mў shāre—
Ĭ stĭll hăd hōpes mў lātĕst hōurs tŏ crōwn,
Ămĭdst thĕse hŭmblĕ bōwers tŏ lāy mĕ dōwn;
Tŏ hŭsbănd ōut līfe's tāpĕr ăt thĕ clōse,
Ănd, keēp thĕ flāme frŏm wāstĭng bў rĕpōse:
Ĭ stĭll hăd hōpes, fŏr prīde ăttĕnds ŭs stĭll,
Ămĭdst thĕ swāins tŏ shōw mў book-lĕarned skĭll,
Ăroŭnd mў fĭre ăn ēvenĭng groŭp tŏ drāw,
Ănd tĕll ŏf āll Ĭ fĕlt, ănd āll Ĭ sāw;
Ănd, ăs ă hāre, whŏm hoŭnds ănd hōrns pŭrsūe,
Pănts tŏ hĭs plāce frŏm whĕnce ăt fĭrst shĕ flĕw.
Ĭ stĭll hăd hōpes, mў lōng vĕxātĭŏns păst,
Hĕre tŏ rĕtŭrn—ănd dīe ăt hōme ăt lăst.
          Oliver Goldsmith—" Deserted Village."

Example (4).

Whăt ĭs't tŏ ŭs, ĭf tāxĕs rīse ŏr făll?
Thănks tŏ ōur fŏrtūne, wĕ păy nōne ăt āll.
Lĕt mŭckwŏrms, whŏ ĭn dĭrtў ācrĕs dēal,
Lămĕnt thŏse hārdshĭps whĭch wĕ cănnŏt feēl.
Hĭs Grāce, whŏ smărts, măy bĕllōw ĭf hĕ plĕase,
Bŭt mŭst Ĭ bĕllōw toō, whŏ sĭt ăt ēase?

MEASURES EXEMPLIFIED.

Bў cŭstŏm sāfe, thĕ pŏĕt's nŭmbĕrs flŏw
Frĕĕ ăs thĕ līght ănd āir sŏme yēars ăgŏ.
Nŏ stătesmăn ē'er wĭll fĭnd ĭt wōrth hĭs pāins
Tŏ tāx ŏur lăbŏrs ănd ĕxcīse ŏur brāins.
Bŭrthĕns līke thēse, vĭle ēarthlў buīldĭngs beār ;
Nŏ trĭbŭte lāid ŏn cāstlĕs īn thĕ āir !
Charles Churchill—"The Poverty of Poets."

Measure, Hexameter.
Rhythm, Iambic.
Formula, bA × 6.
Sign, ◡ — × 6.

EXAMPLE (1).

Bĕsīde thĭs māssĭve gātewăy
  Buĭlt ŭp ĭn yēars gŏne bў,
Ŭpŏn whŏse tōp thĕ clōuds
  Ĭn ĕtĕrnăl shădŏw līe,
Whĭle strēams thĕ ēvenĭng sūnshĭne
  Ŏn thĕ quĭĕt woōd ănd lēa,
Ĭ stānd ănd cālmlў wāit
  Tĭll thĕ hĭngĕs tŭrn fŏr mē.
William Cullen Bryant—"Waiting by the Gate."

EXAMPLE (2).

Ădōre nŏ Gŏd bĕsīdes mĕ, tō prŏvōke mīne eўes ;
Nŏr wŏrshĭp mē ĭn shāpes ănd fŏrms thăt mĕn dĕvīse ;
Wĭth rĕvĕrĕnce ūse mў nāme, nŏr tŭrn mў wŏrds tŏ jĕst ;
Ŏbsĕrve mў Sābbăth wĕll, nŏr dāre prŏfāne mў rēst ;
Hōnŏr ănd dūe ŏbēdĭĕnce tō thў pārĕnts give ;
Nŏr spĭll thĕ guĭltlĕss bloōd, nŏr lĕt thĕ guīltў lĭve ;
Prĕsērve thў bŏdў chāste, ănd fleē thĕ ŭnlāwfŭl bĕd ;
Nŏr stēal thў neīghbŏr's gōld, hĭs gārmĕnt, ŏr hĭs brēad ;
Fŏrbeār tŏ blāst hĭs nāme wĭth fālsehoōd ŏr dĕcēit ;
Nŏr lĕt thў wīshés loōse ŭpŏn hĭs lārge ĕstāte.
Dr. Isaac Watts—"The Ten Commandments Versified."

Example (3).

Whăt āils theĕ, yoŭng Ŏne? whāt? Whȳ pūll sŏ āt thȳ cōrd?
Ĭs ĭt nŏt wĕll wĭth theĕ? wĕll bōth fŏr bĕd ănd bōard?
Thȳ plŏt ŏf grāss ĭs sŏft, ănd greēn ăs grāss căn bē;
Rĕst, lĭttlĕ yoŭng Ŏne, rĕst; whăt ĭs't thăt āilĕth theĕ?
  Wordsworth—"The Pet Lamb."

The iambic hexameter is seldom employed by our poets, except in combination with other measures. It is used to form the last line of the Spenserian stanza.

Measure, Heptameter.
Rhythm, Iambic.
Formula, bA × 7.
Sign, ⌣ — × 7.

This is our regular ballad meter. For greater convenience, owing to its length, it is generally written in alternate lines of four and three feet.

It is a favorite measure, and perhaps more examples may be found in it than almost any other kind.

Dr. Holmes, always a felicitous writer, has few better poems than the one from which we quote the first stanza. It is in ballad meter:

Example (1).

Ŏ fŏr ŏne hōur ŏf yoūthfŭl jōy!
  Gīve băck mȳ twĕntĭĕth sprĭng!
Ĭ'd rāthĕr lāugh ă brīght-hāired bōy
  Thăn rēign ă grāy-bĕard kīng!
  "The Old Man Dreams."

EXAMPLE (2).

The Sōuth-wĭnd brĕathes, ănd lō! yŏŭ thrŏng
    Thĭs rŭggĕd lānd ŏf ōurs:
Ĭ thĭnk thĕ pāle blŭe clōuds ŏf Māy
    Drŏp dōwn, ănd tūrn tŏ flōwers.
Thomas Bailey Aldrich—"The Bluebells of New England."

EXAMPLE (3).

Ăs ōne whŏ cōns ăt ēvĕnĭng ō'er ăn ălbŭm ăll ălōne,
Ănd mūsĕs ōn thĕ făcĕs ŏf thĕ frĭends thăt hĕ hăs knōwn,
Sŏ Ĭ tūrn thĕ lēaves ŏf făncў tĭll, ĭn shădŏwў dĕsīgn,
Ĭ fĭnd thĕ smĭlĭng fēatŭres ŏf ăn ōld sweĕtheărt ŏf mīne.
    James Whitcomb Riley—"An Old Sweetheart."

EXAMPLE (4).

Thĕ mātrŏn ăt hĕr mĭrrŏr, wĭth hĕr hănd ŭpŏn hĕr brōw,
Sĭts gāzĭng ŏn hĕr lŏvelў făce—ăy, lŏvelў ēvĕn nōw ;
Whў dŏth shĕ lēan ŭpŏn hĕr hănd wĭth sūch ă loŏk ŏf cāre ?
Whў stĕals thăt tēar ăcrōss hĕr cheĕks ?—Shĕ seĕs hĕr fĭrst grăy
    hāir.
            Thomas H. Bayly—"The First Gray Hair."

Measure, Iambic.
Rhythm, Octometer.
Formula, bA × 8.
Sign, ⌣ — × 8.

Owing to the length of the lines we usually find this measure written in stanzas of four lines, rhyming alternately :

EXAMPLE (1).

Ĭt wās thĕ tĭme whĕn lĭlĭes blōw,
    Ănd clōuds ăre hĭghĕst ŭp ĭn āir,
Lŏrd Rōnăld brōught ă lĭlў-whĭte dōe
    Tŏ gĭve hĭs coŭsĭn, Lādў Clāre.
        Alfred Tennyson—"Lady Clare."

EXAMPLE (2).

The light of smiles shall fill again
The lids that overflow with tears;
And weary hours of woe and pain
Are promises of happier years.
    Bryant—"Blessed Are They That Mourn."

DACTYLIC.

Verse in dactylic rhythms is not so common as in other rhythms. It is, however, capable of great results. It is a stately rhythm, and one in which some of our best battle hymns are written. Love, pathos, grief and all the tender emotions are expressed in this rhythm with durable effect. Patriotism finds true expression in dactylic accents. Tetrameter verse is the favorite measure of writers of this rhythm. Dactylic with single rhymes end with a caesura or single foot; while double rhymes end with a trochee; full dactylic usually form triple rhymes. Dactylic poetry is seldom pure and regular.

Measure, Dimeter.
Rhythm, Dactylic.
Formula, Abb × 2.
Sign, — ⌣ ⌣ × 2.

EXAMPLE (1).

Little white Lily
  Sat by a Stone,
Drooping and wilting
  Till the sun shone.
Little white Lily
  Sunshine has fed;
Little white Lily
  Is lifting her head.
George Mac Donald—"The White Lily."

Example (2).

Māke nŏ deĕp scrūtĭnў
Īntŏ hĕr mūtĭnў,
Rāsh ănd ŭndūtĭfŭl :
Pāst ăll dĭshōnŏr,
Dĕath hăs lĕft ōn hĕr
Ŏnlў thĕ beaūtĭfŭl.
Thomas Hood—"Bridge of Sīghs."

Example (3).

"Roōm fŏr hĭm īntŏ thĕ
Rānks ŏf hŭmānĭtў;
Gĭve hĭm ă plāce ĭn yoŭr
Kĭngdŏm ŏf vānĭtў!
Wĕlcŏme thĕ strāngĕr wĭth
Kĭndlў ăffēctĭŏn ;
Hōpefŭllў, trūstfŭllў,
Nōt wĭth dĕjēctĭŏn."
"My Boy."

Example (4).

Rĭsĭng ănd lēapĭng,
Sĭnkĭng ănd creēpĭng,
Swĕllĭng ănd sweēpĭng,
Shōwerĭng ănd sprĭngĭng,
Flўĭng ănd flĭngĭng,
Wrīthĭng ănd rĭngĭng,
Ēddyĭng ănd whĭskĭng,
Spōutĭng ănd frĭskĭng,
Tŭrnĭng ănd twĭstĭng,
Ărōund ănd ărōund—
Wĭth ēndlĕss rĕbōund!
Robert Southey—"The Cataract of Lodore."

Example (5).

Hălf ă lĕague, hălf ă lĕague,
Hălf ă lĕague ōnwărd,
Āll ĭn thĕ vălley ŏf Dēath
   Rōde thĕ sĭx hŭndrĕd.
"Fōrwărd, thĕ Līght Brĭgāde!
Chărge fŏr thĕ gŭns," hĕ sāid:
Ĭntŏ thĕ vălley ŏf Dēath
   Rōde thĕ sĭx hŭndrĕd.
   Tennyson—"The Charge of the Light Brigade."

Example (6).

Bīrd ŏf thĕ wĭldĕrnĕss,
Blīthesŏme ănd cŭmbĕrlĕss,
Sweēt bĕ thў mātĭn, ŏ'er moōrlănd ănd lēa!
Ēmblĕm ŏf hăppĭnĕss,
Blēst ĭs thў dwĕllĭng plăce—
Ō, tŏ ăbīde ĭn thĕ dēsĕrt wĭth theē!
Wīld ĭs thў lāy ănd lōud
Fār ĭn thĕ dōwnў clōud,
Lōve gĭves ĭt ēnĕrgў, lōve găve ĭt bīrth.
Whēre, ŏn thў dēwў wīng,
Whēre ărt thŏu jōurnĕyĭng?
Thў lāy ĭs ĭn hēavĕn, thў lōve ĭs ŏn ēarth.

Ō'er fĕll ănd fōuntăin sheēn
Ō'er moŏr ănd mōuntăin greēn,
Ō'er thĕ rĕd strēamĕr thăt hĕrălds thĕ dāy,
Ōvĕr thĕ clōudlĕt dīm,
Ōvĕr thĕ raīnbŏw's rīm,
Mūsĭcăl chĕrŭb, sŏar, sĭngĭng ăwāy!
Thĕn, whĕn thĕ glōamĭng cōmes,
Lōw ĭn thĕ hēathĕr bloōms
Sweēt wĭll thў wĕlcŏme ănd bĕd ŏf lŏve bĕ!
Ēmblĕm ŏf hăppĭnĕss,
Blēst ĭs thў dwĕllĭng plăce—
Ō, tŏ ăbīde ĭn thĕ dēsĕrt wĭth theē!
     James Hogg—"The Sky Lark."

The above is dimeter, trimeter and tetrameter.

MEASURES EXEMPLIFIED.

Measure, Tetrameter.
Rhythm, Dactylic.
Formula, Abb × 4.
Sign, — ◡ ◡ × 4.

EXAMPLE (1).

Cŏ̄vĕr thĕm ōvĕr wĭth beaûtĭfŭl flŏ̄wĕrs ;
Dĕck thĕm wĭth gārlănds, thŏse brōthĕrs ŏf ōurs ;
Lȳĭng sŏ sīlĕnt, bў nĭght ănd bў dāy,
Sleēpĭng thĕ yēars ŏf theĭr mānhoŏd ăwāy :
Yĕars thĕy hăd mārked fŏr thĕ jōys ŏf thĕ brāve ;
Yĕars thĕy mŭst wăste ĭn thĕ slōth ŏf thĕ grāve.
Ăll thĕ brĭght laūrĕls thĕy fōught tŏ māke bloŏ̄m
Fĕll tŏ thĕ ēarth whĕn thĕy wĕnt tŏ thĕ tōmb.
Gīve thĕm thĕ meēd thĕy hăve wŏn ĭn thĕ pāst ;
Gĭve thĕm thĕ hōnŏrs theĭr mĕrĭts fŏrecāst ;
Gĭve thĕm thĕ chăplĕts thĕy wŏn ĭn thĕ strĭfe ;
Gĭve thĕm thĕ laūrĕls thĕy lŏst wĭth theĭr lĭfe.
Cŏ̄vĕr thĕm ōvĕr—yĕs, cŏ̄vĕr thĕm ōvĕr—
Pārĕnt, ănd hūsbănd, ănd brŏther, ănd lŏ̄vĕr :
Crōwn ĭn yoŭr heărt thĕse dĕad hĕ̄roĕs ŏf ōurs,
Ănd cŏ̄vĕr thĕm ōvĕr wĭth beaûtĭfŭl flŏ̄wĕrs.
              Will Carleton—"Cover Them Over."

EXAMPLE (2).

Wĕarў wăy-wāndĕrĕr, lănguĭd ănd sĭck ăt heărt,
  Trăvĕlĭng pāinfŭllў ōvĕr thĕ rŭggĕd rŏad,—
Wĭld-vĭsăged wāndĕrĕr ! Gŏd hĕlp theē, wrĕtchĕd ŏne !
        Robert Southey—"The Soldier's Wife."

EXAMPLE (3).

Hāil tŏ thĕ Chiĕf whŏ ĭn triŭmph ădvāncĕs !
  Hŏnŏred ănd blĕssed bĕ thĕ ĕvĕrgreēn pīne !
Lōng măy thĕ treē, ĭn hĭs bānnĕr thăt glāncĕs
  Floŭrĭsh, thĕ shĕltĕr ănd grāce ŏf oŭr līne !
        Sir Walter Scott—"Boat Song."

Example (4).

Cōme tŏ mĕ, dĕar, ĕre Ĭ dīe ŏf mў sōrrŏw,
Rise ŏn mў gloōm līke thĕ sūn ŏf tŏ-mōrrŏw.
Strōng, swĭft ănd fŏnd ăs thĕ wōrds thăt Ĭ spēak, lŏve
Wĭth ă sōng ŏn yŏur lĭp ănd ă smīle ŏn yŏur cheēk, lŏve.
Cōme, fŏr mў heārt ĭn yŏur ābsĕnce ĭs wēarў—
Hāste, fŏr mў spĭrĭt ĭs sickĕned ănd drēarў—
Cōme tŏ thĕ ārms whĭch ălōne shoŭld cărĕss theĕ,
Cōme tŏ thĕ heārt whĭch ĭs thrōbbĭng tŏ prĕss theĕ!
  Joseph Brennan— "Come to Me, Dearest."

Measure, Hexameter.
Rhythm, Dactylic.
Formula, Abb × 6.
Sign, — ◡ ◡ × 6.

Example (1).

Beaūtĭfŭl wăs thĕ nĭght. Bĕhĭnd thĕ blăck wăll ŏf thĕ fŏrĕst,
Tĭppĭng ĭts sūmmĭt wĭth sĭlvĕr, ărōse thĕ moōn. Ŏn thĕ rĭvĕr
Fĕll hĕre ănd thĕre thrŏŭgh thĕ brănchĕs ă trĕmŭloŭs glēam ŏf thĕ moōnlĭght,
Like thĕ sweĕt thōughts ŏf lŏve ŏn ă dărkĕned ănd dĕvĭoŭs spĭrĭt.
Nĕarĕr ănd rōund ăbōut hĕr, thĕ mănĭfōld flōwers ŏf thĕ gārdĕn
Pōured ŏut thĕir sōuls ĭn ōdŏrs, thăt wĕre thĕir prāyers ănd cŏnfĕssĭŏns
Ŭntŏ thĕ night, ăs ĭt wĕnt ĭts wăy, līke ă sĭlĕnt Cărthūsĭăn.
Fūllĕr ŏf frăgrănce thăn thĕy, ănd ăs hĕavў wĭth shădŏws ănd nĭght dĕws,
Hūng thĕ heārt ŏf thĕ māidĕn. Thĕ cālm ănd thĕ măgĭcăl moōnlĭght
Seĕmed tŏ ĭnūndāte hĕr sōul wĭth ĭndĕfīnāblĕ lōngĭngs,
Ăs, thrŏŭgh thĕ gārdĕn gāte, ănd bĕnĕath thĕ shāde ŏf thĕ ōak treĕs
Păssed shĕ ălōng thĕ păth tŏ thĕ ĕdge ŏf thĕ mĕasūrelĕss prārĭĕs.
  Henry Wadsworth Longfellow—"Evangeline on the Prairie."

ANAPESTIC.

Anapestic measure is growing in favor year by year, and the tumbling meter of King James is one of the beautiful rhythms of modern verse. It is interchangeable with the iambus, as well as other measures, especially the dactylic and amphibrach. An iambus is frequently the first foot of anapestic measure. Anapestic tetrameter is very smooth flowing, a rhythm some of our poets use with admirable effect, producing verse of both melody and vigor. It is well adapted to cheerful and humorous verse.

Measure, Monometer.
Rhythm, Anapestic.
Formula, bbA.
Sign, ⌣ ⌣ —.

Anapestic monometer is rarely met with except where it is used as a refrain or in combination with other measures of verse. It is so near akin to trochaic catalectic dimeter, that it is often extremely difficult to distinguish it from that measure. Anapestic verse is very often mixed, and its measure can only be determined by a careful scansion, and, by the prevailing primary measure or foot.

Example (1).

In thĕ slēigh
Hīe ăwāy!
Hĕre wĕ gō
Ŏn thĕ snōw.

In ă trānce,
Hŏw wĕ dānce
Steĕds ăwāy
Ŏh hŏw gāy!

Mŭsĭc-swĕlls
Ŏf thĕ bĕlls
In thĕ nīght
Gīve dĕlīght.

In ă dāze
Hŏw wĕ gāze
In ă māze
Ăt thĕ slēighs!

Nŏw wĕ rīde,   'Tĭs ă trēat,
Nŏw wĕ glīde,   Ŏn thĕ sleēt—
Swĭft gŏ bȳ   Wĭth yoŭr Sweēt
Hŏw wĕ flȳ !   Tŏ gŏ slēighĭng !
                          "The Sleigh Ride."

EXAMPLE (2).

Thĕn wĕ gŏ
Tŏ ănd frŏ,
Wĭth ŏur knācks
Ăt ŏur bācks,
Tŏ sŭch strēams
Ăs thĕ Thāmes
Ĭf wĕ hăve thĕ lēisŭre.
            Chalkhill—"The Angler."

"The Angler" is a trochaic poem, although these lines are readily scanned as anapestic monometer.

Measure, Dimeter.
Rhythm, Anapestic.
Formula, bbA × 2.
Sign, ⌣ ⌣ — × 2.

EXAMPLE (1).

Hĕ ĭs gōne ! Hĕ ĭs gōne !
   Līke thĕ lĕaf frŏm thĕ treē,
Ŏr thĕ dōwn thăt ĭs blōwn
   Bȳ thĕ wĭnd ŏ'er thĕ lēa.
Hĕ ĭs flĕd, thĕ lĭght-heārtĕd !
   Yĕt ă tĕar mŭst hăve stārtĕd
Tŏ hĭs eȳes, whĕn hĕ pārtĕd
   Frŏm lŏve strĭckĕn mē.
         Motherwell—"He is Gone—He is Gone."

The stanza below from the "Heathen Chinee" is anapestic dimeter, trimeter and tetrameter:

EXAMPLE (2).

Whĭch Ĭ wĭsh tŏ rĕmārk—
Ănd mў lānguăge ĭs plāin—
Thăt fŏr wāys thăt ăre dārk
Ănd fŏr trĭcks thăt ăre vāin,
Thĕ hēathĕn Chĭneë ĭs pĕcūlĭār:
Whĭch thĕ sāme Ĭ woŭld rīse tŏ ĕxplāin.
Bret Harte—"Plain Language from Truthful James."

EXAMPLE (3).

Thĕ blĕssĕd ŏld fīre-plăce! hŏw brīght ĭt ăppēars,
Ăs băck tŏ mў bōyhoŏd Ĭ gāze,
Ŏ'er thĕ dĕsŏlăte wāste ŏf thĕ vănĭshĭng yēars,
Frŏm thĕ gloōm ŏf thĕse lōne lăttĕr-dāys;
Ĭts lĭps ăre ăs rūddў, ĭts heărt ĭs ăs wārm
Tŏ mў făncў tŏnĭght ăs ŏf yōre,
Whĕn wĕ cŭddlĕd ăroūnd ĭt ănd smīled ăt thĕ stŏrm,
Ăs ĭt shōwed ĭts whīte teēth ăt thĕ doōr.
James Newton Matthews—"The Old Fireplace."

This stanza is anapestic trimeter and tetrameter.

Measure, Trimeter.
Rhythm, Anapestic.
Formula, bbA × 3.
Sign, ᴗ ᴗ — × 3.

EXAMPLE (1).

Ĭ ăm mŏnărch ŏf āll Ĭ sŭrvēy,
Mў rĭght thĕre ĭs nŏne tŏ dĭspūte;
Frŏm thĕ cĕntrĕ ăll roūnd tŏ thĕ sēa,
Ĭ ăm lŏrd ŏf thĕ fŏwl ănd thĕ brūte.

O Solitude! where are the charms
　　That sages have seen in thy face?
Better dwell in the midst of alarms
　　Than reign in this horrible place.
　　　　　William Cowper—"Alexander Selkirk."

Example (2).

Oh, Love is a wonderful wizard!
　He can see by his own keen light,
He laughs at the wrath of the tempest,
　He has never a fear of the night.
Two lives that are wedded leagues hold not apart,—
　Love can hear, e'en through thunder, the beat of a heart.
　　　　　Lucy Larcom—"On the Misery Islands."

This stanza is trimeter and tetrameter:

Measure, Tetrameter.
Rhythm, Anapestic.
Formula, bbA × 4.
Sign, ⌣ ⌣ — × 4.

Example (1).

Mr. 'Liakim Smith was a hard-fisted farmer
　　Of moderate wealth,
　　And immoderate health,
Who fifty-odd years in a stub and twist armor
Of callous and tan, had fought like a man
His own dogged progress through trials and cares,
And log-heaps, and brush-heaps, and wild cats and bears,
And agues and fevers, and thistles and briars,
Poor kinsman, rich foeman, false saints, and true liars;
Who oft, like "the man in our town," overwise,
Through the brambles of error had scratched out his eyes,
And when the unwelcome result he had seen,
　　Had altered his notion,
　　Reversing the motion

MEASURES EXEMPLIFIED.

And scratched them both in again, perfect and clean ;
Who had weathered some storms, as a sailor might say,
And tacked to the left and the right of his way,
Till he found himself anchored, past tempests and breakers,
Upon a good farm of a hundred-odd acres.
Will Carleton—"The Three Lovers."

EXAMPLE (2).

When the candles burn low, and the company's gone,
In the silence of night as I sit here alone —
I sit here alone, but we yet are a pair —
My Fanny I see in my cane-bottomed chair.
William Makepeace Thackeray — "The Cane-Bottomed Chair."

EXAMPLE (3).

My heart's in the Highlands, my heart is not here ;
My heart's in the Highlands a-chasing the deer ;
Chasing the wild deer, and following the roe,
My heart's in the Highlands wherever I go.
Farewell to the Highlands, farewell to the North,
The birth-place of valor, the country of worth ;
Wherever I wander, wherever I rove,
The hills of the Highlands forever I love.
Robert Burns—"My Heart's in the Highlands"

EXAMPLE (4).

O young Lochinvar is come out of the west;
Through all the wide border, his steed was the best ;
And save his good broadsword he weapons had none,
He rode all unarmed, and he rode all alone.
So faithful in love and so dauntless in war,
There never was knight like the young Lochinvar.
Sir Walter Scott—"Lochinvar."

Example (5).

Thĕ goŏd shĭp Ărbēllă ĭs lēadĭng thĕ flēet,
Ăwāy tŏ thĕ wĕstwărd thrŏŭgh rāin-stŏrm ănd sleĕt ;
Thĕ whīte clĭffs ŏf Ēnglănd hăve drŏpped oŭt ŏf sīght :
Ăs bĭrds frŏm thĕ wărmth ŏf thĕir nēsts tākĭng flīght
Ĭntŏ wīdĕr hŏrīzŏns ĕach flŭttĕrĭng sāil
Fŏllŏws făst whĕre thĕ Māyflŏwer flēd ŏn thĕ gāle
Wĭth hĕr rēsŏlūte Pĭlgrĭms, ŏn wĭntĕrs bĕfōre ;
Ănd thĕ fĭre ŏf thĕir fāith lĭghts thĕ sēa ănd thĕ shōre.
     Lucy Larcom—"The Lady Arbella."

Measure, Hexameter.
Rhythm, Anapestic.
Formula, bb A × 6.
Sign, ⌣ ⌣ — × 6.

Example (1).

Mў sĭstĕr'll bĕ dŏwn ĭn ă mĭnūte, ănd sāys yoŭ're tŏ wāit, ĭf yoŭ plĕase,
Ănd sāys Ĭ mĭght stāy tĭll shĕ cāme, ĭf Ĭ'd prŏmĭse hĕr nĕvĕr tŏ tēase
Nŏr spĕak tĭll yoŭ spōke tŏ mĕ fĭrst, bŭt thăt's nŏnsĕnse, fŏr hŏw woŭld yoŭ knŏw
Whăt shĕ tōld mĕ tŏ sāy ĭf Ĭ dĭdn't? Dŏn't yoŭ rēallў ănd trūlў thĭnk sō?
    Bret Harte—" Entertaining her Big Sister's Beau."

CHAPTER XI.

IMITATION OF CLASSICAL MEASURES.

MANY of our modern poets have experimented in the classical meters. Cowper, Southey, Kingsley, Swinburne, Longfellow and Tennyson, have all imitated classic measures. The results in most instances are not practical, and have furnished us only with curiosities in literature. There are said to be some twenty-nine Greek and Latin meters. As all Latin and Greek verse depended upon quantity, and English verse depends upon accent, we do not believe classical measures can be successfully adopted in English.

In addition to Latin Pentameters and Hexameters, some English poets have imitated Greek Sapphics and Alcaics. Alkaios was a lyric poet born in Mitylene, the capital of Lesbos, who flourished B. C. 606 years. He was supposed to have been the inventor of the Alcaic Ode, an ode written in the Alcaic meter composed of several strophes, each consisting of four lines. An Alcaic strophe consisted of two Alcaic hendekasyllables, one Alcaic enneasyllable, and one Alcaic decasyllable. The following imitation by the poet laureate of England is given:

> Ŏ mīghtў mōuthĕd ĭnvēntŏr ŏf hārmŏnĭes,
> Ŏ skīlled tŏ sīng ŏf Tīme ŏr Ĕtērnĭtў,
>   Gŏd-gīftĕd ōrgăn-vōice ŏf Ēnglănd,
>   Mīltŏn, ă nāme tŏ rĕsoūnd fŏr āgĕs.
>   *Tennyson*—"Milton."

The Sapphic meter is a kind of verse said to have been invented by Sappho, a Greek poetess, nearly contemporaneous with Alkaios, born at Mitylene, in the Island of Lesbos, B. C. 600. The Sapphic verse consisted of eleven syllables in five feet, of which the first, fourth and fifth are trochees, the second a spondee, and the third a dactyl. This verse, or line, is thrice repeated and followed by an Adonic. The following lines imitate the Sapphic:

> Cōld wăs thĕ nīght-wĭnd, drīftĭng fāst thĕ snōw fĕll,
> Wīde wĕre thĕ dōwns, ănd shēltĕrlĕss ănd nākĕd,
> Whĕn ă poŏr Wāndĕrĕr strŭgglĕd ōn hĕr joūrnĕy,
>   Wĕary̆ ănd wāy-sŏre.
>   *Southey*—"The Widow."

Here is still another imitation of this measure:

> Āll thĕ nĭght slēep cāme nŏt ŭpōn my̆ ey̆elĭds,
> Shĕd nŏt dĕw, nŏr shoŏk nŏr ŭnclōsed ă fĕathĕr,
> Yĕt wĭth lĭps shŭt clōse ănd wĭth ey̆es ŏf īrŏn
>   Stōod ănd bĕhĕld mĕ.
>   *Swinburne*—"Sapphics."

Dr. Watts gives a vivid picture of the last day, in Sapphics:

> Tēars thĕ strŏng pĭllărs ŏf thĕ vāult ŏf hēavĕn,
> Brĕaks ŭp ōld mārblĕ, thĕ rĕpōse ŏf prīncĕs;
> Sēe thĕ grăves ōpĕn, ănd thĕ bōnes ărīsĭng.
>   Flāmes ăll ărōund thĕm!
>   *Watts*—"The Day of Judgment."

Hexameter verse was the heroic verse of the classics. It consists of six feet properly dactyls, the last of which is shortened by one syllable and so became a trochee, or, as the final syllable is long by position, a spondee. This form was not always observed strictly, and the first four feet were indifferently dactyls or spondees, the former being used to produce the idea of rapid, the latter of slow, laborious movement. The fifth foot should always be a dactyl, sometimes, though rarely, it is replaced by a spondee, in which case the fourth foot must be a dactyl.

Ŏvĕr thĕ sēa, păst Crēte, ŏn thĕ Sȳrĭăn shōre tŏ thĕ sōuthwărd,
Dwĕlls ĭn thĕ wĕll-tĭlled lōwlănd ă dārk-hāired Æthĭŏp pēoplĕ,
Skĭllfŭl wĭth nēedlĕ ănd lōom, ănd thĕ ārts ŏf thĕ dȳĕr ănd cārvĕr,
Skĭllfŭl, bŭt fēeblĕ ŏf heārt; fŏr thĕy knōw nŏt thĕ lōrds ŏf
    Ŏlȳmpŭs.
Lŏvĕrs ŏf mēn; nĕithĕr brōad-brōwed Zĕūs, nŏr Pāllăs Ăthēnĕ,
Tēachĕr ŏf wīsdŏm tŏ hērŏes, bĕstōwĕr ŏf mīght ĭn thĕ bāttlĕ;
Shāre nŏt thĕ cūnnĭng ŏf Hērmĕs, nŏr līst tŏ thĕ sōngs ŏf Ăpōllŏ.
                Kingsley—"Andromeda."

Thĕse lāme hĕxāmĕtērs thĕ strōng-wĭnged mūsĭc ŏf Hōmĕr!
Nō—bŭt ă mōst bŭrlĕsque bārbărŏŭs ĕxpĕrĭmĕnt.
Whĕn wăs ă hārshĕr sōund ĕvĕr hēard, yĕ Mūsĕs ŏf Ēnglănd?
Whĕn dĭd ă frŏg cōarsĕr crōak ŭpōn oŭr Hĕlĭcōn?
Hĕxāmĕtĕrs nŏ wōrse thăn dārĭng Gērmănȳ gāve ŭs,
Bărbărŏŭs ĕxpĕrĭmĕnt, bărbărŏŭs hĕxāmĕtĕrs.
                Tennyson—"Hexameters and Pentameters."

Ārt thoŭ sŏ nēar ūntŏ mē, ānd yĕt Ĭ cānnŏt bĕhōld thĕĕ?
Ārt thoŭ sŏ nēar ūntŏ mē, ānd yĕt thȳ vōice dŏes nŏt rēach mē?
Āh! hŏw ōftĕn thȳ fēet hăve trōd thĭs pāth tŏ thĕ prāirĭĕ!
Āh! hŏw ōftĕn thĭne ēyes hăve loōked ŏn thĕ woōdlănds ăroŭnd
    mĕ!
Āh! hŏw ōftĕn bĕnēath thĭs ōak, rĕtūrnĭng frŏm lābŏr,
Thoū hăst lāin dŏwn tŏ rēst ănd to drēam ŏf mē ĭn thȳ slŭmbĕrs!
Whĕn shāll thĕse ĕyes bĕhōld, thĕse ārms bĕ fōldĕd ăboūt thĕe?
Loūd ănd sūddĕn ănd nēar thĕ nōte ŏf ă whĭp-poŏr-wĭll soūndĕd

Like a flute in the woods; and anon, through the neighboring
    thickets,
Farther and farther away it floated and dropped into silence.
"Patience!" whispered the oaks from oracular caverns of dark-
    ness;
And, from the moonlit meadow, a sigh responded, "Tomorrow!"
    Henry Wadsworth Longfellow—"Evangeline."

A Hendecasyllable is a verse of eleven syllables. It does not occur in Horace. In Catullus it sometimes has a trochee or an iambus in the first place.

Example (1)

O you chorus of indolent reviewers,
Irresponsible, indolent reviewers,
Look, I come to the test, a tiny poem
All composed in a meter of Catullus,
All in quantity, careful of my motion,
Like the skater on ice that hardly bears him,
Lest I fall unawares before the people,
Waking laughter in indolent reviewers.
Should I flounder awhile without a tumble
Thro' this metrification of Catullus,
They should speak to me not without a welcome,
All that chorus of indolent reviewers.
Hard, hard, hard is it, only not to tumble,
So fantastical is the dainty meter.
Wherefore slight me not wholly, nor believe me
Too presumptuous, indolent reviewers.
O blatant Magazines, regard me rather—
Since I blush to belaud myself a moment—
As some rare little rose, a piece of inmost
Horticultural art, or half coquette-like
Maiden, not to be greeted unbenignly.
    —*Tennyson*—"Hendecasyllabics."

EXAMPLE (2).

In thĕ mŏnth ŏf thĕ lōng dēclīne ŏf rōsĕs,
Ī, bĕhōldĭng thĕ sŭmmĕr dĕad bĕfōre mĕ,
Sĕt mў fāce tŏ thĕ sēa, ănd jōurnĕyed sĭlĕnt,
Gāzĭng ĕagĕrlў whēre, ăbōve thĕ sēa-mărk,
Flāme ăs fĭerce ăs thĕ fĕrvĭd eўes ŏf līŏns
Hălf-dĭvīdĕd thĕ eўelĭds ŏf thĕ sŭnsĕt;
Tĭll Ĭ hĕard, ăs ĭt wĕre, ă nōise ŏf wātĕrs
Mŏvĭng trĕmŭlŏŭs ūndĕr fĕĕt ŏf āngĕls
Mŭltĭtūdĭnŏŭs, ōut ŏf āll thĕ hĕavĕns;
Knēw thĕ flŭttĕrĭng wĭnd, thĕ flŭttĕred fōlĭăge,
Shākĕn fĭtfŭllў, fŭll ŏf sōund ănd shădŏw;
Ănd săw, trōddĕn ŭpōn bў nōiselĕss āngĕls,
Lōng mўstĕrīŏŭs rēachĕs fĕd wĭth moōnlĭght,
Swēet săd strāits ĭn ă sŏft sŭbsīdĭng chănnĕl,
Blōwn ăbōut bў thĕ lĭps ŏf wĭnds Ĭ knĕw nŏt,
Wĭnds nŏt bŏrn ĭn thĕ nōrth nŏr ănў quărtĕr,
Wĭnds nŏt wărm wĭth thĕ sōuth nŏr ănў sūnshĭne;
Hĕard bĕtwēen thĕm ă vōice ŏf ĕxŭltātĭŏn,
"Lō, thĕ sŭmmĕr ĭs dĕad, thĕ sŭn ĭs fādĕd,
Ĕvĕn līke ăs ă lēaf thĕ yĕar ĭs wĭthĕred,
Āll thĕ frŭits ŏf thĕ dāy frŏm āll hĕr brănchĕs
Gāthĕred, nēithĕr ĭs ānў lĕft tŏ gāthĕr.

Swinburne—"Hendecasyllabics."

What the ingenuity of man may yet invent is hard to tell. We may say therefore, look to the Greek and Latin measures still for models, some ingenious mortal may be richly rewarded.

It is claimed Edgar Allan Poe caught the inspiration of the rhythm of his "The Raven," from Latin lines:

Ōnce ŭpōn ă mĭdnĭght drēarў
Lēc-tŏr căst-ĕ căth-ŏ-lĭc-ĕ
Whīle Ĭ pōndĕred wĕak ănd wēarў.
Āt-quĕ ŏb-sĕs āth-lĕt-ĭc-ĕ.

This same great master of English rhythm in his "Rationale of Verse," also stated, "That if he were permitted to use the Spondee, the Trochee, the Iambus, the Anapest and the Dactyl, together with the Caesura. he would engage to scan correctly any true rhythm human ingenuity could invent." His statement after years of time, who can gainsay?

CHAPTER XII.

POETICAL LICENSES.

Many are the peculiarities and licenses granted to the writers of poetry, not accorded to the writers of prose. These peculiarities add a charm and a freshness to our poetry and are employed freely by the best writers, and this freedom is often necessary to meet the requirements of accent and rhythm, and to it we owe much of the beauty of poetry. There is nothing which adds more grace to our language than these peculiarities of speech, and every student of poetry should become thoroughly familiar with them. While they are recognized violations of the regular rules of speech, they are not so extensive but that they will admit of classification. These peculiarities are usually the conceptions of our master minds, who vary from the regular construction and become, so to speak, inventors of new usages, which afterwards become by common acceptance recognized licenses in our language.

(1) Poetry differs from prose in the fact that every verse or line always commences with a capital letter, as:

    Shăll hē ălōne, whŏm rátiŏnāl wĕ cāll,
    Bĕ blēssed wĭth nōthĭng, ĭf nŏt blēssed wĭth āll?
              Pope — "Essay on Man."

(2) For the sake of brevity or meter the article is not infrequently omitted, as :

> Whăt drēadfŭl plēasūre! Thēre tŏ stănd sŭblime,
> Līke shĭp-wrĕcked mărīnēr ŏn dĕsĕrt cōast!
> *Beattie*—"The Minstrel."

(3) Interjections are oftener employed in poetry than in prose, as :

> Ŏ grāy ŏblĭvĭoŭs Rĭvĕr!
> Ŏ sŭnsĕt-kĭndlĕd Rĭvĕr!
> Dŏ yoū rĕmĕmbĕr ĕvĕr
>   Thĕ eȳes ănd skīes sŏ blūe
> Ŏn ă sŭmmĕr dāy thăt shōne hĕre,
> Whĕn wē wĕre ăll ălōne hĕre,
> Ănd thĕ blūe eȳes wēre toŏ wīse
>   Tŏ spēak thĕ lōve thĕy knĕw?
> *John Hay*—"The River."

(4) The noun "self" is introduced after another noun of the possessive case, as :

> Thŏughtlĕss ŏf beaūtȳ, shĕ wăs beaūtȳ's sĕlf.
> *Thomson*—"The Seasons."

(5) The use of a kind of compound adjective ending in "like," as :

> Thĕ prŏud dĭctātŏr ŏf thĕ *stāte-līke* woōd—
> Ĭ mĕan thĕ sŏvĕreĭgn ŏf ăll plānts, thĕ ōak—
> Droŏps, dies, ănd fālls wĭthŏut thĕ clĕavĕr's strōke.
> *Herrick*—"All Things Decay and Die."

> Whŏ swims wĭth vĭrtŭe, hĕ shăll still bĕ sūre,
> Ŭlȳssĕs-like, ăll tĕmpĕsts tō ĕndūre,
> Ănd 'mĭdst ă thŏusănd gŭlfs tŏ bē sĕcūre.
> *Herrick*—"No Shipwreck of Virtue."

POETICAL LICENSES.

Crowned with trailing plumes of sable, right a-front my standing-
 place
Moved a swarthy ocean-steamer in her storm-resisting grace.
Prophet-like, she clove the waters toward the ancient mother-land,
And I heard her clamorous engine and the echo of command,
While the long Atlantic billows to my feet came rolling on,
With the multitudinous music of a thousand ages gone.
Stedman—"Flood-Tide."

(6) The comparative degree is used joined to the positive before a verb, as :

"Near and more near the intrepid beauty pressed"
Merrick.

(7) The conjunctions "or—or," and "nor—nor" are used as correspondents, as :

Not all the autumn's rustling gold,
Nor sun, nor moon, nor star shall bring
The jocund spirit which of old
Made it an easy joy to sing!
Aldrich—"Song-Time."

The hand of God came to him, and he rose :
 "Go trench the valley; though you may not feel
 Or wind or rain, the waters shall be poured
Throughout the camps in streams. Nor heed the foes,
 For Moab shall be given to your steel,
 The choicest cities spoiled, the fruit trees scored,
The wells choked up, the gardens marred with stones !"
 In awe they heard the potent words. Alas,
For homes foredoomed to fall with evil thrones,
For, as he had foretold, it came to pass!
Joseph O'Conner—"Bring Me a Minister."

(8) The use of "and—and" for "both—and," as :

"And the starlight and moonlight."

(9) The preposition is placed after the object, as:

> I lounge in the ilex shadows,
> I see the lady lean,
> Unclasping her silken girdle,
> The curtain's folds between.
> *Aldrich*—"Nocturne."

(10) Prepositions and their adjuncts are not unfrequently placed before the words on which they depend, as:

> Against your fame with fondness hate combines;
> The rival batters and the lover mines.
> *Samuel Johnson.*

(11) Compound epithets are frequently used, as:

> Hebe's here, May is here!
> The air is fresh and sunny;
> And the *miser-bees* are busy
> Hoarding golden honey.
> *Aldrich*—"May."

> "*Blue-eyed, strange-voiced, sharp-beaked, ill-omened* fowl
> What art thou? 'What I ought to be, an owl.'"

(12) Inversions are very common in poetry, as:

> *Few* and *short* were the prayers we said,
> And we spoke not a word of sorrow;
> But we steadfastly gazed on the face of the dead,
> And we bitterly thought of the morrow.
> *Charles Wolfe*—"Burial of Sir John Moore."

(13) Superfluous pronouns are freely used, as:

> There came a burst of thunder sound;
> The boy,—oh! where was he?
> Ask of the winds, that far around
> With fragments strewed the sea.
> *Felicia Hemans*—"Casabianca."

POETICAL LICENSES. 181

(14) Foreign idioms are not unfrequently used, as :

"Fŏr nŏt tŏ hāve beĕn dīpped ĭn Lēthĕ lāke
Coŭld sāve thĕ sōn ŏf Thĕtĭs *frŏm tŏ dīe.*"

(15) The adjective is placed after the noun, as :

"Ăcrōss thĕ mēadŏws bāre ănd brōwn."

(16) The adjective is placed before the verb "to be," as:

"Sweĕt ĭs thĕ breăth ŏf vērnăl shōwers."

(17) The antecedent is not infrequently omitted, as :

Whŏ nēvĕr fāsts, nŏ bānquĕt e'er ĕnjōys,
Whŏ nēvĕr tōils ŏr wātchĕs, nēvĕr sleĕps.
Armstrong.

(18) The relative is omitted, as :

"'Tĭs Fāncў ĭn hĕr fĭerў cār,
Trănspōrts mĕ tō thĕ thĭckĕst wār."

(19) The verb precedes the nominative, as :

Thĕn *shoŏk* thĕ hĭlls wĭth thŭndĕr rīvĕn,
Thĕn *rūshed* thĕ steĕds tŏ bāttlĕ drīvĕn,
Ănd loŭdĕr thăn thĕ bōlts ŏf hĕavĕn,
Făr *flāshed* thĕ rēd ărtĭllĕrў.
Thomas Campbell—"Hohenlinden."

(20) The verb follows the accusative, as :

Hĭs *prāyer* hĕ *sāith*, thĭs hōlў mān.
Keats.

(21) The infinitive is placed before the word on which it depends, as:

> Whĕn fĭrst thў sīre, *tŏ sĕnd* ŏn ēarth
> Vĭrtūe, hĭs dārlĭng chĭld, dĕsīgned.
> *Thomas Gray.*

(22) The use of the first and third persons in the imperative mood, as:

> *Bĕ* mān's pĕcūliăr *wŏrk* hĭs sōle dĕlīght.
> *Beattie.*

> *Tŭrn wĕ* ă mōmĕnt fāncў's răpĭd flīght.
> *Thomson.*

(23) The pronoun is expressed with the imperative, as:

> "Hŏpe *thŏu* ĭn Gŏd."

(24) The object precedes the verb, as:

> Lănds hĕ coŭld mēasūre, tīmes ănd tīdes prĕsāge.
> *Goldsmith*—"Deserted Village."

(25) Adverbs are placed before the words which they modify, as:

> Thĕ plōwmăn hōmewărd plōds hĭs wēarў wāy.
> *Gray's Elegy.*

(26) The introductory adverb is not unfrequently omitted, as:

> Wăs nāught ărŏund bŭt ĭmăgĕs ŏf rēst.
> *Thomson.*

POETICAL LICENSES.

(27) The use of personal pronouns and afterwards introducing their nouns, as :

> İt cūrled nŏt Tweēd ălōne, thăt *breēze*.
> *Scott.*

(28) The use of the second person singular oftener than prose writers, as :

> Bŭt *thŏu*, ŏf tēmplĕs ōld, ŏr āltărs nēw,
> *Stāndĕst* ălōne—wĭth nōthĭng līke tŏ theē.
> *Lord Byron.*

> Ŏ Lūcĭfēr, thŏu sōn ŏf mōrn,
> Ălīke ŏf Hēaven ănd mān thĕ fōe;
> Hēaven, mĕn, ănd āll,
> Nŏw prĕss thў fāll,
> Ănd sīnk thĕ lōwĕst ōf thĕ lōw.
> *Oliver Goldsmith*—"The Captivity."

(29) The use of antiquated words and modes of expression, as :

> Jŏhn Gīlpĭn wăs ă cītĭzēn
> Ŏf crēdĭt ānd rĕnōwn,
> Ă trāin-bănd cāptăin *ēke* wăs hē
> Ŏf fāmoŭs Lōndŏn tōwn.
> *Cowper*—"The Diverting History of John Gilpin."

(30) The use of many words not used by prose writers or that are used but rarely :

(i) Nouns, as—benison, boon, emprise, fane, guerdon, guise, ire, ken, lore, meed, sire, steed, welkin, yore.

(ii) Adjectives, as—azure, blithe, boon, dank, darkling, darksome, doughty, dun, fell, rife, rapt, rueful, sear, sylvan, twain, wan.

(iii) Verbs, as—appall, astound, brook, cower, doff, ken, wend, ween, trow.

(iv) Adverbs, as—oft, haply, inly, blithely, cheerily, deftly, felly, rifely, starkly.

(v) Prepositions, as—adown, aloft, aloof, anear, aneath, askant, aslant, aslope, atween, atwixt, besouth, traverse, thorough, sans.

(34) The formation of many adjectives in y, not common, as :

Dimply, dusky, gleamy, heapy, moony, paly, sheety, stilly, spiry, steepy, towery, vasty, writhy.

PART SECOND.

CHAPTER I.

FIGURES OF SPEECH COMMON TO POETRY.

FIGURES OF ETYMOLOGY.

APHERESIS.

The cutting off of one or more letters from the beginning of a word, as:

'Neath for beneath, 'gan for began, 'gainst for against 'thout for without, 'ghast for aghast, 'mazed for amazed, 'fore for before, 'feeble for enfeeble, 'dure for endure, 'venge for avenge, 'Nelope for Penelope, 'sdained for disdained, 'Frisco for San Francisco, woe's for woe is, he's for he is, what's for what is, 'twas for it was, I'll for I will, she's gone for she is gone, devil's for devil is, she'll for she will, world's for world is, I'm for I am, you're for you are, there's for there is, I'd for I would, soul's for soul is.

> The glow-worm shows the matin to be near,
> And 'gins to pale his ineffectual fire.
> *Shakespeare*—"Hamlet, Act 5."

> The moon's the earth's enamoured bride;
> True to him in her very changes,
> To other stars she never ranges:
> Though, crossed by him, sometimes she dips
> Her light in short, offended pride,
> And faints to an eclipse.
> *Campbell*—"Moonlight."

Apocope

Is the elision of a letter or letters at the end of a word, as:

Tho' for though, th' for the, t'other for the other, thro' for through, Pont' for Pontus, Lucrece for Lucretia, obstruct for obstruction, Per for Persia, Ind for India, Adon for Adonis, conduct for conductor, amaze for amazement, Moroc for Morocco, addict for addicted, Pat for Patrick, wretch for wretched, sads for saddens, sult for sultry, swelt for swelter, potates for potatoes, after for afterwards.

>Woe! woe! each heart shall bleed—shall break!
>She would have hung upon his neck,
> Had he come but yester-even;
>And he had clasped those peerless charms
>That shall never, never fill his arms,
> Or meet him but in heaven.
>   *Campbell*—"The Brave Roland."

>But time will teach the Russ, ev'n conquering War
>Has handmaid arts.
>   *Campbell*—"The Power of Russia."

Epenthesis.

Is the inserting of a letter or letters in the middle of a word, as:

>The wearied sentinel
>At eve may overlook the crouching foe,
>Till, ere his hand can sound the alarum bell,
>He sinks beneath the unexpected blow;
>Before the whisker of grimalkin fell,
> When slumbering on her post, the mouse may go;
>But woman, wakeful woman's never weary;
>Above all, when she waits—to thump her deary.
>   *R. H. Barham.*

"U" is inserted in "alarum." The "y" at the end of the word "dear-y" furnishes also a fine example of Annexation or Paragoge.

PARAGOGE.

Is the annexing of an expletive syllable to a word. A satire on Sir John Suckling furnishes us a fine example of this figure. Sir John Suckling was a courtier and poet at the court at the time of King Charles I, in the seventeenth century. He was well educated and refined in his taste for that day, writing the purest and brightest poetry of his time. Sir John, in response to a call from his majesty, the King, raised a troop of one hundred men and equipped them at a cost of sixty thousand dollars. Gaily caparisoned as were his troops, they ran off the field at the first approach of the Scotch covenanters in their first and only skirmish. Some one given to satire thus describes Sir John. It will be noticed annexation assists the ridicule intended with pleasing effect:

"Sir John, he got him an ambling nag,
 To Scotland for to ride-a,
With a hundred horse more, all his own he swore,
 To guard him on every side-a."

Another stanza runs thus:

"The ladies ran all to the windows to see
 So gallant and warlike his sight-a,
And as he pressed by they cried with a sigh,
 'Sir John why will you go fight-a?'"

PROSTHESIS.

The prefixing of one or more letters to the beginning of a word, as:

Amid for mid, yclept, yclad, ypowdered.

> Lĕt fāll ădōwn hĭs sīlvĕr bēard sŏme tēars.
> *Thomson.*

> Thĕ grōund wăs greēn, y̆pōwĕred wĭth thĕ dāisy̆.
> *Chaucer.*

SYNCOPE.

Is the elision of a letter or letters from the middle of a word, as:

Ca't for called, r'ally for really, med'cine for medicine, e'en for even or evening, o'er for over, conq'ring for conquering, s'en night for seven night, ha' penny for half penny, de'il for devil.

> Fĭrst, thĕn, ă wōmăn will, ŏr wŏn't, dĕpēnd ŏn't;
> Ĭf shĕ wĭll dō't, shĕ wĭll; ănd thĕre's ăn ēnd ŏn't.
> Bŭt ĭf shĕ wŏn't, sĭnce sāfe ănd sōund yŏur trŭst ĭs,
> Fĕar ĭs ăffrōnt, ănd jēalŏŭsy̆ ŭnjŭst ĭs.
> *Hill*—"Woman."

SYNAERESIS.

Is the joining together of two syllables with one, as:

I'll for I will, 'tis for it is, spok'st for spokest.

> Ōnly̆ ă lĭttlĕ mōre
> Ĭ hăve tŏ wrīte,
> Thĕn Ĭ'll gĭve ō'er,
> Ănd bĭd thĕ wŏrld gŏŏd-nīght.

'Tis būt ă flȳĭng minŭte
That Ĭ mŭst stāy,
Ŏr lĭngĕr ĭn ĭt;
And thēn Ĭ mūst ăwāy.
Herrick.

TMESIS.

The inserting of a word between the parts of a compound or between two words which should be united if they stood together, as:

Yoŭ sāy tŏ mē-wărds yoŭr ăffēctiŏn's strōng;
Prăy lōve mĕ ă lĭttlĕ, sō yoŭ lōve mĕ lōng.
Slōwlȳ gŏes fārre; thĕ mĕane ĭs bĕst; dĕsīre
Grŏwn viŏlēnt, dŏ's ēithĕr dīe, ŏr tīre.
Herrick.

FIGURES OF SYNTAX.

ELLIPSIS.

An omission; a figure by which one or more words are omitted, which the hearer or reader can supply, and which are necessary to a full construction of a sentence. Words thus omitted are said to be understood. It is a figure very common in the language, and serves to avoid repetitions. When, however, the ellipsis would have a tendency to obscure the meaning or weaken the force of the sentence it should be avoided. The ellipsis may be of the substantive, adjective, article, pronoun, verb, adverb, preposition or conjunction. The following is an excellent illustration of this figure :

Ōne mŏre ŭnfōrtŭnăte,
Wēarȳ ŏf brĕath;
Rāshlȳ ĭmpōrtŭnăte,
Gōne tŏ hĕr dĕath.
Hood—"Bridge of Sighs."

In the following couplet the antecedent pronoun is omitted, as:

> Who has no inward beauty, none perceives,
> Though all around be beautiful.
> Richard Henry Dana.

One of our greatest American poets in his conception of the wild mystic, furnishes in the stanza following an instance of the omission of the verb:

> Once upon a midnight dreary, while I pondered weak and weary
> Over many a quaint and curious volume of forgotten lore,
> While I nodded nearly napping, suddenly there came a tapping,
> As of some one gently rapping, rapping at my chamber door;
> Only this and nothing more.
> Edgar Allan Poe—"The Raven."

The subject of the verb is often omitted, as in the following stanza:

> Did the green isles
> Detain thee long? Or 'mid the palmy groves
> Of the bright South, where Nature ever smiles,
> Didst sing thy loves
> *Pickering*.

The following will serve as an example of the omission of the participle:

> His knowledge measured to his state and place,
> His time a moment, and a point his space.
> *Alexander Pope*.

An Ellipsis of the adverb:

> She shows a body rather than a life;
> A statue than a brother.
> *Shakespeare*—"Anthony and Cleopatra."

FIGURES OF SPEECH.

ENALLAGE.

Is the use of one part of speech, or of one modification for another.

(1) Substituting a noun for an adjective :

From thy Glory-throne.
Palgrave.

Glory-throne used instead of glorious throne, Seraph-sound for Seraphic sound, Carthage-queen for Carthagenian queen.

(2) A phrase for a noun :

Come, cuddle your head on my shoulder, dear,
  Your head like the golden-rod,
And we will go sailing away from here
  To the beautiful Land of Nod.
Away from life's hurry, and flurry, and worry,
  Away from earth's shadows and gloom,
To a world of fair weather we'll float off together,
  Where roses are always in bloom.
  Ella Wheeler Wilcox—"The Beautiful Land of Nod."

" Land of Nod " is here substituted for the noun "sleep."

Had she told me fifty shillings,
  I might (and wouldn't you?)
Have referred to that dress in a way folks express
  By an eloquent dash or two ;
But the guileful little creature
  Knew well her tactics when
She casually said that that dream in red
  Had cost but two pounds ten.
    Eugene Field—"The Tea-Gown."

(3) The use of an adverb for a noun :

> Tō thĕ lānd ŏf thĕ hĕreāftĕr.
> *Longfellow*—" Hiawatha."

The adverb " hereafter " used as a noun, viz : to heaven.

> Ă bĕttĕr Whĕre tŏ fīnd.
> *Shakespeare.*

Where instead of place or home.

(4) Noun for a verb :

> " I'll *queēn ĭt* nō ĭnch fārthĕr."

Viz : I'll walk or go no inch farther.

> Bĕdāwn ŏur skȳ.
> *Shakespeare.*

Dawn, a noun, changed to a verb by prefix be-dawn.

Noun for a verb :

> Crīmsŏned wĭth flōwĕrs ănd dārk wĭth lĕafȳ shāde.
> *Vaughan.*

(5) An adjective for a noun :

> Thȳ pāth ĭs hīgh ŭp ĭn hĕavĕn ; wĕ cānnŏt gāze
> Ŏn thĕ *ĭntēnse ŏf līght* thăt gĭrds thȳ cār.
> *Percival*—" Apostrophe to the Sun."

Viz : the sun.

(6) An adjective for a verb :

> Ĭt *lānks* thĕ cheĕk ănd pāles thĕ frĕshĕst sīght.
> *Giles Fletcher.*

> Thĭs dāy wĭll *gĕntlĕ* his cŏndĭtiŏn.
> *Shakespeare.*

(7) An eighth variety is to compare with -er and -est adjectives that are compared by more and most, or vice versa.

Tŏ hēar yoŭr mōst sweĕt mūsĭc mĭrăclē.
Mrs. E. B. Browning—"Seraphim."

(8) An adjective for an adverb :

Bŭt sŏft! mĕthĭnks Ĭ scēnt thĕ mōrnĭng's āir.
Shakespeare—"Hamlet, Act 1, Scene 5."

Whĕn sōft wăs thĕ sūn.
"Piers Plowman."
Soft for softly.

(9) A noun and a preposition for an adjective.

Ă thīng ŏf beaūtȳ īs ă jōy fŏrēvĕr.
Keats.
Of beauty for a beauteous thing.

(10) A preposition for an adjective :

Wĭth thĕ spleēn
Ŏf āll thĕ *ŭndĕr* fiĕnds.
Shakespeare.

(11) An adverb for a pronoun :

Whēre ăgāinst
Mȳ grăined āsh ă hŭndrĕd tīmes hăth brōke.
Shakespeare.

(12) A preposition is used for a noun :

Ŏ nŏt līke mē
Fŏr mĭne's bĕyōnd Beyōnd.
Shakespeare.

(13) Adverb and a preposition in place of a preposition:

> Fŏr thăt Ī ăm sŏme twĕlve ŏr fōurteĕn moŏnshīnes *Lăg ŏf* ă brŏthĕr.
> *Shakespeare.*

(14) A verb is used as a noun:

> Wĭth ēverȳ gāle ănd vārȳ ŏf thĕir māstĕrs.
> *Shakespeare.*

(15) An adjective used as a participle:

> Lĕt thē *blŏat* kĭng tĕmpt yoū.
> *Shakespeare.*

(16) Usages similar to "Meseems:"

> Mĕthĭnks hĕr pātiĕnt sōns bĕfōre mĕ stănd.
> *Goldsmith*—"Traveler."

(17) Change of prepositions. Using "of" instead of "by:"

> Ī ăm sŏ wrăpt, ănd thŏrŏughlȳ lăpt
> Ŏf jŏllȳ goŏd āle ănd ōld.
> *John Still.*

(18) Participles are turned into adjectives and actions ascribed to them which do not belong to them, as:

> Whĕre smilĭng sprĭng ĭts ēarliĕst vĭsĭt pāid,
> Ănd pārtĭng sŭmmĕr's lĭngerĭng bloŏms dĕlāyed.
> *Goldsmith*—"Deserted Village."

> Ănd păssĭng rĭch wĭth fŏrtȳ pōunds ă yēar.
> *Goldsmith*—"Deserted Village."

(19) The use of transitive verbs as intransitive, as :

This minstrĕl-gōd, wĕll-plēased, ămid thĕ chōir
Stoŏd prōud tŏ *hymn*, ănd tūne hĭs yoūthfŭl lȳre.
                                                            Pope.

(20) The use of intransitive verbs as transitive, as :

Lăng ăftĕr kĕnned ŏn Cārrĭck shōre;
Fŏr mŏnў ă bēast tŏ *dēad* shĕ shŏt,
Ănd *pĕrĭshed* mŏnў ă bŏnnĭe bōat.
                                        Burns—"Tam O'Shanter."

Stĭll ĭn hărmōnĭoŭs ĭntĕrcōurse, thĕy *lĭved*
Thē rūrăl dāy, ănd *tālked* thĕ flōwĭng heārt.
                                                            Thomson.

(21) The use of the auxiliary after its principal, as :

Thĕ mān whŏ sŭffĕrs, lŏudlў māy cŏmplāin;
Ănd *rāge* hĕ *māy*, bŭt hē shăll rāge ĭn vāin.
                                                            Pope.

(22) The use of can, could and would as principal verbs transitive, as :

Whăt wŏuld thĭs mān? Nŏw ŭpwărd will hĕ sōar,
Ănd, littlĕ lĕss thăn āngĕl, wŏuld bĕ mōre.
                                                            Pope.

HYPERBATON OR INVERSION.

A figurative construction inverting the natural and proper order from words and sentences. The following stanza furnishes us with a fine example :

> În Englănd rivĕrs āll ăre māles,
>   Fŏr instance, Fāthĕr Thāmes ;
> Whŏĕvĕr în Cŏlŭmbiă sāils
>   Fĭnds thĕm mămsĕlles ănd dāmes.
> Yĕs, thĕre thĕ sŏftĕr sĕx prĕsīdes—
>   Ăquātĭc, Ĭ ăssūre yoŭ ;
> Ănd Mrs. Sippў rŏlls hĕr tīdes
>   Rĕspōnsĭve tō Mĭss Soŭrĭ.
>   *James Smith.*

Milton furnishes us a fine example of an inversion at the very commencement of his great epic :

> Ŏf mān's fĭrst dĭsŏbēdĭĕnce ănd thĕ frūit
> Ŏf thăt fŏrbĭddĕn treē, whŏse mōrtăl tāste
> Brŏught dēath intō thĕ wōrld ănd āll ŏur wōe,
> Sĭng, hĕavenlў Mŭse.
>   "Paradise Lost."

PLEONASM.

The use in speaking or writing of more words than are necessary to express the thought. From Thomas Hood we have the following, in the second line Pleonasm can be detected:

> Ănd whĕn Ĭ spĕak, mў vŏice ĭs weāk ;
>   Bŭt hĕrs, shĕ mǎkes ă gŏng of ĭt ;
> Fŏr Ĭ ăm smāll ănd shĕ ĭs tāll,
>   Ănd thāt's thĕ shŏrt ănd lŏng of ĭt.

SYLLEPSIS.

A figure of speech by which we conceive the sense of words otherwise than the words import, and construe them according to the intention of the author—the taking of words in two senses at once, the literal and the metaphorical. The following is an example of this figure :

> Whĭle Prŏvĭdĕnce sŭppŏrts,
> Lĕt sāints sĕcūrelў dwĕll ;
> Thăt hănd whĭch beārs ăll Nătŭre ūp,
> Shăll guide hĭs chĭldrĕn wĕll.
> *Philip Doddridge.*

FIGURES OF RHETORIC.

ALLEGORY.

Is the narration of fictitious events, designed to represent and illustrate important realities. It is continued metaphor, representing objects and events that are intened to be symbolical of other objects and events having usually moral and spiritual character.

The following beautiful allegory by Longfellow, starting with the metaphorical representation of the state as a ship, expands the metaphor into a complete description :

> Thŏu toō, săil ŏn, Ŏ Shĭp ŏf Stāte !
> Săil ŏn, Ŏ Ūnĭŏn, strŏng ănd greāt !
> Hŭmănĭtў, wĭth ăll ĭts fēars,
> Wĭth āll ĭts hōpes ŏf fūtŭre yēars,
> Ĭs hăngĭng brĕathlĕss ŏn thў fāte !
> Wĕ knŏw whăt Māstĕr lāid thў keēl,
> Whăt Wŏrkmĕn wrōught thў ribs ŏf steēl,
> Whŏ māde ĕach māst, ănd sāil, ănd rōpe,
> Whăt ānvĭls rāng, whăt hămmĕrs bĕat,
> Ĭn whăt ă fōrge ănd whăt ă hēat
> Wĕre shāped thĕ ănchŏrs ŏf thў hōpe !
> Fĕar nŏt ĕach sŭddĕn sŏund ănd shŏck—
> 'Tĭs ŏf thĕ wāve ănd nŏt thĕ rŏck ;

'Tis but the flapping of the sail,
And not a rent made by the gale!
In spite of rock and tempest's roar,
In spite of false lights on the shore,
Sail on, nor fear to breast the sea!
Our hearts, our hopes, are all with thee,
Our hearts, our hopes, our prayers, our tears,
Our faith triumphant o'er our fears,
Are all with thee! are all with thee!

APOSTROPHE.

Literally a turning away from the natural course of one's thoughts or ideas to address the absent or dead as if present, former ages, future ages, some person or thing. It is closely allied to Personification with which it is often combined. Objects personified, however, are not addressed; objects apostrophized are addressed.

Roll on, thou deep and dark blue ocean,—roll!
Ten thousand fleets sweep over thee In vain;
Man marks the earth with ruin,—his control
Stops with the shore;—upon the watery plain
The wrecks are all thy deed, nor doth remain
A shadow of man's ravage, save his own,
When, for a moment, like a drop of rain,
He sinks into thy depths with bubbling groan,
Without a grave, unknelled, uncoffined, and unknown.
Byron—" Childe Harold.

Roll on, ye stars! Exult in youthful prime;
Mark with bright curves the printless steps of Time.
Near and more near your beamy cars approach,
And lessening orbs on lessening orbs encroach.
Flowers of the sky! ye too to age must yield,
Frail as your silken sisters of the field!

Star after star from heaven's high arch shall rush,
Suns sink on suns, and systems systems crush,
Till o'er the wreck, emerging from the storm,
Immortal nature lifts her changeful form;
Mounts from her funeral pyre on wings of flame,
And soars and shines, another and the same.
Erasmus Darwin.

Ay, tear her tattered ensign down!
  Long has it waved on high,
And many an eye has danced to see
  That banner in the sky;
Beneath it rung the battle-shout,
  And burst the cannon's roar;
The meteor of the ocean air
  Shall sweep the clouds no more!
Holmes—"Old Ironsides."

Hail, holy Light, offspring of Heaven first-born!
Or of the Eternal co-eternal beam
May I express thee unblamed? since God is light,
And never but in unapproached light
Dwelt from eternity, dwelt then in thee,
Bright effluence of bright essence increate!
Or hear'st thou rather pure ethereal stream,
Whose fountain who shall tell?
Milton—"Paradise Lost."

ANAPHORA.

Is the repetition of a word at the beginning of several clauses of a sentence. It is thus repeated that the mind may be more distinctly impressed with the idea or thought, as:

(1).

All nature is but art, unknown to thee ;
All chance, direction, which thou canst not see ;
All discord, harmony not understood ;
All partial evil, universal good ;
And spite of pride, in erring reason's spite,
One truth is clear, Whatever is, is right.
                      Pope—" Essay on Man."

(2).

Sometimes the linnet piped his song ;
  Sometimes the throstle whistled strong ;
Sometimes the sparhawk, wheeled along,
  Hushed all the groves from fear of wrong.
       Tennyson—" Sir Launcelot and Queen Guinevere."

(3).

There is a rest for all things. On still nights
  There is a folding of a million wings—
The swarming honey-bees in unknown woods,
The speckled butterflies, and downy broods
    In dizzy poplar heights ;
Rest for innumerable nameless things,
Rest for the creatures underneath the Sea,
  And in the Earth, and in the starry Air—
Why will it not unburden me of care ?
It comes to meaner things than my despair.
O weary, weary night, that brings no rest to me !
              Aldrich—" Invocation to Sleep."

ANTITHESIS.

A contrast by which each of the contrasted things is rendered more striking :

On parent knees, a naked new-born child,
Weeping thou sat'st, while all around thee smiled ;
So live, that sinking in thy last, long sleep,
Thou then may'st smile, while all around thee weep.
Sir William Jones.

EPANALEPSIS.

Is a figure by which a sentence ends with the same word with which it begins :

(1).

Fare thee well, and if forever,
  Still forever fare thee well ;
Even though unforgiving never
  'Gainst thee shall my heart rebel.
Byron—" To His Wife."

(2).

They questioned each the other
What Brahma's answer meant.
Said Vivochumu, " Brother,
Through Brahma the great Mother
Hath spoken her intent :
"*Man* ends as he began,—
The shadow on the water is all there is of *man!*"
Richard Henry Stoddard.—" Brahma's Answer."

EPIGRAM.

It is a statement in which there is an apparent contradiction between the form of the expression and the meaning really intended. The force of the epigram lies in the pleasant surprise attendant upon the perception of the real meaning :

(1).

My wŏndĕr ĭs rĕăllў bŏundlĕss,
  Thăt ămŏng thĕ queĕr cāsĕs wĕ trў,
Ă lānd cāse shŏuld ŏftĕn bĕ grŏundlĕss,
  Ănd ă wātĕr-cāse ālwăys bĕ drў!
      Saxe—"On a Famous Water-Suit."

(2).

Swăns sīng bĕfŏre thĕy dīe, 'twĕre nō băd thĭng
Dĭd cĕrtăin pĕrsŏns dīe bĕfŏre thĕy sīng.
      S. T. Coleridge.

EPIZEUXIS.

The repetition of a word or words for the sake of emphasis:

(1).

Thĕ Īsles ŏf Greēce, thĕ ĪSLES ŎF GREĒCE,
Whĕre bŭrnĭng Săpphŏ lōved ănd sŭng,
Whĕre grĕw thĕ ārts ŏf wār ănd peāce,
Whĕre Dĕlŏs rōse ănd Phoĕbŭs sprŭng—
Ĕtĕrnăl sŭmmĕr gīlds thĕm yĕt,
Bŭt āll ĕxcĕpt thĕir sūn ĭs sĕt.
      Byron.

(2).

An example of double affirmation:

"Fālselў, fālselў hăve yĕ dōne,
Ŏ mōthĕr," shĕ sāid, "Ĭf thĭs bĕ trūe
Tŏ keĕp thĕ bĕst măn ŭndĕr thĕ sŭn
Sŏ mănў yēars frŏm hĭs dūe."
      Tennyson—"Lady Clare."

(3).

Laugh, ănd thĕ wōrld lāughs wĭth yoŭ,
  Weēp, ănd yoŭ weēp ălōne;
Fŏr thĕ sād ōld ēarth mŭst bōrrŏw ĭts mĭrth,
  Bŭt hăs trōublĕ ĕnoūgh ŏf ĭts ōwn.
Sĭng, ănd thĕ hĭlls wĭll ānswĕr,
  Sĭgh, ĭt ĭs lōst ŏn thĕ āir;
Thĕ ēchŏes bōund tŏ ă jōyfŭl sōund,
  Bŭt shrĭnk frŏm vōicĭng cāre.
                Ella Wheeler Wilcox—"Solitude."

(4).

"Thĕ fāult wăs mine, thĕ fāult wăs mīne"—
Whў ām Ĭ sĭttĭng hēre sŏ stūnned ănd stĭll,
Plŭckĭng thĕ hărmlĕss wĭld-flŏwer ōn thĕ hĭll?
Ĭt ĭs thĭs gŭiltў hănd!
                Tennyson—"Maud."

(5).

  Mŭst yĕ wāit? Mŭst yĕ wāit?
Tĭll thĕy răvăge hĕr gărdĕns ŏf ōrănge ănd pālm,
  Tĭll hĕr heārt ĭs dūst, tĭll hĕr strĕngth ĭs wātĕr?
Mŭst yĕ seē thĕm trămplĕ hĕr, ănd bĕ cālm
  Ăs priĕsts whĕn ă vĭrgĭn ĭs lēd tŏ slāughtĕr?
Shăll thĕy smīte thĕ mărvĕl ŏf ăll lănds,—
  Thĕ Nātiŏn's lōngĭng, thĕ ēarth's cŏmplētenĕss,—
Ŏn hĕr rĕd mŏuth drŏppĭng mўrrh, hĕr hănds
  Fĭlled wĭth frūităge ănd spīce ănd sweētnĕss?
  Mŭst yĕ wāit?
                Stedman—"Cuba."

EROTESIS OR INTERROGATION.

Is an animated or passionate interrogation. Interrogation in its primary sense is the asking of a question, and an answer would be expected. When declarative sentences are expressed in the interrogative form, no answer is expected ; for the statement is made thereby more emphatic and convincing.

The negative interrogation affirms—an affirmative denies. An interrogative sentence should always be followed by a question mark.

> Căn stōrĭĕd ūrn, ŏr ānĭmātĕd būst,
> Băck tō ĭts mănsiŏn căll thĕ fleētĭng brēath ?
> Căn hōnŏr's vōice prŏvōke thĕ sĭlĕnt dūst,
> Ŏr flăttery̆ soōthe thĕ dūll cōld ēar ŏf dēath ?
> *Gray*—"Elegy."

ECPHONESIS.

Is an animated or passionate exclamation, generally indicated by such interjections as O ! oh ! ah ! alas !

(1).

> Ŏ my̆ sŏul's jŏy,
> If ăftĕr ĕvery̆ tĕmpĕst cōmes sŭch cālms,
> Māy thĕ wĭnds blōw tĭll thĕy hăve wākĕned dēath !
> *Shakespeare*—"Othello."

Pope illustrates well one of the ruling passions that continue not only throughout life but even unto death :

(2).

> "Ŏdĭoŭs ! Ĭn woōlĕn ! 'Twŏuld ă sāint prŏvōke !"
> Wĕre thĕ lăst wŏrds thăt poōr Nărcĭssă spōke.
> "Nŏ, lĕt ă chărmĭng chĭntz ănd Brŭssĕls lāce
> Wrăp my̆ cōld lĭmbs, ănd shāde my̆ lĭfelĕss fāce.
> Ōne wōuld nŏt, sūre, bĕ frĭghtfŭl whĕn ŏne's dĕad ;
> Ănd, Bĕtty̆, gĭve thĭs cheēk ă lĭttlĕ rĕd."

"I give ănd Ĭ dĕvīse," ŏld Eūclĭŏ sāid
Ănd sīghed, "mў lānds ănd tēnĕmēnts tŏ Nĕd."
"Yoŭr mōnĕy, sĭr?" "Mў mōnĕy, sĭr? Whăt! āll?
Whў, ĭf Ĭ mūst (thĕn wēpt), Ĭ gīve tŏ Pāul—"
"Thĕ mānŏr, sĭr?" "Thĕ mānŏr? Hōld!" hĕ crīed;
"Nŏt thăt—Ĭ cānnŏt pārt wĭth thāt!" ănd dīed.

(3).

Ă hōrse! ă hōrse! Mў kīngdŏm fōr ă hōrse!
Shakespeare—"King Richard III."

EUPHEMISM.

Is the suppression of a harsh or obnoxious word or phrase, by substituting a word or phrase in its place that is delicate, yet expressing the same meaning:

(1).

Wŏrn ŏut wĭth ānguĭsh, tōil, ănd cōld, ănd hūngĕr,
Dōwn sŭnk thĕ wāndĕrĕr; sleēp hăd sēized hĕr sēnsĕs.
Thēre dĭd thĕ trāvĕlĕr fĭnd hĕr ĭn thĕ mōrnĭng:
    Gōd hăd rĕlēased hĕr.
            Southey—"The Widow."

From Burns we have the following:

(2).

Ăn hōnĕst wăbstĕr tō hĭs trāde,
Whăse wife's twă nēives wĕre scārce weĕl-brĕd.

(3).

Ŏ, féar nŏt ĭn ă wŏrld līke thĭs,
Ănd thŏu shălt knŏw ĕre lŏng,—
Knŏw hŏw sŭblīme ă thĭng ĭt ĭs
Tŏ sŭffĕr ānd bĕ strŏng.
        Longfellow—"The Light of the Stars."

HEARING.

Is a figure akin to vision. The speaking doubtfully of some sound that has been heard at the present or just before apparently indistinct, but which proves to be the distant roar of cannon, of thunder, or something real. Byron's Waterloo, taken from Childe Harold, is one of the finest examples of the figure :

> Dĭd yē nŏt hēar ĭt? Nō! 'twăs būt thĕ wĭnd,
> Ŏr thĕ căr răttlĭng ō'er thĕ stŏnў strēet ;
> Ŏn wĭth thĕ dānce! Lĕt jŏy bĕ ūncŏnfīned ;
> Nŏ slēep tĭll mōrn, whĕn Youth ănd Plēasŭre meēt
> Tŏ chāse thĕ glōwĭng hōurs wĭth flȳĭng feĕt.
> Būt hărk ! Thăt hĕavy sōund brĕaks ĭn ŏnce mōre,
> Ăs if thĕ clōuds ĭts ēchŏ wōuld rĕpēat ;
> And nēarĕr, clēarĕr, dēadlĭĕr thăn bĕfōre !
> Ărm ! ārm ! Ĭt īs, ĭt īs thĕ cănnŏn's ŏpenĭng rōar !
>
> Canto III, Stanza XXII.

HYPERBOLE.

Is inflated or exaggerated speech ; so great is the exaggeration that it cannot be expected to be believed by the reader or hearer. It is an expression of strong passion, and is often made use of by the poet and the orator. Impulsive natures make great use of this figure of speech. Everything with them is magnificent ! splendid ! sublime ! awful ! Abraham Cowley has translated from the Greek poet Anacreon, this beautiful hyperbole entitled, "The Grasshopper" :

> Hăppў ĭnsĕct ! whăt căn bē
> Ĭn hăppĭnĕss cŏmpāred tŏ theē ?
> Fĕd wĭth noŭrĭshmĕnt dĭvīne,
> Thĕ dĕwў mŏrnĭng's gĕntlĕ wīne !
> Nātŭre wāits ŭpŏn theĕ still,
> Ănd thў vĕrdănt cŭp dŏes fĭll ;

'Tis filled wherever thou dost tread,
Nature's self's thy Ganymede.
Thou dost drink, and dance and sing,
Happier than the happiest king!
All the fields which thou dost see,
All the plants belong to thee ;
All the summer hours produce,
Fertile made with early juice.
Man for thee does sow and plough,
Farmer he, and landlord thou!
Thou dost innocently joy,
Nor does thy luxury destroy.
The shepherd gladly heareth thee,
More harmonious than he.
The country hinds with gladness hear,
Prophet of the ripened year!
Thee Phoebus loves and does inspire ;
Phoebus is himself thy sire,
To thee, of all things upon the earth,
Life is no longer than thy mirth.
Happy insect ! happy thou
Dost neither age nor winter know ;
But when thou'st drunk and danced and sung
Thy fill, the flowery leaves among,
(Voluptuous and wise withal,
Epicurean animal !)
Sated with thy summer feast,
Thou retir'st to endless rest.

" Ye stars! which are the poetry of heaven!
If in your bright leaves we would read the fate
Of men and empires,—'tis to be forgiven,
That in our aspirations to be great,
Our destinies o'erleap their mortal state,
And claim a kindred with you ; for ye are
A beauty and a mystery, and create
In us such love and reverence from afar,
That fortune, fame, power, life, have named themselves a star."
             Byron—"Childe Harold."

IRONY.

A figure of telling effect when properly used. It is used to express directly the opposite of what it is intended shall be understood. It is used effectively in Whittier's "The Prisoner for Debt," a poem of great merit:

>What has the gray-haired prisoner done?
> Has murder stained his hands with gore?
>Not so; his crime's a fouler one;
> GOD MADE THE OLD MAN POOR!
>For this he shares a felon's cell,—
>The fittest earthly type of hell!
>For this, the boon for which he poured
>His young blood on the invader's sword,
>And counted light the fearful cost,—
>His blood-gained liberty is lost!
>
>And so, for such a place of rest,
> Old prisoner, dropped thy blood as rain
>On Concord's field, and Bunker's crest,
> And Saratoga's plain?
>Look forth, thou man of many scars,
>Through thy dim dungeon's iron bars;
>It must be joy, in sooth to see
>Yon monument upreared to thee,—
>Piled granite and a prison cell,
>The land repays thy service well!
>
>Go, ring the bells and fire the guns,
> And fling the starry banners out;
>Shout "Freedom!" till your lisping ones
> Give back their cradle-shout;
>Let boastful eloquence declaim
>Of honor, liberty and fame;
>Still let the poet's strain be heard,
>With glory for each second word,
>And everything with breath agree
>To praise "our glorious liberty!"

But when the patron cannon jars
  That prison's cold and gloomy wall,
And through its gates the stripes and stars
  Rise on the wind, and fall,—
Think ye that prisoner's aged ear
Rejoices in the general cheer?
Think ye his dim and failing eye
Is kindled at your pageantry?
Sorrowing of soul, and chained of limb,
What is your carnival to him?

Down with the LAW that binds him thus!
  Unworthy freemen, let it find
No refuge from the withering curse
  Of God and human kind!
Open the prison's living tomb,
And usher from its brooding gloom
The victims of your savage code
To the free sun and air of God;
No longer dare as crime to brand
The chastening of the Almighty's hand.

LITOTES.

A diminution or softening of statement, for the purpose of avoiding censure, or of expressing more strongly what is intended ; a figure in which the affirmative is expressed by the negative of the contrary ; thus, "a citizen of no mean city" means "of an illustrious or important city."

It is the opposite of hyperbole.

The following from one who was unsurpassed as a prose writer, and who was a very clever poet, illustrates this figure.

The Mŏuntăin ănd thĕ Squĭrrĕl
Hăd ă quărrĕl ;
Ănd thĕ Mŏuntăin călled thĕ Squĭrrĕl "Lĭttlĕ Prĭg."
Bŭn rĕplīed,
"Yoŭ ăre doŭbtlĕss vĕry̆ bĭg ;
Bŭt ăll sŏrts ŏf things ănd weăthĕr
Mŭst bĕ tākĕn ĭn tŏgēthĕr
Tŏ māke ŭp ă yĕar
Ănd ă sphēre ;
Ănd Ī thĭnk Ĭt nō dĭsgrāce
Tŏ ŏccŭpy̆ my̆ plăce.
Ĭf Ī'm nŏt sŏ lārge ăs yoŭ,
Yoŭ ăre nŏt sŏ smăll ăs Ī,
Ănd nŏt hălf sŏ spry̆.
Ī'll nŏt dĕny̆ yoŭ māke
Ă vĕry̆ prĕtty̆ squĭrrĕl trăck :
Tălĕnts dĭffĕr ; āll ĭs wĭsely̆ pŭt,—
Ĭf Ī cānnŏt cărry̆ fŏrĕsts ōn my̆ băck,
Nĕithĕr căn yoŭ crăck ă nŭt."

Emerson—"A Fable."

METONYMY.

A change of noun or substantive, is a figure in which the name of one object is put for some other object. The relation is always that of causes, effects, or adjuncts.

(1) Substituting a noun that expresses the cause, for the noun that expresses the effect :

Ă time thĕre wăs, ĕre Ĕnglănd's griĕfs bĕgān
When ēvery̆ roōd ŏf groŭnd māintāined ĭts măn.
Goldsmith—"The Deserted Village."

"Ground" is here used for what the ground produces, viz : food.

Ŏ fŏr ă bēakĕr fŭll ŏf thĕ wărm Soŭth !
Keats—"Lines to the Nightingale."

"South" is here used for the rich wines produced in sunny lands.

> Robed in the long night of her deep hair.
> *Tennyson.*

"Night," the cause of darkness, is put for "darkness," the effect.

(2) Substituting the noun expressing the effect for the noun used to express the cause, being the converse of the first proposition:

> Swift as an arrow flies the leaden death.
> *James Harvey*—"Thereon and Aspasia."

"Death," the effect of the bullet, is put for the bullet itself.

(3) A substantive denoting the place is substituted for a substantive denoting the inhabitants:

> At length the world, renewed by calm repose,
> Was strong for toil; the dappled morn arose.
> *Parnell*—"The Hermit."

"World" is used for "inhabitant."

> "What land is so barbarous injustice to allow?"

"Land" is used to express "race" or "people."

(4) The sign is used for that of which it is the symbol or signifies:

> His banner leads the spears no more amid the hills of Spain.
> *Felicia Hemans.*

"Spears" is used for "soldiers."

As, too, "the olive branch," instead of "peace;" the "throne," the "purple," the "scepter" instead of "kingly power."

> The path by which we twain did go,
>   Which led by tracks that pleased us well,
>   Through four sweet years arose and fell,
> From flower to flower, from snow to snow.
>
> But where the path we walked began
>   To slant the fifth autumnal slope,
>   As we descended, following Hope,
> There sat the Shadow feared of man.
>
> Tennyson.

"Flower," "snow" and "shadow" as used here are emblematic of "Summer," "Winter" and "Death."

(5) Substituting the abstract for the concrete term, and vice versa:

> There *Honor* comes, a pilgrim gray,
>   To deck the turf that wraps their clay;
> And *Freedom* shall a while repair
>   To dwell a weeping hermit there.
>
> Collins.

"Honor" is used to denote an individual of merit. A man of honor full of ripe years.

> I have found out a gift for my fair;
>   I have found where the wood-pigeons breed;
> But let me the plunder forbear—
>   She would say 'twas a barbarous deed,
> For he ne'er could be true, she averred,
>   Who could rob a poor bird of its young:
> And I loved her the more when I heard
>   Such *tenderness* fall from her tongue.
>
> <div align="right"><i>Shenstone</i>—"A Pastoral."</div>

Here the word "tenderness" is used to express "kind feelings."

(6) Substituting the container for what is contained.

"Ŏur shīps nĕxt ōpĕned fīre."

Here the word "ships" is used to designate "sailors."

"Hĕ ĭs fōnd ŏf thĕ *bōttlĕ*."

Viz : he is fond of "drink."

"Yoŭr pŭrse ŏr yoŭr lîfe."

Viz : your money.

"Whĕre will yoŭ fĭnd ănōthĕr brĕast līke hĭs?"

"Breast" is here used for the spirit that animated it.

(7) Substituting the substantive that denotes the thing supporting for the substantive that denotes the thing supported, as:

Field for battle, table for eatables on it, altar for sacrifice.

(8) Substituting the name of the thing possessed for the possessor, as :

"Thĕ wār-whoŏp shăll wāke thĕ sleēp ŏf thĕ crādlĕ."

Viz : the voice of men en route to battle.

Drōve thĕ brĭstlĕd lĭps bĕfōre hĭm."
Shakespeare—"Coriolanus."

Viz : Drove indetermined men.

(9) Substituting the possessor for the possessed :

"Lĕt ŭs brōwse ŏn thĕ fĭelds coŏl wĭth dĕw."
Virgil—"Georgics."

"Us" is used here for "our flocks."

(10) Substituting the instrument for the user :

"Light hăs sprĕad, ănd ĕvĕn bāyonĕts think"

"Bayonets," the instrument or thing used is here substituted for "soldiers" or men who use bayonets.

"Fŭll fĭftў thōusănd mŭskĕts bright,
Lĕd bӯ ŏld wārriŏrs trāined ĭn fĭght."

"Muskets oright" used for "soldiers."

(11) Substituting the noun denoting the material for the thing made of that material :

Like ă tĕmpĕst dōwn thĕ rĭdgĕs
Swĕpt thĕ hŭrrĭcāne ŏf steĕl ;
Rōse thĕ slōgăn ŏf MăcDōnăld,
Flāshed thĕ brōad swŏrd ŏf Lŏchiĕl.
Aytoun—"Battle of Killiecrankie."

"Steel" here means "swords."

Thĕ wind ĭs pīpĭng lōud, mӯ bŏys,
Thĕ lightenĭng flăshĕs freĕ ;
Whĭle thĕ hŏllŏw ōak ŏur pălăce ĭs,
Ŏur hĕrĭtăge thĕ sēa.
Allan Cunningham.

"The hollow oak" is here used to represent "a ship."

Hood has also given us a fine example similar to the one above, in the following :

> Thĕ ōakĕn cēll
> Shăll lōdge hĭm wēll
> Whŏse scēptrĕ rūled ă rēalm.
>   "A Dream in the Woods."

It is very easy for one to guess the meaning of the word "oaken cell" in the above quotation.

(12) Substituting the noun for the period of time during which certain events occured for the events :

> Sŏ hāve Ĭ wŏrn ŏut mānў sleēplĕss nīghts,
> Ănd wādĕd deēp throŭgh mănў ă bloōdў dāy.
>   *Homer.*

"Nights" here is used to designate a period of time, viz : "many sleepless nights" in place of "a given number of days." The same is true of day in the next verse or line ; it is a noun used to express a fact, viz : waded through a bloody battle or through war.

(13) Substituting the place for the occurrence that happened there :

> Bŭt Lĭndĕn sāw ănōthĕr sīght,
> Whĕn thē drŭm bēat, ăt dĕad ŏf nīght,
> Cŏmmāndĭng fīres ŏf dēath tŏ līght
>   Thĕ dārknĕss ōf hĕr scēnĕrў.
>   *Thomas Campbell—*"Hohenlinden."

Here Linden, the place, is used for the occurrence that happened there, viz : The Battle of Hohenlinden.

> Ăgĭncōurt, Ăgĭncōurt!
> Knōw yĕ nŏt Ăgĭncōurt,
> Whēre wĕ wŏn fiēld ănd fōrt?
> Frĕnch flĕd lĭke wōmĕn
> Bў hănd ănd ēke bў wătĕr;
> Nĕvĕr wăs seēn sŭch slăughtĕr
> Māde bў ŏur bōwmĕn.
> *Drayton*—" Agincourt."

Here "Agincourt," the place, is used for the occurrence that happened there, viz: The Battle of Agincourt in 1415.

ECHO.

A returning of what has already been uttered; is another form of repetition:

(1).

> Būt thĕ Pāst ănd āll ĭts beaūtў,
> Whĭthĕr hăs ĭt flĕd ăwāy?
> Hărk! thĕ mōurnfŭl ēchŏes sāy—
> "Flēd ăwāy!"
> *Adelaide Anne Procter.*

(2)

> Būt thĕ drŭm
> Ĕchŏed "Cōme!"
> *Brete Harte.*

ONOMATOPŒIA.

Is the use of a word or a phrase formed to imitate the sound of the thing signified, as:

> Thĕ mōan ŏf dōves ĭn ĭmmĕmōriăl ēlms
> Ănd mŭrmurĭng ŏf ĭnnŭmĕrāblĕ beēs.
> *Tennyson.*

The breezy call of incense-breathing morn,
The swallow twittering from the straw-built shed,
The cock's shrill clarion, or the echoing horn,
No more shall rouse them from their lowly bed.
            Gray—"Elegy"

But soon obscured with smoke, all heaven appeared,
From those deep-throated engines belched, whose roar
Embowelled with outrageous noise the air,
And all her entrails tore, disgorging foul
Their devilish glut, chained thunderbolts and hail
Of iron globes.
            Milton—"Paradise Lost."

            Here it comes sparkling,
            And there it lies darkling;
            Here smoking and frothing,
            Its tumult and wrath in,
        It hastens along, conflicting strong;
            Now striking and raging,
            As if a war waging,
        Its caverns and rocks among,
            Rising and leaping,
            Sinking and creeping,
            Swelling and flinging,
            Showering and springing,
            Eddying and whisking,
            Spouting and frisking,
            Turning and twisting
                Around and around;
            Collecting, disjecting,
                With endless rebound;
            Smiting and fighting,
            A sight to delight in,
            Confounding, astounding,
        Dizzying and deafening the ear with its sound.
        Robert Southey—"The Cataract of Lodore."

PARALEIPSIS.

A pretended or apparent omission; a figure by which a speaker pretends to pass by what at the same time he really mentions, as:

> Her kindness and her worth to spy,
> You need but gaze on Ellen's eye;
> Not Katrine, in her mirror blue,
> Gives back the shaggy banks more true,
> Than every free-born glance confessed
> The guileless movements of her breast;
> Whether joy danced in her dark eye,
> Or woe or pity claimed a sigh,
> Or filial love was glowing there,
> Or meek devotion poured a prayer,
> Or tale of injury called forth,
> The indignant spirit of the North,
> One only passion unrevealed,
> With maiden pride the maid concealed,
> Yet not less purely felt the flame—
> O need I tell that passion's name?
>   *Scott*—"The Lady of the Lake."

PERSONIFICATION.

Is a figure by which the absent are introduced as present and by which inanimate objects and abstract ideas are represented as living. Personification is a species of Metaphor:

> There is a Reaper whose name is Death,
>   And, with his sickle keen,
> He reaps the bearded grain at a breath,
>   And the flowers that grow between.
>   *Longfellow*—"The Reaper and the Flowers."

To you, fair phantoms in the sun,
　Whom merry Spring discovers,
With blue-birds for your laureates,
　And honey-bees for lovers.
　　　Aldrich—"The Blue-Bells of New England."

His was the spell o'er hearts
　Which only acting lends,—
The youngest of the sister Arts,
　Where all their beauty blends;

For ill can Poetry express
　Full many a tone of thought sublime,
And Painting, mute and motionless,
　Steals but a glance of time.
But by the mighty actor brought,
　Illusion's perfect triumphs come,—
Verse ceases to be airy thought,
　And Sculpture to be dumb.
　　　Campbell—"To J. P. Kemble."

REFRAIN, OR CHANT.

A kind of musical repetition.

Hast thou a golden day, a starlit night,
　Mirth, and music, and love without alloy?
Leave no drop undrunken of thy delight:
Sorrow and shadow follow on thy joy,
　　'Tis all in a lifetime.
　　Edmund Clarence Stedman—"All In a Lifetime."

John Gibson Lockhart also furnishes in his translations of Spanish ballads, another fine illustration:

The Moorish king rides up and down
Through Grenada's royal town;
From Elvira's gates to those
Of Bivarambla on he goes:
　Woe is me, Alhama!"

SIMILE.

Is an express comparison; usually introduced by like, as, and so:

(1).

Life ĭs līke ă tāle
Ĕndĕd ēre 'tĭs tōld.
Aldrich—"Dirge."

(2).

Măn, like thĕ gĕnerŏŭs vīne, sŭppōrtĕd līves;
Thĕ strĕngth hĕ gāins ĭs frŏm thĕ ĕmbrāce hĕ gīves.
Pope.

(3).

Bŭt plĕasŭres āre līke pŏppĭes sprĕad,—
Yoŭ sēize thĕ flŏwer, ĭts bloōm ĭs shĕd;
Ŏr like thĕ snŏwfăll in thĕ rĭvĕr,
Ă mōmĕnt whīte—thĕn mĕlts fŏrĕvĕr;
Ŏr like thĕ bŏrĕălĭs rāce,
Thăt flĭt ĕre yoŭ căn pōint thĕir plāce;
Ŏr like thĕ rāinbŏw's lŏvelў fōrm,
Ĕvănĭshĭng ămĭd thĕ stŏrm.
Burns—"Tam O'Shanter."

(4).

Thĕ dāy ĭs dōne, ănd thĕ dărknĕss
Făls frŏm thĕ wīngs ŏf Nĭght,
Ăs ă fĕathĕr ĭs wăftĕd dōwnwărd
Frŏm ăn ēaglĕ ĭn hĭs flĭght.
Longfellow—"The Day is Done."

SYNECDOCHE.

Is the figure by which the whole of a thing is taken for the part, or a part for the whole, as, the genus for the species, or the species for the genus. It comprehends more or less in the expression than the word which is employed literally signifies.

The noun "sail" is used instead of the noun "ship"—a part of the ship for the whole :

> A sail! a sail! a prŏmĭsed prize tŏ hōpe,
> Hĕr nātiŏn's flāg—hŏw spēaks thĕ tĕlĕscōpe?
> Nŏ prize, ălās! bŭt yĕt ă wĕlcŏme sail.
> *Byron.*

The force of this figure consists of the greater vividness with which the part or species is realized.

In Pickering's ballad we have the following lines where this figure of speech is found, where one wreath is put for the many, that make the whirl, or storm :

> "Cŏme in, ăuld Cārl, I'll steĕr my̆ fire,
> I'll māke ĭt bleēze ă bŏnnĭe flāme ;
> Yoŭr bluĭd ĭs thĭn, yĕ've tĭnt thĕ gāte,
> Yĕ shoŭldnă strāy săe făr frăe hāme."

> "Năe hāme hăve Ĭ," thĕ mĭnstrĕl sāid ;
> " Săd pārty̆ strĭfe ŏ'ertūrned my̆ hā' ;
> And weēpĭng āt thĕ clōse ŏf life,
> Ĭ wāndĕr throŭgh ă *wrĕath ŏf snāw.*"

TROPE.

An important figure defined as a figurative use of a word; a word or expression used in a different sense from that which it properly possesses, or a word changed from its original signification to another for the sake of life or emphasis to an idea, as when we call a shrewd man a fox. Tropes are chiefly of four kinds: Metaphor, Metonymy, Synecdoche, and Irony, but to these may be added Allegory, Prosopopœia, Antonomasia, and perhaps some others.

The word Trope comes from the Greek word *tropos*, which means a turning.

A change of noun is termed a Metonymy, a change of adjective is termed a Trope.

The following are illustrations:

(1).

Now fades the glimmering landscape on the sight,
   And all the air a solemn stillness holds,
Save where the beetle wheels his droning flight,
   And *drowsy tinklings* lull the distant folds.
Gray's Elegy.

(2).

Away! away! to Athunree!
Where, downward when the sun shall fall
The raven's wing shall be your pall!
'And not a vassal shall unlace
The visor from your *dying* face!
Campbell—"Curse of O'Connor's Child."

(3).

She wept to leave the *fond* roof where
   She had been loved so long;
Though glad the peal upon the air,
   And gay the bridal throng.
Miss Landon—"Adieu to a Bride."

(4).

At last the closing season browns the plain,
And *ripe October* gathers in the grain.
        Joel Barlow—"The Hasty Pudding."

(5).

Fountain-heads and pathless groves—
Places which *pale passion* loves.
        Francis Beaumont.

(6).

When the humid shadows hover
  Over all the starry spheres,
And the *melancholy darkness*
  Gently weeps in rainy tears,
What a bliss to press the pillow
  Of a cottage chamber-bed,
And to listen to the patter
  Of the soft rain overhead.
        Coates Kinney—"Rain on the Roof."

(7).

'Tis pleasant, by the cheerful hearth, to hear
Of tempests and the dangers of the deep;
And pause at times and feel that we are safe,
Then listen to the *perilous* tale again.
        Southey—"Modoc."

(8).

Mother, thy child is blessed;
And though his presence may be lost to thee,
And vacant leave thy breast,
And missed *a sweet load* from thy parent knee;
Though tones familiar from thine ear have passed,
Thou'lt meet thy first-born with the Lord at last.
        Willis G. Clark.

(9).

> Shĕ hēars thĕ cānnŏn's *dĕadly* rāttlĕ.
> *Washington Allston*—"Spanish Maid."

(10).

> *Pūrplĕ* drĕssĕs, thĕ weārĭng ŏf which ĭs brīghtĕr thăn ānў stār.
> *Horace*—"Odes."

(11).

> Thĕ dōgs făr kīndĕr thăn thĕir *pūrplĕ* māstĕr.
> "Lazarus and Dives."

(12)

> Ŏthĕrs frŏm thĕ *dāwnĭng* hills
> Loōked ăroŭnd.
> *Milton*—"Paradise Lost."

The "hills" are but the receivers of the light—they are not "dawning hills" save when the "dawning light" shines upon them.

VISION.

Is the expression of powerful emotion, akin to Apostrophe. It is a figure in which the past or future is conceived for the present. It is appropriate to animated description, as it produces the effect of an ideal presence. Thomas Campbell's "Lochiel's Warning" illustrates this figure:

> Lōchiĕl, Lōchiĕl! bĕwāre ŏf thĕ dāy
> Whĕn thĕ Lōwlănds shăll meēt theĕ ĭn băttlĕ ărrāy!
> Fŏr ă fiĕld ŏf thĕ dĕad rŭshĕs rĕd ŏn mў sight,
> Ănd thĕ clăns ŏf Cŭllōdĕn ăre scăttĕred ĭn fight.
> Thĕy rāllў, thĕy bleĕd, fŏr thĕir kīngdŏm ănd crŏwn;—
> Wŏe; wŏe tŏ thĕ rīdĕrs thăt trămplĕ thĕm dŏwn!
> Prŏud Cŭmbĕrlănd prăncĕs, ĭnsŭltĭng thĕ slāin,
> Ănd thĕir hoŏf-bĕatĕn bōsŏms ăre trŏd tŏ thĕ plāin.

PART THIRD.

CHAPTER I.

OF THE VARIOUS KINDS OF POETRY.

WE cannot better introduce our chapter "On the Various Kinds of Poetry" than by giving Fontenelle's celebrated allegory on "The Empire of Poetry." It is professedly one of the finest metaphorical descriptions that has ever been written.

THE EMPIRE OF POETRY.

This Empire is a very large and populous country. It is divided, like some of the countries of the Continent, into the Higher and Lower Regions. The Upper Region is inhabited by grave, melancholy and sullen people, who, like other mountaineers, speak a language very different from that of the inhabitants of the valleys. The trees in this part of the country are very tall, having their tops in the clouds. Their horses are superior to those of Barbary, being fleeter than the winds. Their women are so beautiful as to eclipse the star of day. The great city which you see in the maps, beyond the lofty mountains, is the capital of this province, and is called Epic. It is built on a sandy and ungrateful soil, which few take the pains to cultivate. The length of the city is many days' journey, and it is otherwise of a tiresome extent. On leaving its gate, we always meet with men who are killing one another; whereas, when we pass through Romance, which forms the suburbs of Epic, and which is larger than the city itself, we meet with groups of happy people, who are hastening to the shrine of Hymen.

The mountains of Tragedy are also in the province of Upper Poetry. They are very steep, with dangerous precipices; and, in consequence, many of its people build their habitations at the bottom of the hills, and imagine themselves high enough. There have been found on these mountains some very beautiful ruins of ancient cities, and from time to time, the materials are carried lower to build new cities; for they are now never built nearly so high as they seem to have been in former times.

The Lower Poetry is very similar to the swamps of Holland. Burlesque is the capital, which is situated amid stagnant pools. Princes speak there as if they had sprung from the dung-hill, and all the inhabitants are buffoons from their birth. Comedy is a city which is built on a pleasant spot; but it is too near to Burlesque, and its trade with this place has injured the manners of the inhabitants.

I beg you will notice, in the map, those vast solitudes which lie between High and Low Poetry. They are called the Deserts of Common Sense. There is not a single city in the whole of this extensive country, and only a few cottages scattered at a distance from one another. The interior of the country is beautiful and fertile, but you need not wonder that there are so few that choose to reside in it; for the entrance is very rugged on all sides, the roads are narrow and difficult, and there are seldom any guides to be found capable of conducting strangers.

Besides, this country borders on a province where every person prefers to remain, because it appears to be very agreeable, and saves the trouble of penetrating into the Deserts of Common Sense. It is the province of False

Thoughts. Here we always tread on flowers; everything seems enchanting. But its general inconvenience is, that the ground is not solid; the foot is always sinking in the mire, however careful one may be. Elegy is the capital. Here the people do nothing but complain; but it is said that they find a pleasure in their complaints. The city is surrounded with woods and rocks, where the inhabitant walks alone, making them the confidants of his secrets, of the discovery of which he is so much afraid that he often conjures those woods and rocks never to betray them.

The Empire of Poetry is watered by two rivers: One is the River of Rhyme, which has its source at the foot of the Mountains of Reverie. The tops of some of these mountains are so elevated that they pierce the clouds. Those are called the Points of Sublime Thoughts.

Many climb there by extraordinary efforts; but almost the whole tumble down again, and excite, by their fall, the ridicule of those who admired them at first without knowing why. There are large platforms almost at the bottom of these mountains, which are called the Terraces of Low Thoughts. There are always a great number of people walking on them. At the end of these terraces are the Caverns of Deep Reverie. Those who descend into them do so insensibly, being so much enwrapt in their meditations that they enter the cavern before they are aware. These Caverns are perfect labyrinths, and the difficulty of getting out again could scarcely be believed by those who have not been there. Above the terraces we sometimes meet with men walking in easy paths, which are called the Paths of Natural Thoughts; and these gentlemen ridicule equally those who try to scale the Points of Sublime Thoughts as well as those who grovel on the terraces below. They would be in the right if they could keep undeviatingly in the Paths of Natural Thoughts, but they fall almost instantly into a snare by entering into a splendid palace which is at a very little distance. It is the Palace of Badinage. Scarely have they entered it, when, in place of the natural thoughts which they formerly had, they dwell upon such only as are mean and vulgar. Those, however, who never abandon the Paths of Natural Thoughts are the most rational of all. They aspire no higher than they ought, and their thoughts are never at variance with sound judgment.

Besides the River Rhyme, which I have described as issuing from the foot of the mountains, there is another called the River of Reason. These two rivers are at a great distance from one another, and, as they have different courses, they could not be made to communicate except by canals, which cost a great deal of labor; for these canals of communication could not be formed at all places, because there is only one part of the River Rhyme which is in the neighborhood of the River Reason; and hence many cities situated on the Rhyme, such as Roundelay and Ballad, could have no commerce with the Reason, whatever pains might be taken for the purpose.

Further, it would be necessary that these canals should cross the Deserts of Common Sense, as you will see by the map, and that is almost an unknown country. The Rhyme is a large river, whose course is crooked and unequal, and, on account of its numerous falls, it is extremely difficult to navigate. On the contrary, the Reason is very straight and regular, but does not carry vessels of every burden.

There is in the Land of Poetry a very obscure forest, where the rays of the sun never enter. It is the Forest of Bombast. The trees are close, spreading, and twined into each other. The forest is so ancient that it has become a sort of sacrilege to prune its trees, and there is no probability that the ground will ever be cleared. A few steps into this forest and we lose our road, without dreaming that we have gone astray. It is full of imperceptible labyrinths, from which no one ever returns. The Reason is lost in the forest.

The extensive province of Imitation is very sterile. It produces nothing. The inhabitants are extremely poor, and are obliged to glean in the richer fields of the neighboring provinces; and some even make fortunes by this beggarly occupation.

The Empire of Poetry is very cold toward the north, and consequently this quarter is the most populous. There are the cities of Anagram and Acrostic, with several others of a similar description.

Finally, in that sea which bounds the States of Poetry, there is the Island of Satire, surrounded by bitter waves. The salt from the water is very strong and dark-colored. The greater part of the brooks of this island resemble the Nile in this, that their sources are unknown; but it is particularly remarkable that there is not one of them whose waters are fresh. A part of the same sea is called the Archipelago of Trifles. The French term is l' Archipel des Bagatelles, and their voyagers are well acquainted with those islands. Nature seems to have thrown them up in sport, as she did those of the Egean Sea. The principal islands are the Madrigal, the Song, and the Impromptu. No lands can be lighter than those islands, for they float upon the waters.

FONTENELLE.

The painter gives color to his study, and his tints and tone colors are varied according as the master possesses science in his art, and as genius has given him ability and industry necessary to great effort. The poet paints with another brush. Figures of Rhetoric are his colors, and nature furnishes him with similes, metaphors, and personifications. He should abound in imagery, and his words should be descriptive of external objects which are on every side. His efforts should be to please, and he is allowed greater freedom than any other writer. Man is always interested in his fellow man; hence, character, fortitude, devotion, affection, aspiration, and passion, are all elements that may enter into the poem. From the earliest ages down to the present, poetry has held a place in the human heart. Rude songs descriptive of war and peace, love and affection, hymns to the gods, and poems celebrating the achievements of heroes are among the first productions of all nations. Traditional odes are found among the rudest tribes. Poetry has always been a pleasing form of literature, and has been assiduously cultivated at all times. The higher the grade of civilization the greater has been the appreciation of the poet's efforts. His efforts should always be to attain the ideal. He has the whole world of reality to select from. He should seek to surpass nature in his creative imagination. The true poet is a creator, sensitive to all the scenes and impressions around him; his eye should catch that which the ordinary observer passes by; and his ear should be attuned to every sound about him. The picturesque, the ideal, and the real are all his. To fancy he gives form and color, and his expressions should contain a delicacy, richness and warmth of feeling and beauty, that should ever be a pleasure to mankind. His ideas, figures, characters, scenes, and language should all harmonize. His lines should carry the reader throughout the poem without a jar or interruption. Words should be selected for their beauty of sound and association; and the effort should alone be to attain the highest form of expression known to elevated thought and diction.

CLASSIFICATION OF POETRY.

It is very difficult to classify all poems. Poems may be found that are susceptible of various classification; others will be found that will hardly take their places in any list. Poetry may be divided, however, into six general heads:

1. Lyrical.
2. Pastoral.
3. Didactic.
4. Epic.
5. Dramatic.
6. Satirical.

These six species may be again subdivided as follows:

THE LYRIC.

1. Songs, { Sacred. Secular.
2. Odes.
3. Ballads.
4. Elegy, (Epitaph).
5. Sonnet.
6. Epigram.

THE PASTORAL.

1. Eclogue.
2. Idyl.

THE DIDACTIC.

1. Philosophical.
2. Meditative.

THE EPIC.

1. Grand Epic.
2. Mock Epic.
3. Metrical Romance.
4. Metrical Tale.

The Drama.

1. Tragedy, (Prologue).
2. Comedy, (Epilogue, Envoy).
3. Farce.
4. Mask, Travesty or Mock Heroic.
5. Melodrama.
6. Burletta.

The Satire.

1. Moral.
2. Personal.
3. Political.

To the above classification we may be allowed to add some other heads which properly speaking belong to some of the classes above enumerated. They are, however, figures and forms different from the ordinary:

1. Dialectic.
2. Nonsensical.
3. Versicles.

OBJECTIVE AND SUBJECTIVE POETRY.

We should ask ourselves when we begin to write poetry whether what we write should be objective or subjective. The mental forces at work in writing Cowper's "Task" or Wordsworth's "Excursion," both eminently subjective,—are different from the mental forces at work in writing Longfellow's "Psalm of Life" or "The Day is Done," or Brennan's "Come to Me, Dearest," which are objective poems. In objective poetry the structure is light and airy, lit up as by the gay light of electricity, and the teachings merely suggestive; the other structure—subjective poetry—is strong and ponderous, grave and staid, and its writers may be termed teachers of their own experiences, thoughts and feelings. Subjective poetry is mostly written in the iambic rhythm and comprises not only poems of beauty, but poems of strength and grandeur. Objective poetry is more frequently written in the trochaic, anapestic and dactylic rhythms,—light, tripping, airy, suggestive, and yet possessed of more outward beauty than any other class of poetry. Objective poetry expresses not facts, but fancies; yet these fancies must have facts for a basis. Conciseness in poetry is a virtue—often a necessity, and the writer of anapestic and dactylic verse cannot cram his lines like the writer of iambic verse, or they would be harsh and rugged. Then again, consonants dominate the vowels in our language, and the writer of anapestic and dactylic verse should make it unobtrusively alliterative, and thus artfully bevel the corners by the smoothing process of alliteration. Bring the liquids into use.

THE LYRIC.

The lyric poets form the largest class of singers. They are a kingdom unto themselves, and often they are too much engaged with their own feelings and emotions to have sympathy with the world about them. The lyric poet loves his muse, however, and feels that the muse loves him, and, like the bird, he warbles his joys and sorrows, his fears and aspirations, and the world is made better and brighter by his song. Lyric poetry is gaining rapidly in popular favor; it today has more worshippers at its shrine than either the dramatic or epic, and goes hand in hand with the metrical romance.

SECULAR SONGS.

Secular songs that have endured for all time claim some notice. The poets of every age and clime have sung and will continue to sing of the beauties about them. Especially do they sing of love, that mightiest of all the passions. Facts and fancies, love and romances, sentiment and reflection, have all been food for the poet's imagination. What a world of melody and rhythm today delights human kind, written for us by the singers of all ages. Today we are delighted constantly by some new words set to popular music. Today our song writers are as sentimental, as true to nature and as skilled as the writers of any other age. It is, however, the old songs,—the songs of days gone by—of the long ago, that we naturally go back to and inquire after.

Burns, Bayly, Byron, Lover, Moore, Caroline Norton, Whittier, Longfellow, Holmes, and Tennyson have all written words that will be ever enduring.

Bishop, Balfe, Claribel, Foster, Sullivan, and Winner have written music that have immortalized not only the words but the authors of both words and music. Ever have music and poetry been twin sisters. The world would be not beautiful without them. They are both a passion burning in the human soul that makes the cold, bleak world warm with their inspirations. All peoples love songs. The rudest savages have songs of love and of war, of home and of country, of peace and of religion. The wild Cossack delights in his songs and sings of and to his love, with the same tenderness as the cultivated European.

Ireland has ever been famous for her song writers. The Welsh and Scots have given to the world the sweetest of music. Germany has contributed her part. The singers of all kindreds and of every clime have produced words and music which solace mankind. Let it not be supposed, however, that the popular song that has frequently handed the name of the author down to posterity is but the work of an idle moment.

Thomas Moore's "Last Rose of Summer" is one of the most widely popular songs. Its sale in this country alone is estimated at over two million copies. It cost Moore deep meditation. He wrote the song for an old air, "The Groves of Blarney." He tells us he was weeks composing just one of its lines before he succeeded in obtaining words that were suitable. Moore's Irish Melodies are full of the sweetest of songs—songs that will be more and more appreciated in the future by a refined and cultivated public. None can, however, touch the popular heart more than the one we have just alluded to, a song of but three stanzas of eight lines each, written in anapestic rhythm. "The Last Rose of Summer" will be as popular with future generations as it has been with past ones, and had Moore never written anything else his name would be immortalized. We select the last stanza :

> Sŏ soōn mȧy I fŏllŏw,
>   Whĕn friĕndshĭps dĕcāy,
> Ăs frŏm lōve's shĭnĭng cĭrclĕ
>   Thĕ gĕms drŏp ăwāy !
> Whĕn trŭe heārts ăre wĭthĕred,
>   Ănd fōnd ŏnes ăre flōwn,
> Ŏh ! whŏ woŭld ĭnhābĭt
>   Thĭs blĕak wŏrld ălōne?

Many accounts are given of how "Home, Sweet Home" came to be written. John Howard Payne, its author, was an American poet and playwright who had received a fair education and who made his living by his pen and on the stage. Like many actors, as well as writers, he was a spendthrift and became stranded in Paris, France, the world's gay capitol. While all the world below was gayety and pleasure, he was the occupant of a poorly furnished room in the topmost story of a house in the Palais-Royale. Without friends, and temporarily without money, naturally enough these words suggested themselves to him :

> 'Mĭd plĕasŭres ănd pālăcĕs thōugh wĕ mǎy rōam,
> Bĕ ĭt ĕvĕr sŏ hŭmblĕ thĕre's nō plăce līke hōme ;
> Ă chārm frŏm thĕ skīes seĕms tŏ hāllŏw ŭs thĕre,
> Whĭch, seĕk thrŏugh thĕ wōrld, ĭs nĕ'er mĕt wĭth ĕlsewhēre.
> Hōme ! Hōme ! sweĕt, sweĕt hōme !
> Thĕre's nō plăce līke hōme !
> Ŏh, thĕre's nō plăce līke hōme !

The words found a response in every heart. Over one hundred thousand copies of the song were sold the first year of its publication. Although Payne was never benefitted a penny thereby, it immortalized him. Its music is an old Calabrian air familiar to the peasant folk of Sicily. Sir Henry Bishop, who arranged the music, tells us that he obtained the air from an old army officer who served in Sicily. The rhythm of the poem is anapestic tetrameter.

Stephen Collins Foster,* author of "The Old Kentucky

---

* Stephen Collins Foster was born July 4, 1826, in Pennsylvania. He was a delicate child, and throughout life was of a quiet and retiring disposition. At the early age of thirteen he composed, "Sadly to My Heart Appealing," and at sixteen years of age, "Open Thy Lattice, Love." In after years he gave to the world, "Old Uncle Ned," "O Susanna," "Massa's in the Cold Ground," "Old Dog Tray," "Gentle Annie," and ' Come Where My Love Lies Dreaming." Foster not only composed the words, but the music to most of his songs. His was a peculiar musical talent, which has been recognized by musical celebrities, and his airs have been incorporated by many into concert fantasias. He died as he had lived, in neglect and poverty, at the early age of thirty-seven, in 1864, in New York City. It is a sad commentary upon life to know the songs of this gifted writer are daily sung in almost every household, and still continue to delight the public on both sides of the Atlantic, and yet, no monument marks the last resting place of the author of " The Old Folks at Home."

Home," was a writer of still another class of songs indigenous to the United States. They are negro melodies, sad and quaint, and many of them will last forever. "The Old Folks at Home" in both words and air cannot be surpassed. Its rhythm is iambic:

> Way down upon de Swanee Ribber,
>   Far, far away—
> Dare's wha my heart is turning ebber-
>   Dare's wha de old folks stay.
> All up and down de whole creation,
>   Sadly I roam;
> Still longing for de old plantation,
>   And for de old folks at home.
>
> All de world am sad and dreary,
>   Eb'rywhere I roam;
> Oh, darkeys, how my heart grows weary,
>   Far from de old folks at home.
>
> All round de little farm I wandered,
>   When I was young;
> Den many happy days I squandered,
>   Many de songs I sung.
> When I was playing wid my brudder,
>   Happy was I;
> Oh! take me to my kind old mudder!
>   Dare let me live and die!
>
> One little hut among de bushes—
>   One dat I love—
> Still sadly to my memory rushes,
>   No matter where I rove.
> When will I see de bees a-humming,
>   All round de comb?
> When will I hear de banjo tumming
>   Down in my good old home?

Henry Russell is the author of "A Life on the Ocean Wave." It is one of the most popular of the many beautiful songs of the sea. The British Admiralty adopted it as the march of the Royal Marines. It is iambic trimeter. We select the first stanza:

> Ă life ŏn thĕ ōcĕan wāve,
>   Ă hōme ŏn thĕ rōllĭng deēp,
> Whĕre thĕ scāttĕred wătĕrs rāve,
>   Ănd thĕ wīnds thĕir rĕvĕls keēp!
> Līke ăn ēaglĕ cāged, Ĭ pine,
>   Ŏn thĭs dŭll, ŭnchāngĭng shōre;
> Ŏh! gīve mĕ thĕ flāshĭng brīne,
>   Thĕ sprāy ănd thĕ tēmpĕst rōar!

"The Bay of Biscay," by John Davy, and "Black-Eyed Susan," by John Gay, both favorites in their day, are still popular sea songs.

A little romance is attached to one the prettiest of the old Scotch songs. Annie Laurie was no myth. She was born on the 16th day of December, 1682. Her father was Sir Robert Laurie of Maxwelton, who lived on the opposite side of the river Nith, from Dumfries, Scotland. William Douglass wooed, but never won her. His song describing her beauty and his passion for her will render her name immortal. The fickle Annie preferred, however, to become the wife of Sir Robert Ferguson, who possessed riches as well as a name. The music of the song was composed by Lady Jane Scott, and both words and music will live for generations to come. We give the original words as they were first written, as numerous changes have been made to them since that time. The rhythm is iambic.

Māxwēltŏn bānks ăre bŏnnĭe,
  Whĕre ĕarlў fā's thĕ dĕw ;
Whĕre mē ănd Ānnĭe Lāurĭe
  Măde ūp thĕ prŏmĭse trŭe;
Măde ūp thĕ prŏmĭse trŭe,
  Ănd nĕvĕr fŏrgēt wĭll Ī ;
Ănd fŏr bŏnnĭe Ānnĭe Lāurĭe
  Ĭ'll lāy mĕ dōwn ănd dĭe.

Shĕ's bāckĭt līke thĕ pēacŏck,
  Shĕ's brĕistĭt līke thĕ swān,
Shĕ's jĭmp ăbōut thĕ mĭddlĕ,
  Hĕr wāist yĕ weēl mĭcht spān ;
Hĕr wāist yĕ weēl mĭcht spān,
  Ănd shĕ hās ă rōllĭng ēye ;
Ănd fŏr bŏnnĭe Ānnĭe Lāurĭe
  Ĭ'll lāy mĕ dōwn ănd dĭe.

The poets of the Emerald Isle will ever be held in high esteem in the memories and hearts of all nations. The songs of her writers have a fervency and pathos that are unsurpassable. The old song from which we select the second stanza is ever dear to the heart of her countryman. This song is selected not only on account of the admirable words but also for the reason they are written in dactylic rhythm — dactylic tetrameter:

Ŏvĕr thĕ greēn sĕa, Māvoŭrneĕn, Māvoŭrneĕn,
Lŏng shŏne thĕ whīte săil thăt bōre theĕ ăwāy,
Rĭdĭng thĕ whīte wăves thăt făir sūmmĕr mōr-ĭn',
Jŭst līke ă Māyflŏwer ăflōat ŏn thĕ bāy.
Oh, bŭt mў heārt sănk whĕn clōuds cămĕ bĕtweēn ŭs,
Līke ă grĕy cŭrtăin ŏf răin fāllĭng dōwn,
Hĭd frŏm mў sād ĕyes thĕ păth ŏ'er thĕ ōceăn,
Făr, făr ăwāy whĕre mў cōlleĕn hăd flōwn,

Thĕn cŏme băck tŏ Ĕrĭn, Māvoŭrneĕn, Māvoŭrneĕn,
Cŏme băck ăgāin tŏ thĕ lănd ŏf thў birth;
Cŏme băck tŏ Ĕrĭn, Māvoŭrneĕn, Māvoŭrneĕn,
Ănd ĭt's Kĭllārnĕy shăll rĭng wĭth ŏur mĭrth.

Claribel—" Come Back to Erin."

It requires only true manhood which is born of cultivation and civilization to appreciate anything which is beautiful, either of art or nature. And even the careless, the indifferent, and the impatient lover of business will frequently turn aside and listen to such delicious songs of love as "Ever of Thee I'm Fondly Dreaming," by Linley, "Her Bright Smile Haunts Me Still," by Carpenter, or "Love Not," by Caroline Norton.

The field of song is one of the finest, and every poet has entered it, and many have told in song their tales of joy or woe that will never die. Burns sang of his "Highland Mary," and nothing in all of his wonderful productions is superior to it. "Mary of Argyle" by Nelson, is a beautiful song. It is mixed iambic and anapestic meter, but the prevailing foot is iambic. We select the first stanza :

Ĭ hăve hĕard thĕ māvĭs sĭngĭng
    Hĭs lōve-sŏng tō thĕ mŏrn ;
Ĭ hăve sĕen thĕ dĕw-drŏps clĭngĭng
    Tŏ thĕ rōse jŭst nĕwlў bōrn ;
Bŭt ă swēetĕr sŏng hăs chĕered mĕ
    Ăt thĕ ēvenĭng's gĕntlĕ clōse,
Ănd Ĭ've sĕen ăn eўe stĭll brĭghtĕr
    Thăn thĕ dĕw-drŏp ōn thĕ rōse ;
'Twăs thў vōice, mў gĕntlĕ Mārў,
    Ănd thĭne ārtlĕss, wĭnnĭng smile,
Thăt māde thĭs wŏrld ăn Ĕdĕn,
    Bŏnnў Mārў ŏf Ărgўle.

"Only Friends and Nothing More," by Septimus Winner, one of the famous song writers of the New World, is a very pretty song. Alice Hawthorne who is accredited with the words was Winner's mother—Hawthorne being her maiden name. Out of respect for his mother, her talented and gifted son has named her as the authoress of some of the most charming and delightful of songs. One, "The Mocking-Bird," is world renowned, on account of the delicious melody of the music, and also the words of the song.

The stanza selected from "Only Friends and Nothing More," is iambic rhythm.

> Wĕ mĕt ăs manў hăve bĕfōre
> Nŏr wished nŏr hōped tŏ mēet ăgāin ;
> Nĕ'er drēamĭng ōf ŏur fāte ĭn stōre
> Wĭth dăys ŏf plĕasŭre ōr ŏf pāin.
> Wĕ mĕt ăgāin wĭth right gŏod will
> Yĕt paūsed whĕn pārtĭng āt thĕ dōor ;
> Wĕ lĭngĕred wĭth ă sīgh, bŭt stĭll
> Ăs ōnlў friĕnds ănd nōthĭng mōre.
> Wĕ lĭngĕred wĭth ă sīgh, bŭt stĭll
> Ăs ōnlў friĕnds ănd nōthĭng mōre.

Old songs that still live and are in touch with the popular heart are many, but the quaint ones, the expressive ones, those that possess a distinctiveness of their own, are not so numerous as one would suppose. An old English song, a war song, entitled "I Will Hang My Harp on a Willow Tree," is such an one. The measure is mixed, but the iambus is the prevailing foot. The anapest, however, is also found in almost every line. We select the first stanza:

> I'll hăng mў hārp ŏn ă wĭllŏw trēe,
>   Ĭ'll ŏff tŏ thĕ wărs ăgāin ;
> Mў pēacefŭl hōme hăs nŏ chărm fŏr mē,
>   Thĕ băttlĕfiĕld nŏ pāin ;
> Thĕ Lādў Ĭ lōve wĭll sōon bĕ ă brīde,
>   Wĭth ă dĭădĕm ŏn hĕr brŏw.
> Ŏh ! whў dĭd shĕ flăttĕr mў bōyĭsh prĭde,
>   Shĕ's gōĭng tŏ lĕave mĕ nŏw,
> Ŏh ! whў dĭd shĕ flăttĕr mў bōyĭsh prĭde,
>   Shĕ's gōĭng tŏ lĕave mĕ nŏw.

The four stanzas composing this grand old song are all first-class, although a little different from the war music of the present time. There is, however, something about the air that is fine, and music and words will still continue to find old as well as young admirers.

The Civil War of the United States produced many great songs—songs that stir the souls of men. Charles S. Hall's "John Brown's Body" will still go marching on. It caught the public feeling of the North—the public sentiment. "Dixie," the great song of the South was composed by Gen. Albert N. Pike, the music by Dan D. Emmett. The music found a general response, not only in the South, but also in the North, and every school boy sang the song. The words are iambic rhythm, and there is genuine music in every word, as well as every note.

"Bonnie Blue Flag" was also one of the great songs of the South, and was written by H. McCarthy. It is mixed iambic and anapestic measure, the iambic foot prevailing. No song of the South was, however, greater in words and music than "My Maryland," written in 1861 by James R. Randall. We select the third stanza :

> Thŏu wĭlt nŏt cōwĕr ĭn thĕ dūst,
> Mārȳlānd, mȳ Mārȳlānd!
> Thȳ glēamĭng swōrd shăll nĕvĕr rūst,
> Mārȳlānd, mȳ Mārȳlānd!
> Rĕmēmbĕr Cārrŏll's sācrĕd trūst,
> Rĕmēmbĕr Hōwărd's wărlĭke thrūst,
> Ănd āll thȳ slŭmbĕrĕrs wĭth thĕ jūst,
> Mārȳlānd, mȳ Mārȳlānd!

We remember while a boy in college hearing Chaplain Charles C. McCabe, who had just been released from a Southern prison and was visiting at the home of that great and good uncle of his, Prof. L. D. McCabe, of the Ohio Wesleyan University, sing the "Battle Hymn of the Republic." The song is by one of the grandest of womankind, Julia Ward Howe. Nothing we have ever heard found a greater response. As Chaplain McCabe's voice went up it thrilled the very soul. The chorus was caught by all present, and men and women sang in the old William Street Church upon that occasion who never sang before. The song is in the iambic rhythm. We select the first stanza.

Mĭne eȳes hăve sēen thĕ glōrȳ ŏf thĕ cōmĭng ŏf thĕ Lŏrd;
Hĕ ĭs trămplĭng ōut thĕ vĭntăge whēre thĕ grāpes ŏf wrăth ăre
  stōred:
Hĕ hăth lōosed thĕ fātefŭl lĭghtnĭng ŏf Hĭs tĕrrĭblē swĭft swōrd.
Hĭs trūth ĭs mārchĭng ōn.

Song writing, while it may not be the greatest conception of the poet's mind, is one that may serve to keep his memory green. It requires feeling, tenderness and sympathy to write the sweet songs that must endure forever.

SACRED SONGS.

How often have we listened in former days to good old hymns, designated by the minister as Long Meter, Short Meter, or Particular Meter. We did not then understand, or could we tell just what was meant by it. When, however, some good brother would start the tune, we could distinguish and recognize the old familiar sound; for in those days tunes were scarce. When we heard the following iambic stanza:

> Ŏ whēre shăll rēst bĕ foūnd,
>   Rĕst fōr thĕ wēarў sōul?
> 'Twĕre vāin thĕ ōceăn's dĕpths tŏ sōund,
>   Ŏr piērce tŏ ēithĕr pōle.
>
> Montgomery.

it was not difficult for us to distinguish the tune from the following, which the same brother, who always led the singing, would start, written in trochaic rhythm:

8s 7s.

> Cōme, thŏu Fōunt ŏf ēverў blĕssĭng,
>   Tūne mў heārt tŏ sĭng thў grāce.
> Strēams ŏf mērcў nĕvĕr cēasĭng,
>   Cāll fŏr sōngs ŏf lōudĕst prāise.
> Tēach mĕ sōme mĕlōdĭoŭs sōnnĕt,
>   Sūng bў flāmĭng tōngues ăbōve:
> Prāise thĕ mōunt—Ĭ'm fīxed ŭpŏn ĭt;
>   Mōunt ŏf thў rĕdeēmĭng lōve!
>
> Robinson.

Our ear soon taught us that this was Particular or Odd Meter. We could distinguish it from the first, known as short measure, or from this stanza in iambics, when the same good brother would start the tune again, and drawl its slow length on to the end :

> Deĕm nŏt thăt thēy ăre blēst ălōne
> Whŏse dāys ă pēacefŭl tēnŏr keēp ;
> Thĕ ănoīntĕd Sōn ŏf Gōd mākes knōwn
> Ă blēssĭng fōr thĕ ēyes thăt weēp.
>
> *Bryant.*

This hymn was designated as Long Meter. These measures were also to be distinguished from the following stanza in iambics, as

> Ĭ lōve tŏ steāl ăwhile ăwāy
> Frŏm ēverȳ cūmberĭng cāre,
> Ănd spēnd thĕ hŏurs ŏf sēttĭng dāy
> Ĭn hŭmblĕ, grātefŭl prāyer.
>
> *Mrs. Brown.*

This was known as common measure. The Wesleys, John and Charles, and Dr. Watts, have made these measures familiar, and all remember the old hymns we learned at church, and are thankful for what they taught us. A stanza of four iambic lines, the first, second and fourth being trimeters ; the third line, tetrameter, is designated as Short Meter.

A stanza of four iambic lines, the first and third being tetrameter, the second and fourth trimeter, is known as Common Meter.

A stanza of four lines, rhyming in couplets, or alternately, in iambic tetrameter, is Long Meter. Particular or Odd Meter was formerly used to denote all other kinds of meter, as distinguishable from L. M., S. M., C. M., etc. We have also what is known as the Hallelujah Meter, a stanza of six iambic lines, the first four being trimeter; the last two tetrameter, or the last two lines may be separated into four lines, containing two iambics each, as

> All hail! the glorious morn,
>   That saw our Saviour rise,
> With victory bright adorned,
>   And triumph in his eyes;
> Ye saints, extol your risen Lord,
>   And sing his praise with sweet accord.
> "Psalms and Hymns."

Long Particular Meter is still another form of the stanza in which some of our hymns are written. The stanza is iambic. The six lines are tetrameter, the third and sixth rhyming together, the others rhyming in couplets, as

> Let mortals tremble and adore
> A God of such resistless power,
>   Nor dare indulge their feeble rage;
> Vain are your thoughts, and weak your hands,
> But his eternal counsel stands,
>   And rules the world from age to age.
> "Psalms and Hymns."

All the above stanzas but one are written in iambics. The second stanza is in trochaic measure. The iambic is a favorite measure for hymns.

OTHER METERS.

But we have many beautiful hymns in other measures. Many hymns are designated as 8s and 7s, 7s, 6s and 8s, 8s

OF THE VARIOUS KINDS OF POETRY. 251

and 7s and 4s, 11s, 12s, etc. This simply has reference to the number of syllables contained in the line or verse of the stanza.

A common form of our hymns is the trochaic tetrameter, lines of eight and seven syllables rhyming alternately. The line of seven syllables being catalectic. This form in our hymn books is denominated the 8s and 7s.

It would be much better were we to name it properly—trochaic tetrameter.

Hymns written in trochaic, dactylic, or anapestic meter are however, designated only by figures, giving us no clue to the rhythm. Were the name of the meter added, as, 11s, anapestic tetrameter, our hymns would be properly designated.

The following stanza of an old hymn is in anapestic rhythm, 6s and 9s :

> "Ŏ hŏw hāppў ăre thēy
> Whŏ thĕ Sāviŏŭr ŏbēy,
> Ănd hăve lāid ŭp thĕir trēasŭre ăbōve!
> Ŏ whăt tōngue căn ĕxprĕss
> Thĕ sweĕt cōmfŏrt ănd peāce
> Ŏf ă sōul ĭn ĭts ēarlĭĕst lōve?"
>
> *C. Wesley.*

The first, second, fourth and fifth lines are anapestic dimeter, the third and sixth anapestic tetrameter.

Our hymns have been greatly improved in recent years; not only have many new and beautiful ones been added, but the music has been vastly improved. We remember hearing an eminent divine once say, "The church has all the good hymns, but the de'il has all the best tunes." This can no longer be said. Hymnology has kept pace with the times. Such benefactors as Philip Phillips, Ira D. Sankey, P. P. Bliss and many others have revolutionized church hymns and church music. Some of our hymns are the most beautiful of songs. The slow and sorrowful iambics of the long, short and common meters are being replaced by sweet strains in trochaic, anapestic and dactylic rhythms. What can be more beautiful than the tender and pathetic hymn, written by Frances Laughton Mace. It is trochaic tetrameter. We give the first stanza :

>Ŏnlў wāitĭng tĭll thĕ shădŏws
> Āre ă littlĕ lōngĕr grŏwn ;
>Ŏnlў wāitĭng, tĭll thĕ glĭmmĕr
> Ŏf thĕ dāy's lăst bĕam hăs flŏwn ;
>Tĭll thĕ night ŏf eārth ĭs fădĕd
> Frŏm thĕ heārt ŏnce fŭll ŏf dāy ;
>Tĭll thĕ stārs ŏf hēavĕn ăre breākĭng
> Throŭgh thĕ twĭlĭght sŏft ănd grāy.
>   "Only Waiting."

Another woman, Sarah Flower Adams, has written for us another beautiful hymn. It is mixed measure, the iambic being the prevailing foot. The first, third, fifth and sixth lines are iambic trimeter ; the second, fourth and seventh lines, iambic dimeter. We give the first stanza :

>Nĕarĕr mў Gōd, tŏ theē,
> Nĕarĕr tŏ theē !
>Ĕ'en thŏugh ĭt bĕ ă crōss
> Thăt rāisĕth mĕ ;
>Stĭll āll mў sōng shăll bĕ
>Neārĕr mў Gōd, tŏ theē
> Nĕarĕr tŏ theē !
>   "Nearer My God to Thee."

Bishop Heber is the author of a beautiful hymn in dactylic rhythm. It is the 11s and 10s, dactylic tetrameter. We give the first stanza :

> Brightĕst ănd bĕst ŏf thĕ sŏns ŏf thĕ mŏrnĭng,
> Dāwn ĭn ŏur dārknĕss ănd lēnd ŭs thĭne āid ;
> Stār ŏf thĕ Ēast, thĕ hŏrīzŏn ădōrnĭng,
> Guīde whĕre ŏur ĭnfănt Rĕdeēmĕr ĭs lāid.

"The Beautiful River" is still another of our hymns that will be sung until the children of earth are gathered on the other shore. It is trochaic tetrameter. We give the first stanza :

> Shāll wĕ gāthĕr āt thĕ rĭvĕr
> Whēre brĭght āngĕl feĕt hăve trōd ;
> Wĭth ĭts crȳstăl tīde fŏrēvĕr
> Flōwĭng bȳ thĕ thrōne ŏf Gŏd ?

CHORUS—
> Yēs, wĕ'll gāthĕr āt thĕ rĭvĕr,
> Thĕ beaūtĭfŭl, thĕ beaūtĭfŭl rĭvĕr—
> Gāthĕr wĭth thĕ sāints ăt thĕ rĭvĕr,
> Thāt flōws bȳ thĕ thrōne ŏf Gŏd.
>
> *Rev. Robert Lowry.*

The "Sweet By and By," a hymn in anapestic rhythm, is another of our popular hymns. We give the second stanza :

> Wĕ shăll sĭng ŏn thăt beaūtĭfŭl shōre
> Thĕ mĕlōdĭoŭs sōngs ŏf thĕ blēst,
> Ănd ŏur spĭrĭts shăll sōrrŏw nŏ mōre
> Nŏt ă sĭgh fŏr thĕ blĕssĭng ŏf rĕst.

CHORUS—
   In thĕ sweēt bȳ-ănd-bȳ,
      Wĕ shăll meēt ŏn thăt beaūtĭfŭl shōre,
   Ĭn thĕ sweēt bȳ-ănd-bȳ,
      Wĕ shăll meēt ŏn thăt beaūtĭfŭl shōre.
                              S. Filmore Bennett.

While many beautiful hymns have been written, and old ones arranged to new music, there is a charm that lingers around many old ones, and they will never die. We mention "Old Hundred," written by Dr. Isaac Watts, it being a paraphrase of the one hundredth Psalm, the music by G. Franc, 1554; "Jesus, Lover of My Soul," Rev. Charles Wesley, 1740, the music by Simeon B. Marsh in 1798; "Rock of Ages," written by Rev. A. M. Toplady, 1776, and set to music 1830 by Dr. Thomas Hastings; "Sweet Hour of Prayer," written in 1846 by Rev. W. H. Walford, arranged to music in 1859 by W. H. Bradbury.

Many are the hymns that have survived for over one hundred years, and are fresh in the minds of the people today.

THE ODE.

Odes are of four kinds Sacred, Heroic, Moral and Amatory. The ode is one of the most elevated forms of lyric compositions. Ode, derived from the Greek, meaning song, originally meant any poem adapted to be sung. The ode is, however, to be distinguished from the song. It is the loftiest form of lyrical poetry, embodying as it does the most elevating thoughts and most intense emotions of the writer. It is usually written in an abrupt, concise and energetic style. The meters are often irregular and are not arranged by any fixed stanzaic law, but by a deeper law— that feeling which guides the soul of inspiration on and on, in rapt emotion, regardless of the demands of the stanza. Poetry may, however, lose immensely by not being governed by a fixed stanzaic law for much of its beauty depends upon the fixed regularity of its rhyme. Odes are, however, irregular, and call forth the highest art of the poet in adapting the meters and cadences to the ever varying changes of sentiment and imaginative thought.

THE SACRED ODE.

Byron's Hebrew Melodies and Moore's Sacred Melodies contain fine specimens of lyrical beauty. Milton's ode on the "Nativity" is still another fine example:

> Ănd ōn thăt cheēk ănd ō'er thăt brōw
> Sŏ sōft, sŏ cālm, sŏ ēlŏquĕnt,
> Thĕ smiles thăt wīn, thĕ tīnts thăt glōw,
> Bŭt tēll ŏf dāys ĭn goōdnĕss spēnt,—
> Ă mīnd ăt pēace wĭth āll bĕlōw,
> Ă heārt whōse lōve ĭs ĭnnŏcĕnt.
> *Byron*—"She Walks in Beauty."

THE MORAL ODE.

Odes of this nature express sentiment suggested by friendship, humanity of heart, and patriotism. Lanier's "Ode to the Johns Hopkins University" is an example in iambic:

And hēre, Ŏ finer Pāllăs, lōng rĕmāin,—
Sĭt ŏn thēse Mărўlănd hĭlls, ănd fĭx thў rēign,
And frāme ă fāirĕr Āthēns thān ŏf yōre
   Ĭn thēse blĕst bōunds ŏf Bāltĭmōre,—
   Hĕre, whĕre thĕ clĭmătes meĕt
Thăt ēach măy māke thĕ ŏthĕr's lăck cŏmplēte,—
Whĕre Flŏrĭdă's sŏft Făvŏniăn āirs bĕguile
Thĕ nĭppĭng Nōrth,—whĕre Nătŭre's pŏwĕrs smīle,—
Whĕre Chĕsăpēake hŏlds frănklў fōrth hĕr hānds
Sprĕad wide wĭth ĭnvĭtătĭon tō āll lănds.—
Whĕre nŏw thĕ ēagĕr pēoplĕ yēarn tŏ fĭnd
Thĕ ōrgănĭzĭng hănd thăt fāst măy bĭnd
Loŏse strāws ŏf āimlĕss ăspĭrătĭon fāin
   Ĭn shēaves ŏf sĕrvĭceāblĕ grāin,—
   Hĕre, ōld ănd nĕw ĭn ōne,
Thrŏugh nōblĕr cўclĕs rōund ă rĭchĕr sūn
   Ŏ'er-rūle ŏur mŏdĕrn wāys,
Ŏ blĕst Mĭnĕrvă ŏf thēse lārgĕr dāys!

THE AMATORY ODE.

It is better known as a love song. Most English and American poets have contributed to this great class of literature. Goethe, Schiller and Heine are the most celebrated of the German writers who have contributed to this species of poetry. The Madrigal is a little amorous poem that may be properly classed under this head. Byron's "Maid of Athens," Tennyson's "Maud," and Burns' "Highland Mary" are among the finest specimens of our love songs, expressing refined sentiment and tender affection:

    Ŏ, săd ăre thĕy whŏ knōw nŏt lōve,
      Bŭt, făr frŏm păssiŏn's tēars ănd smīles,
    Drĭft dŏwn ă moŏnlĕss sēa ănd pāss
      Thĕ sĭlvĕr cōasts ŏf fāirў ĭsles.
Thomas Bailey Aldrich—"Sad Are They Who Know Not Love."

THE HEROIC ODE.

Odes of this species celebrate and sing the praises of heroes and are mostly occupied with martial exploits. Lowell's "Commemoration Ode" and Coleridge's "Ode to France" are specimens of this species :

Ŏur făthĕrs fōught fŏr Lībĕrtȳ,
Thĕy strŭgglĕd lōng ănd wĕll,
Hīstorȳ ŏf thĕir deēds căn tĕll—
Bŭt dĭd thĕy lēave ŭs freē ?
  Lowell—"Fourth of July Ode."

'Twăs āt thĕ rōyăl fĕast, fŏr Pĕrsĭă wŏn
By Philĭp's wărlĭke sŏn ;
Ălōft ĭn ăwfŭl stāte
Thĕ Gŏdlīke hĕrŏ sāte
Ŏn hīs ĭmpērĭăl thrōne ;
Hĭs vālĭănt peērs wĕre plāced ăroūnd,
Thĕir brōws wĭth rōsĕs ānd wĭth mȳrtlĕs boūnd
(Sŏ should dĕsĕrt ĭn ārms bĕ crōwned.)
Thĕ lōvelȳ Thăis, bȳ hĭs sīde,
Săte like ă bloŏmĭng Ēastĕrn brīde
Ĭn flōwĕr ŏf youth ănd beaūty's pride.
  Hăppȳ, hăppȳ, hăppȳ pāir !
    Nōne bŭt thĕ brāve,
    Nōne bŭt thĕ brāve,
  Nōne bŭt thĕ brāve dĕsĕrves thĕ fāir.
CHORUS—
  Hăppȳ, hăppȳ, hăppȳ pāir !
    Nōne bŭt thĕ brāve,
    Nōne bŭt thĕ brāve,
  Nōne bŭt thĕ brāve dĕsĕrves thĕ fāir.
John Dryden—"Alexander's Feast ; or, the Power of Music."

Thŭs brīght fŏrĕvĕr māy shĕ keēp
  Hĕr fīres ŏf tōlĕrănt Freēdŏm bŭrnĭng,
Tĭll wār's rĕd ēyes ăre chārmed tŏ sleēp
  Ănd bĕlls rĭng hōme thĕ bōys rĕtŭrnĭng.
    John Hay—"Centennial,"

THE BALLAD.

It is only in very enlightened communities that books are readily accessible. Metrical composition, therefore, which, in a highly civilized nation, is a mere luxury, is, in nations imperfectly civilized, almost a necessary of life, and is valued less on account of the pleasure which it gives to the ear, than on account of the help which it gives to the memory. A man who can invent or embellish an interesting story, and put it into a form which others may easily retain in their recollection, will be always highly esteemed by a people eager for amusement and information, but destitute of libraries. Such is the origin of ballad-poetry, a species of composition which scarcely ever fails to spring up and flourish in every society, at a certain point in the progress towards refinement. Tacitus informs us that songs were the only memorials of the past which the ancient Germans possessed. We learn from Lucan and from Ammianus Marcellinus that the brave actions of the ancient Gauls were commemorated in the verses of Bards. During many ages, and through many revolutions, minstrelsy retained its influence over both Teutonic and the Celtic race. The vengeance exacted by the spouse of Attila for the murder of Siegfried was celebrated in rhymes, of which Germany is still justly proud.

The exploits of Athelstane were commemorated by the Anglo-Saxons, and those of Canute by the Danes, in rude poems, of which a few fragments have come down to us. The chants of the Welsh harpers, preserved, through ages of darkness, a faint and doubtful memory of Arthur. In the Highlands of Scotland may still be gleaned some relics of the old songs about Cuthullin and Fingal. The long struggle of the Servians against the Ottoman power was recorded in lays full of martial spirit.

We learn from Herrera that when a Peruvian Inca died, men of skill were appointed to celebrate him in verses, which all the people learned by heart and sang in public on days of festival. The feats of Kurroglou, the great freebooter of Turkistan, recounted in ballads composed by himself, are known in every village of Northern Persia.

Captain Beechey heard the Bards of the Sandwich Islands recite the heroic achievements of Tamehameha, the most illustrious of their kings. Mungo Park found in the heart of Africa a class of singing men, the only annalists of their rude tribes, and heard them tell the story of the victory which Damel, the negro prince of the Jaloffs, won over Abdulkader, the Musselman tyrant of Foota Torra. This species of poetry attained a high degree of excellence among the Castilians, before they began to copy Tuscan patterns. It attained a still higher degree of excellence among the English and the Lowland Scotch, during the fourteenth, fifteenth, and sixteenth centuries. But it reached its full perfection in ancient Greece; for there can be no doubt that the great Homeric poems are generically ballads, though widely distinguished from all other ballads, and indeed from almost all other human compositions, by transcendent sublimity and beauty.

         LORD MACAULAY.

Among the modern poets, Schiller, Goethe, Hood, Cowper, Carleton, Tennyson, Lang and Dobson have written some of the finest ballads. William Cowper's "John Gilpin's Ride," is a ballad known to almost every one.

Thomas Campbell ranks as one of the best of English writers, and few ballads have been more popular with the general reader than "Lord Ullin's Daughter." Thomas Hood was an inimitable writer, one who could spin puns and take even the bright side of life when adversity was his almost constant companion. His "Faithless Nelly Gray" is a ballad that will ever be remembered, and his work abounds with good things in this species of poetry. Oliver Wendell Holmes has also given to the world some excellent ballads.

Our common English ballads record in easy verse incidents and adventures. Here is a stanza of one of the earlier ballads :

CHEVY CHASE.

"Thĕ drivĕrs throūgh thĕ woŏds wĕnt
   Fŏr tŏ rōuse thĕ deēr,
Bōwmăn hŏvĕred ŭpōn thĕ bĕnt[1]
   Wīth theīr broăd ārrŏws cleār,
Thĕn thĕ wild deĕr throūgh thĕ woŏds wĕnt
   Ŏn ēverȳ side fŭll sheār,[2]
Greȳhoŭnds throūgh thĕ grōve glĕnt[3]
   Fŏr tŏ kill thĕse deēr."

[1] Upland. [2] Many. [3] Chased.

The ballad of today is in higher favor than poems of a didactic character. The ballads of the present day are not merely simple narratives without any symbolical meaning; they are artistic tales, in conception grand, and in execution perfect, and are frequently of an exceedingly high order. Schiller's ballads are among his best poems, and he, without doubt, was second to none of Germany's great poetic geniuses. "The Diver" is one of his most fascinating ballads. With admirable art the poet has heightened the effect of one of the best German stories by ornamenting the poem with those graces of description which were ever at his command. He selects anapestic rhythm, which he uses with such metrical beauty that from the commencement until the conclusion the reader is carried along entranced by the simple style of recital of which Schiller was a master. We select three stanzas :

> Then outspake the daughter in tender emotion—
> "Ah! father, my father, what more can there rest?
> Enough of this sport with the pitiless ocean—
> He has served thee as none would, thyself hast confest.
> If nothing can slake thy wild thirst of desire,
> Let thy knights put to shame the exploit of the squire!"
>
> The King seized the goblet, he swung it on high,
>   And whirling, it fell in the roar of the tide ;
> "But bring back that goblet again to my eye,
>   And I'll hold thee the dearest that rides by my side ;
> And thine arms shall embrace as thy bride, I decree,
> The maiden whose pity now pleadeth for thee."
>
> And heaven, as he listened, spoke out from the space,
>   And the hope that makes heroes shot flame from his eyes ;
> He gazed on the blush in that beautiful face—
> It pales—at the feet of her father she lies !
> How priceless the guerdon!—a moment, a breath,
> And headlong he plunges to life and to death.

John Hay is the author of "Jim Bludsoe," "Banty Tim," and "Little Breeches," three excellent ballads in dialect. Mr. Hay is a fascinating author of both prose and poetry, whose verse has an air of polished personality. We have selected the following stanza from "Banty Tim," originally published in *Harper's Magazine*.

Lŏrd! hŏw thĕ hŏt sŭn wēnt fŏr ŭs,
　And br'īled ănd blīstĕred ănd būrned!
Hŏw thĕ Rĕbĕl būllĕts whīzzed rŏund ŭs
　Whĕn ă cūss ĭn hĭs dēath-grĭp tūrned!
Tĭll ălŏng tōwărd dŭsk Ĭ seēn ă thĭng
　Ĭ could n't bĕliēve fŏr ă spĕll :
Thăt nĭggĕr—thăt Tĭm—wăs ă crāwlĭn' tŏ mē
　Throŭgh thăt fīre-proŏf, gīlt-ĕdged hĕll!

Oliver Wendell Holmes has written a ballad of early New England life entitled, "Agnes," from which we have selected the following stanza :

Thĕ ōld, ōld stŏrў,—fāir ănd yoŭng,
　And fŏnd,—ănd nŏt toŏ wīse,—
Thăt mātrŏns tĕll wĭth shărpĕned tōngue
　Tŏ māids wĭth dŏwncăst eўes.

Of Tennyson's ballads, "Locksley's Hall," "Lady Clare" "The Lord of Burleigh," and "Edward Gray" are the finest. No prettier ballad adorns the English language than "Lady Clare:"

Ĭt wăs thĕ tīme whĕn līlĭes blōw,
　And clŏuds ăre hīghĕst ŭp ĭn āir,
Lŏrd Rōnăld brŏught ă līlў-whīte dōe
　Tŏ gĭve hĭs coŭsĭn, Lādў Clāre.

THE ELEGY.

To be able to move the affections should be the greatest aim and effort of the poet. To be able to touch the heart-strings of mankind is a rare gift and power, and he who succeeds in doing so is a benefactor of mankind. One of our most delightful writers, who has given to the world dialect poetry that has pleased all mankind, refused the offer of a large sum in the lecture field, that he might continue to write poems and give to the world his book offerings. He said there was a little monitor within his breast that told him this was a duty he owed to mankind. It is not, however, altogether his poems in dialect that makes Riley one of the most lovable of poets. He owes a greater part of his popularity to his power to reach the human heart in depicting the scenes of daily life, which he seizes upon and makes the themes of his poetry. Brush away the dialect from Riley's poems and you still have thoughts and expressions that glitter like polished diamonds, and which carry you entranced throughout the reading, on account of the deep feeling that pervades his every thought. His lines are full of tender sympathy, simple pathos, and emotion, that finds a ready response in the hearts of men who cannot write, but who feel and see and know well that which is written, and are ready critics, capable of pronouncing just verdicts. To this class of readers Riley owes his wide popularity. His poetry is not unlike Gray, Burns, Moore, and Cowper, of the past generation; and it ranks with Longfellow, Tennyson, Whittier, Bryant, Holmes, and Lowell, of the present generation in its elegiac character. The elegy combines simplicity and pathos; and a tenderness that frequently springs from an overpowering melancholy. Elegiac poetry must necessarily be begotten of the finest impulse of the human soul. It is always of the mournful and somewhat contemplative class of poetry. It appeals directly to the sympathies of mankind. It may or it may not express grief, yet a tone of melancholy always pervades the sentiment, frequently born of the burning heart-throbs of despair that seizes upon the gifted sons of song, from whose wretchedness, and sorrow, and intense feelings thousands of readers receive joy and delight.

Elegiac poetry is various in character. The grief that one heart expresses another pours out in a manner entirely different, although both show and express the tenderness and pathos of a sensitive and fine nature. Let us make a few selections from James Whitcomb Riley:

> Whĕn Bĕssĭe dīed—
> Wĕ wrīthed ĭn prāyer ŭnsătĭsfīed;
> Wĕ bĕgged ŏf Gŏd, ănd Hē dĭd smīle
> Ĭn sīlĕnce ōn ŭs āll thĕ whīle;
> Ănd wĕ dĭd seē Hĭm, thrŏugh ŏur tēars,
> Ĕnfōldĭng thăt fāir fōrm ŏf hĕrs,
> Shĕ lāughĭng băck ăgāinst Hĭs lōve
> Thĕ kĭssĕs wĕ hăd nōthĭng ŏf—
> Ănd dēath tŏ ūs Hĕ still dĕnīed,
> Whĕn Bĕssĭe dīed.
> "When Bessie Died."

What can be more expressive than the stanza selected from the poem entitled, "Little Mahala Ashcraft?" We select the fourth stanza. Its lines are iambic heptameter:

> Thĕy's sōrrŏw ĭn thĕ wāvĭn' lĕaves ŏf āll thĕ ăpplĕ-treēs;
> Ănd sōrrŏw ĭn thĕ hārvĕst-shēaves, ănd sōrrŏw ĭn thĕ breēze;
> Ănd sōrrŏw ĭn thĕ twĭttĕr ŏf thĕ swāllĕrs 'rōund thĕ shĕd;
> Ănd āll thĕ sōng hĕr rĕd-bĭrd sīngs ĭs "Lĭttlĕ Hālў's dĕad!"

"A Leave Taking" is a poem full of that rare beauty peculiar to the writings of Riley—human nature vividly portrayed:

> Ĭ kĭss thĕ eỹes
> Ŏn ēithĕr lĭd,
> Whĕre hĕr lŏve līes
> Fŏrēvĕr hĭd.
>
> Ĭ cēase mў weēpĭng
> Ănd smīle ănd sāy:
> Ĭ wĭll bĕ sleēpĭng
> Thŭs, sŏme dāy!

How beautiful these lines. Every word comes from the depths of deep thought, sad and reflective:

> Then the face of a Mother looks back, through the mist
> Of the tears that are welling; and, lucent with light,
> I see the dear smile of the lips I have kissed
> As she knelt by my cradle, at morning and night;
> But my arms are outheld, with a yearning too wild
> For any but God in His love to inspire,
> As she pleads at the foot of His throne for her child,—
> As I sit in silence and gaze in the fire.
>
> Riley—"Envoy."

"In the Dark" is another pathetic poem from which we have selected two stanzas:

> And I think of the smiling faces
> That used to watch and wait,
> Till the click of the clock was answered
> By the click of the opening gate—
>
> They are not there now in the evening—
> Morning or noon—not there;
> Yet I know that they keep their vigil,
> And wait for me Somewhere.

The poet Coleridge has defined an elegy to be that form of poetry natural to the reflective mind. It may treat of any subject, but must treat of no subject for itself, but, always and exclusively with reference to the poet himself.

Riley's peculiar genius is such that while he may have many imitators there can never be but one Riley. If we read his poems as the swallow skims the air, we might be led to say there is nothing but frivolity and fun in all his writings. This is not true, however. While many of his poems abound in the pleasantries of life and are mirth-provoking, few writers deal more directly with the sad perversities of life:

> Nŏw—săd pĕrvĕrsĭtў ! Mў thēme
>   Ŏf rārĕst, pūrĕst jŏy
> Ĭs whēn, ĭn fāncў blĕst, Ĭ drēam
>   Ĭ ām ă lĭttlĕ bŏy.
>   *Riley*—"Envoy."

From deep sorrow ofttimes comes great joy,—for out of sorrow or sadness may come joy to the sons of song, after the teardrops have been wiped away from the soulful eye. The misfortunes that seemingly are the inheritance of some of our great men of letters, have given the staid old world an inheritance in the writings of these gifted sons that delights and benefits mankind, even though these treasures are frequently wrung from their very heart's blood. The blindness of Milton gave the world some of the rarest of poetic gems. The melancholy of Gray gave the world an elegy that has never been equaled. The great elegiac effort of Tennyson, "In Memoriam," at the death of his friend, Arthur Hallam, is the echoings of a sad and sorrowful heart. Tennyson who was afflicted from his infancy with a lack of good eyesight, never mingled with the gay festivous world or dealt with its frivolities. To him the death of a friend like Sir Arthur meant something, and he sorrowed over his loss, and sorrowing gave to the world "In Memoriam :"

> Ĭ sōmetĭmes hōld ĭt hălf ă sĭn
>   Tŏ pūt ĭn wŏrds thĕ grĭĕf Ĭ feēl :
>   Fŏr wŏrds, lĭke Nātŭre, hălf rĕvēal
> Ănd hălf cŏncēal thĕ Sōul wĭthīn.

OF THE VARIOUS KINDS OF POETRY.

> Bŭt, fŏr thĕ ŭnquĭĕt heãrt ănd brāin,
> Ă ūse ĭn mēasūred lănguăge lies ;
> Thĕ sād mĕchănĭc ēxĕrcīse,
> Lĭke dūll nărcŏtĭcs, nŭmbĭng pāin.
>
> Ĭn wõrds, lĭke weēds, Ĭ'll wrāp mĕ õ'er,
> Lĭke cōarsĕst clōthĕs ăgāinst thĕ cōld ;
> Bŭt thāt lărge grĭĕf whĭch thēse ĕnfōld
> Ĭs gīven ĭn ōutlĭne ānd nŏ mōre.
>
> *Tennyson*—" In Memoriam."

William Cullen Bryant wrote "Thanatopsis" at the age of eighteen years. His own version of how it came to be written is here given : "Wandering in the primeval forest over the floor of which were scattered the gigantic trunks of fallen trees, mouldering for long years, and suggesting an indefinitely remote antiquity, and where silent rivulets swept along through the carpets of dead leaves, the spoil of thousands of summers, the poem 'Thanatopsis' was composed." Richard Henry Dana, who was then one of the brilliant young editors of the *North American Review*, and who was himself a gifted poet, saw beauty in the lines and gave the poem to the world,—its author's fame was made. Many beautiful lines of the elegiac character have since come from his pen. In "October, 1866," Bryant tenderly embalms the memory of one to whom he once addressed "Oh Fairest of the Rural Maids." Frances Fairchild was the person to whom he addressed his song, and whom he wedded and afterwards lived with for nearly half a century. We select the eighth stanza of "October, 1866 : "

> Ĭ gāze ĭn sādnĕss, īt dĕlīghts mĕ nŏt
> Tŏ loōk ŏn beaūtў whĭch thŏu cănst nŏt seē ;
> Ănd, wēert thŏu bў mў side, thĕ drēarĭĕst spōt
> Wĕre, Ō, hŏw fār mŏre beaūtĭfūl tŏ me.

These lines of "Thanatopsis," from which we quote, are a vivid picture of man's destiny.

> Cŏmes ā stĭll vōice :—Yĕt ā fĕw dāys, ănd theē
> Thĕ āll-bĕhōldĭng sūn shăll seē nŏ mōre
> Ĭn āll hĭs cōurse ; nŏr yĕt ĭn thĕ cŏld grōund,
> Whĕre thў pāle fŏrm wăs lāid, wĭth mānў tēars,
> Nŏr ĭn thĕ ĕmbrāce ŏf ōcĕan, shāll ĕxīst
> Thў īmăge. Ēarth, thăt noŭrĭshed theē, shăll clāim
> Thў grŏwth, tŏ bē rĕsōlved tŏ ēarth ăgāin ;
> Ănd, lŏst ĕach hūmăn trăce, sŭrrĕndĕrĭng ŭp
> Thĭne ĭndĭvĭdŭal bēĭng, shălt thŏu gō
> Tŏ mīx fŏrĕvĕr with thĕ ēlĕmēnts ;
> Tŏ bē ă brŏthĕr tŏ thĕ ĭnsēnsĭblĕ rŏck,
> Ănd tŏ thĕ slŭggĭsh clŏd, whĭch thĕ rŭde swāin
> Tŭrns wĭth hĭs shăre, ănd trēads ŭpŏn. Thĕ ōak
> Shăll sēnd hĭs roŏts ăbrōad, ănd pĭerce thў mōld.

Robert Burns was one of Nature's darlings. No poet, past or present, has so truly depicted the joys and sorrows, the needs and wrongs, the follies, as well as the passions and virtues of mankind. In Burns the people of Scotland found a true representative, especially that strong race of middle life, from whence have sprung many of the sturdiest and best men. Burns, however, owes much of his lasting popularity to elegiac verse. It is said of Burns that he was grave, serious, contemplative, possessing a thoughtful mind. While he was the poet of the lowly and espoused their cause on all occasions, it is a mistake to esteem Burns

> "Thĕ sĭmplĕ Bārd, rŏugh āt thĕ rŭstĭc plōugh."

He was reserved and dignified in his demeanor and commanded the greatest respect among the very best literary men of his time. He was fairly educated, having received good instruction in all the common branches, sufficient to enable him to write, and write correctly. Is it a wonder then, that one possessed of his high qualities, could write such lines of ideal beauty, born of study, genius and inspiration?

> Yĕ bănks ănd brāes ŏ' bŏnnĭe Doōn,
>   Hŏw căn yĕ bloōm săe frĕsh ănd fāir;
> Hŏw căn yĕ chănt. yĕ lĭttlĕ bĭrds,
>   Ănd Ĭ săe wĕarў fū' ŏ' cāre!
> Thŏu'lt breāk mў heārt, thŏu wārblĭng bĭrd,
>   Thăt wăntŏns throūgh thĕ flōwerĭng thŏrn;
> Thŏu mĭnds mĕ ō' dĕpārtĕd jōys,
>   Dĕpārtĕd—nēvĕr tō rĕtūrn!
>
> Ăft hāe Ĭ rōved bў bŏnnў Doōn,
>   Tŏ seē thĕ rōse ănd woōdbĭne twĭne;
> Ănd ĭlkă bĭrd săng ō' ĭts lūve,
>   Ănd fŏndlў săe dĭd Ĭ ŏ' mĭne.
> Wĭ' lĭghtsŏme heārt Ĭ pōu'd ă rōse,
>   Fŭ' sweēt ŭpōn ĭts thōrnў treē;
> Ănd mў fāuse lūvĕr stōle mў rōse,
>   Bŭt āh! hĕ lĕft thĕ thŏrn wĭ' mē.
>   *Burns*—"The Banks of Doon."

Burns tells us in no mistaken strain, how dearly his friend, Captain Matthew Henderson, was esteemed for his good fellowship. His elegy, to use his own language, "is a tribute to the memory of a man I loved much." We select the fifth stanza:

> Mŏurn, lĭttlĕ hārebĕlls ō'er thĕ lĕa!
> Yĕ stātelў fōxglŏves fāir tŏ seē!
> Yĕ woōdbĭnes, hăngĭng bŏnnĭlie,
>   Ĭn scēntĕd bōwers!
> Yĕ rōsĕs ōn yŏur thōrnў treē,
>   Thĕ fĭrst ŏ' flōwers!
>   "Lines on M. Henderson."

Noble and pathetic are the lines in memory of Mary Campbell, one whom Burns had loved. The words are sweet music, penned by a sad heart three years after the death of his Mary, in October, 1789, on the anniversary of her death.

> Thou lingering star, with lessening ray,
>   That lovest to greet the early morn,
> Again thou usherest in the day
>   My Mary from my soul was torn.
> O Mary! dear departed shade!
>   Where is thy place of blissful rest?
> Seest thou thy lover lowly laid?
>   Hearest thou the groans that rend his breast?
>
> That sacred hour can I forget,
>   Can I forget the hallowed grove,
> Where by the winding Ayr we met,
>   To live one day of parting love!
> Eternity will not efface
>   Those records dear of transports past,
> Thy image at our last embrace,—
>   Ah! little thought we 'twas our last!
>
> Ayr, gurgling, kissed his pebbled shore,
>   O'erhung with wild woods, thickening green;
> The fragrant birch, and hawthorn hoar,
>   Twined amorous round the raptured scene;
> The flowers sprang wanton to be prest,
>   The birds sang love on every spray—
> Till too, too soon, the glowing west
>   Proclaimed the speed of winged day.
>
> Still o'er these scenes my memory wakes,
>   And fondly broods with miser care;
> Time but th' impression stronger makes,
>   As streams their channels deeper wear.

Ŏ Mārў! dēar dĕpārtĕd shāde!
Whĕre īs thў plāce ŏf blīssfŭl rĕst?
Sĕest thōu thў lŏvĕr lōwlў lāid?
Hĕarēst thōu thĕ grōans thăt rēnd hĭs brĕast?
　　　　　　　　　" To Mary in Heaven."

We could multiply examples from Burns, but one more will suffice, a stanza in memory of "Highland Mary," —Mary Campbell of Dunoon, on the Firth of Clyde.

Thў crȳstăl strĕam, Āftŏn, hŏw lōvelў ĭt glīdes,
Ănd winds bў thĕ cōt whĕre mў Mārў rĕsīdes;
Hŏw wāntŏn thў wātĕrs hĕr snōwў feĕt lāve,
Ăs gāthĕrĭng sweĕt flōwerĕts shĕ stēms thў clĕar wāve.
　　　　　　　　　" Flow Gently, Sweet Afton."

Emerson, while he may not rank with our most celebrated poets, has left a volume of poetry that finds a high place in literature. He is universally conceded to be one of the first of prose writers; and we may add, to him the world is also indebted for poetry that must always be held in high esteem for its elevated thoughts. Emerson was a thinker. His poetry, therefore, is not of that dreamy nature peculiar to many of our most gifted artists in song. His poetry is refined, elegant and subtle, calm and serene. His poems are not characterized by that peculiar fever-heat which belongs only to the masters. To Emerson, however, we must credit one of the best of elegies. It was in memory of his lost child—his "hyacinthine boy." It was born of the sorrow that brings mankind to tears. It was born of that sorrow only those can feel and realize who have lost one most near and dear. It was born of that sorrow where teardrops cease to flow, and the sorrowing heart ceases to be comforted; and torn and rent, gives voice to its feelings in elegiac verse,—verse that beats time to the aching heart-throbs, and tells its story in an outburst of sorrow.

> Ŏ chīld ŏf pārădīse,
> Bŏy whŏ măde dĕar hĭs făthĕr's hōme,
> Ĭn whōse deĕp eȳes
> Mĕn rĕad thĕ wĕlfăre ŏf thĕ tinies tŏ cōme,
> Ĭ ām toŏ mŭch bĕrĕft :
> Thĕ wŏrld dĭshōnŏred thōu hăst lĕft.
> Ŏ trŭth's ănd nătūre's cōstlȳ lie !
> Ŏ trūstĕd brōkĕn prŏphĕcȳ !
> Ŏ richĕst fŏrtŭne sōurlȳ crōssed !
> Bŏrn fŏr thĕ fūtŭre, tō thĕ fūtŭre lōst !
> *Emerson*—"Threnody."

It was Lord Macaulay, we believe, who said Gray would go down to posterity with a thinner volume of verse than any other one of our great poets. Gray was a timid youth, one so fearful seemingly of mankind, that he was almost a recluse. Gray had a fine sensitive nature ; his fiber was more of heaven than of earth, and he was ill fitted to cope with anything rude or boisterous. His fellow students accused him of being over fastidious, but his nature and organization was higher and he could ill enjoy their vulgar sports. Though not a writer of a great number of poems Gray has written what might be termed the greatest of all poems, his "Elegy Written In a Country Churchyard," completed and published in 1751. The favor in which it was received surprised even its author, who said sarcastically, that it was owing entirely to the subject, and that the public would have received it equally well in prose. There is no poem in the English language more decidedly popular. It appeals to a feeling all but universal,—applicable to all ranks and classes of society. The poem exhibits the highest poetic sensibility and the most cultivated taste. No poem in the English language is more figurative, nor is there any of greater metrical beauty. The popularity which it first attained, today continues unabated. The original manuscript bequeathed by the poet to his friend, Mr. Mason, is still in existence. It sold in 1845 for five hundred dollars; in 1854 it was again placed upon the market, bringing the fabulous sum of six hundred and fifty-five dollars. The original manuscript was written with a crow-quill, a favorite pen of the author, on four sides of a double half sheet of yellow foolscap, in a neat, legible hand. Gray had but one enemy in life—the gout, from which he died. He lived contentedly and in comparative ease, devoting his time to travel and books, of which he was ever fond. A delicate, handsome, effeminate soul, he lived and died one of the greatest of literary geniuses. The entire elegy is here given :

The cūrfĕw tōlls thĕ knēll ŏf pārtĭng dāy,
　The lōwĭng hērd wĭnds slōwlў ō'er thĕ lēa,
The plōughmăn hōmewărd plōds hĭs wēarў wāy,
　And lēaves thĕ wōrld tŏ dārknĕss ănd tŏ mĕ.

Nŏw fādes thĕ glĭmmerĭng lāndscăpe ōn thĕ sīght,
　And āll thĕ āir ă sōlĕmn stĭllnĕss hōlds,
Săve whēre thĕ beētlĕ wheēls hĭs drōnĭng flĭght,
　And drōwsў tĭnklĭngs lūll thĕ dĭstănt fōlds :

Săve thăt, frŏm yōndĕr īvў-māntlĕd tōwer,
　The mōpĭng ōwl dŏes tŏ thĕ moōn cŏmplāin
Ŏf sūch ăs, wāndĕrĭng neār hĕr sēcrĕt bōwer,
　Mŏlĕst hĕr āncĭĕnt sōlĭtărў rēign.

Bĕneāth thōse rūggĕd ēlms, thăt yēw-treĕ's shāde,
　Whĕre hēaves thĕ tūrf ĭn mānў ă mōuldĕrĭng heāp,
Ĕach ĭn hĭs nārrŏw cĕll fŏrēvĕr lāid,
　The rūde fŏrefāthĕrs ŏf thĕ hāmlĕt sleĕp.

The breezy call of incense-breathing morn,
  The swallow twittering from the straw-built shed,
The cock's shrill clarion, or the echoing horn,
  No more shall rouse them from their lowly bed.

For them no more the blazing hearth shall burn,
  Or busy housewife ply her evening care;
No children run to lisp their sire's return,
  Or climb his knees the envied kiss to share.

Oft did the harvest to their sickle yield,
  Their furrow oft the stubborn glebe has broke;
How jocund did they drive their team afield!
  How bowed the woods beneath their sturdy stroke!

Let not ambition mock their useful toil,
  Their homely joys, and destiny obscure;
Nor grandeur hear with a disdainful smile
  The short and simple annals of the poor.

The boast of heraldry, the pomp of power,
  And all that beauty, all that wealth e'er gave,
Await alike the inevitable hour;
  The paths of glory lead but to the grave.

Nor you, ye proud, impute to these the fault,
  If memory o'er their tomb no trophies raise,
Where through the long-drawn aisle and fretted vault
  The pealing anthem swells the note of praise.

Can storied urn, or animated bust,
  Back to its mansion call the fleeting breath?
Can honor's voice provoke the silent dust,
  Or flattery soothe the dull cold ear of death?

Perhaps in this neglected spot is laid
  Some heart once pregnant with celestial fire;
Hands that the rod of empire might have swayed,
  Or waked to ecstasy the living lyre;

But Knowledge to their eyes her ample page
　Rich with the spoils of time did ne'er unroll;
Chill penury repressed their noble rage,
　And froze the genial current of the soul.

Full many a gem of purest ray serene
　The dark unfathom'ed caves of ocean bear;
Full many a flower is born to blush unseen,
　And waste its sweetness on the desert air.

Some village Hampden, that, with dauntless breast,
　The little tyrant of his fields withstood,
Some mute inglorious Milton here may rest,
　Some Cromwell guiltless of his country's blood.

The applause of listening senates to command,
　The threats of pain and ruin to despise,
To scatter plenty o'er a smiling land,
　And read their history in a nation's eyes,

Their lot forbade: nor circumscribed alone
　Their growing virtues, but their crimes confined;
Forbade to wade through slaughter to a throne,
　And shut the gates of mercy on mankind,

The struggling pangs of conscious truth to hide,
　To quench the blushes of ingenuous shame,
Or heap the shrine of luxury and pride
　With incense kindled at the Muse's flame.

Far from the madding crowd's ignoble strife,
　Their sober wishes never learned to stray;
Along the cool sequestered vale of life
　They kept the noiseless tenor of their way.

Yet even these bones from insult to protect,
　Some frail memorial still, erected nigh,
With uncouth rhymes and shapeless sculpture decked,
　Implores the passing tribute of a sigh.

Thĕir nāme, thĕir yēars, spĕlt bў th' ŭnlĕttĕrĕd Mūse,
  Thĕ plāce ŏf fāme ănd ēlĕgў sŭpplў :
Ănd mānў ă hōlў tĕxt ăround shĕ strēws,
  Thăt tēach thĕ rūstĭc mōrălist tŏ die.

Fŏr whō, tŏ dŭmb fŏrgĕtfŭlnĕss ă prēy,
  Thĭs plĕasĭng ānxĭous bēĭng ē'er rĕsīgned,
Lĕft thĕ wărm prĕcĭncts ŏf thĕ cheērfŭl dāy,
  Nŏr cāst ŏne lōngĭng, lĭngerĭng loōk bĕhĭnd?

Ŏn sŏme fŏnd brēast thĕ pārtĭng sōul rĕlīes,
  Sŏme pioŭs drŏps thĕ clōsĭng eўe rĕquīres ;
Ē'en frŏm thĕ tōmb thĕ vōice ŏf nātūre crīes,
  Ē'en ĭn ŏur āshĕs live thĕir wōntĕd fīres.

Fŏr theē, whŏ, mĭndfŭl ŏf th' ŭnhōnŏred dĕad,
  Dŏst ĭn thĕse lines thĕir ārtlĕss tāle rĕlāte :
Ĭf chănce, bў lōnelў cŏntĕmplātiŏn lĕd,
  Sŏme kĭndrĕd spĭrĭt shăll ĭnquīre thў fāte,—

Hāplў sŏme hōarў-hēadĕd swain māy sāy :
  Ŏft hăve wĕ seēn hĭm ăt thĕ peēp ŏf dāwn
Brūshĭng wĭth hāstў stĕps thĕ dēws ăwāy,
  Tŏ meēt thĕ sūn ŭpŏn thĕ ŭplănd lăwn.

Thĕre āt thĕ foŏt ŏf yŏndĕr nŏddĭng beēch,
  Thăt wrēathes ĭts ōld făntāstĭc roōts sŏ hĭgh,
Hĭs lĭstlĕss lĕngth ăt noōntīde would hĕ strĕtch,
  Ănd pōre ŭpŏn thĕ brook thăt băbblĕs bў.

Hărd bў yŏn woŏd, nŏw smīlĭng, ăs ĭn scōrn,
  Mŭttĕrĭng hĭs wāywărd făncĭes, hĕ would rōve ;
Nŏw droōpĭng, wōefŭl-wān, līke ōne fŏrlōrn,
  Ŏr crāzed wĭth cāre, ŏr crŏssed ĭn hōpelĕss lōve.

Ŏne mōrn Ĭ mĭssed hĭm ŏn thĕ 'cŭstŏmed hĭll,
  Ălŏng thĕ hēath, ănd neār hĭs făvorĭte treē ;
Ănōthĕr cāme ; nŏr yĕt bĕsīde thĕ rĭll,
  Nŏr ŭp thĕ lăwn, nŏr ăt thĕ wood wăs hĕ :

The nĕxt, wĭth dīrgĕs dūe, ĭn sād ărrāy,
  Slŏw throŭgh thĕ chūrch-wăy pāth wĕ sāw hĭm bōrne:—
Ăpprōach ănd rēad (fŏr thōu cănst rēad) thĕ lāy
  Grāved ŏn thĕ stōne bĕnēath yŏn āgĕd thōrn.

THE EPITAPH.

Hĕre rĕsts hĭs hĕad ŭpŏn thĕ lāp ŏf ēarth
  Ă yoŭth tŏ fōrtŭne ānd tŏ fāme ŭnknōwn:
Fāir Sciĕnce frŏwned nŏt ŏn hĭs hūmblĕ bīrth,
  Ănd Mĕlănchōlў mārked hĭm fŏr hĕr ōwn.

Lărge wās hĭs bōuntў, ānd hĭs sōul sĭncēre;
  Hĕaven dĭd ă rĕcŏmpēnse ăs lārgelў sĕnd;
Hĕ gāve tŏ mīserў (āll hĕ hād) ă tĕar,
  Hĕ gāined frŏm Hēaven ('twăs āll hĕ wīshed) ă friĕnd.

Nŏ fārthĕr seēk hĭs mĕrĭts tō dĭsclōse,
  Ŏr drāw hĭs frāiltĭes frŏm thĕir drēad ăbōde,
(Thĕre thĕy ălīke ĭn trĕmblĭng hōpe rĕpōse),
  Thĕ bōsŏm ŏf hĭs Fāthĕr ănd hĭs Gōd.

It was Wolfe, the hero of Quebec, on the eve of that decisive battle, gliding down the St. Lawrence in the darkness of midnight with his fellow officers in a boat, who repeated the elegy to them. At the close of the recitation said he: "Now, gentlemen, I would rather be the author of that poem than take Quebec!" In a few hours afterwards Wolfe had taken Quebec. Yet the path of glory led but to the grave.

The elegy properly speaking may be classed as lyric poetry. Many other beautiful elegies might be given. Shelley's "Adonais" on the death of his friend and brother bard, John Keats, is one of the finest in the English language.

John Milton's "Lycidas," commemorative of the virtues of

his friend, Edmund King; Collins' "Dirge in Cymbeline," and Burns' "Man Was Made To Mourn," are all fine specimens of elegiac verse. The elegy is one of the grandest of all departments in the realm of poetical literature.

THE EPITAPH.

An Epitaph is an inscription on a monument in honor or memory of the dead. Many of these inscriptions were formerly written in quaint and curious verse. Our ancestors were given to epitaphic writing more than the writers of the present day. Another definition given is, a eulogy in prose or verse composed without any intent to be engraven on a monument; hence an epitaph may be termed a brief descriptive poem commemorative of the virtues of the dead. An epitaphic stanza in iambics:

> Ĕre sīn coŭld blīght ŏr sōrrŏw fāde,
>   Dĕath cāme wĭth friēndlў cāre;
> Thĕ ōpenĭng būd tŏ Hēaven cŏnvēyed,
>   Ănd bāde ĭt blossŏm thĕre.
>   *Samuel Taylor Coleridge*—"Epĭtaph On An Infant."

The following epitaph is also in iambic rhythm:

> Stŏp, mōrtăl! Hĕre thў brŏthĕr lies—
>   Thĕ Pŏĕt ŏf thĕ Poōr.
> Hĭs boŏks wĕre rĭvĕrs, woŏds, ănd skies,
>   Thĕ mēadŏw ānd thĕ moōr;
> Hĭs tēachĕrs wĕre thĕ tŏrn heărt's wāil,
>   Thĕ tўrănt ānd thĕ slāve,
> Thĕ streĕt, thĕ făctŏrў, thĕ gaōl,
>   Thĕ pălăce—ānd thĕ grāve!
> Sĭn mĕt thў brŏthĕr ĕverўwhĕre!
>   Ănd ĭs thў brŏthĕr blāmed?
> Frŏm pāssiŏn, dāngĕr, dŏubt, ănd cāre,
>   Hĕ nŏ ĕxĕmptiŏn clāimed.
>   *Ebenezer Elliott*—"A Poet's Epitaph."

The following is an elegant epitaph in trochaic rhythm :

Ŭndĕrnēath thĭs mārblĕ hēarse
Līes thĕ sŭbjĕct ōf ăll vērse,
Sȳdnĕy's sĭstĕr,—Pēmbrŏke's mōthĕr.
Dĕath, ĕre thōu hăst slāin ănōthĕr
Fāir ănd wīse ănd goŏd ăs shē,
Tīme shăll thrōw ă dărt ăt theē!

Mārblĕ pīles lĕt nō măn rāise
Tō hĕr nāme ĭn āftĕr dāys;
Sōme kĭnd wōmăn, bōrn ăs shē,
Rēadĭng thĭs, lĭke Nĭŏbē
Shăll tŭrn mārblĕ, ănd bĕcōme
Bōth hĕr mōurnĕr ānd hĕr tōmb.
    Ben Jonson—"Epitaph on the Countess of Pembroke."

The stanzas following are in iambic rhythm :

Ĭs thēre ă whim-ĭnspīrĕd foōl,
Ŏwre fāst fŏr thōught, ŏwre hōt fŏr rūle,
Ŏwre blāte tŏ seēk, ŏwre prōud tŏ snoōl;
    Lĕt hĭm drăw nēar,
Ănd ōwre thĭs grăssȳ hēap sĭng doōl,
    Ănd drăp ă tēar.

Ĭs thēre ă bārd ŏf rūstĭc sōng,
Whŏ, nōtelĕss, stēals thĕ crōwd ămōng,
Thăt weēklȳ thĭs āreă thrōng;
    Ŏ, pāss nŏt bȳ;
Bŭt, wĭth ă frātĕr-feēlĭng strōng,
    Hĕre hĕave ă sĭgh!

Ĭs thēre ă mān whŏse jūdgmĕnt clēar
Căn ōthĕrs tēach thĕ cōurse tŏ steēr,
Yĕt rŭns hĭmsēlf lĭfe's măd cărĕer,
    Wĭld ās thĕ wăve;
Hĕre pāuse, ănd, thrŏugh thĕ stārtĭng tĕar,
    Sŭrvēy thĭs grăve.

Thĕ poŏr ĭnhăbĭtănt bĕlōw
Wăs quĭck tŏ lēarn ănd wīse tŏ knōw,
Ănd keēnlў fĕlt thĕ frĭēndlў glōw,
 Ănd sōbĕr flāme ;
Bŭt thŏughtlĕss fōllĭes lāid hĭm lōw,
 Ănd stāined hĭs nāme !

Rĕadĕr, ăttĕnd,—whēthĕr thў sōul
Sŏars fāncў's flīghts bĕyōnd thĕ pōle,
Ŏr dārklў grūbs thĭs ēarthlў hōle,
 Ĭn lōw pŭrsūit ;
Knōw, prūdĕnt, cāutiŏŭs sĕlf-cŏntrōl
 Ĭs wīsdŏm's roōt.
  Robert Burns—" A Bard's Epitaph."

The lines following, in iambic rhythm, were written August 20th, 1755:

Bĕnēath thĕ stōne brăve Brăddŏck lies,
Whŏ ālwăys hātĕd cōwărdĭce,
Bŭt fĕll ă săvăge săcrĭfĭce ;
 Ămĭdst hĭs Ĭndĭăn fōes.
Ĭ chărge yoŭ, hĕrŏes, ŏf thĕ grōund,
Tŏ guārd hĭs dărk păvĭlĭŏn rōund,
Ănd keēp ŏff āll ŏbtrūdĭng sōund,
 Ănd chĕrĭsh his rĕpōse.

Sleĕp, sleĕp, Ĭ sāy, brăve, vălĭănt măn,
Bŏld dĕath, ăt lāst, hăs bĭd theĕ stănd,
Ănd tō rĕsīgn thў greăt cŏmmănd,
 Ănd căncĕl thў cŏmmĭssĭŏn ;
Ălthōugh thŏu dĭdst nŏt mŭch ĭnclīne,
Thў pōst ănd hōnŏrs tō rĕsīgn,
Nŏw īrŏn slŭmbĕr dŏth cŏnfīne ;
 Nŏne ēnvĭes thў cŏndĭtĭŏn.
  Tilden—" An Epitaph for Braddock."

*THE PASTORAL.

Pastoral poetry, strictly speaking, is that which celebrates rustic or rural life or deals with the objects of external nature. In times gone by pastoral poetry was used to depict shepherd life by means of narratives, songs and dialogues. The pastoral poems of Virgil were called Eclogues. An Eclogue is a pastoral in which shepherds are represented as conversing. Theocritus wrote pastoral poems termed Idyls. An Idyl is a short descriptive pastoral. The term Idyllic poetry is now applied to the pastoral. This variety of poetry is very popular, and meets with a just appreciation by the public. Pastoral poetry depicts all the beauties of rural life,—mountain scenery, lowland vales, majestic rivers, expansive lakes, rifting clouds, birds, beasts, insects, flowers, and rural scenes; and rural sports in all their various phases, are subjects of this kind of poetry. Poems of nature are classed under this head, as the following iambic lines :

(1).

How beautiful is the rain !
After the dust and heat,
In the broad and fiery street,
In the narrow lane,
How beautiful is the rain !

How it clatters along the roofs,
Like the tramp of hoofs !
How it gushes and struggles out
From the throat of the overflowing spout !

---

*For THE SONNET, see page 107. THE EPIGRAM, see page 203.

Ăcrŏss thĕ wīndŏw-pāne
Ĭt pōurs ănd pōurs ;
Ănd swīft ănd wīde,
Wĭth ă mŭddў tĭde,
Lĭke ă rĭvĕr dōwn thĕ gŭttĕr rōars
Thĕ rāin, thĕ wĕlcŏme rāin !
Thĕ sĭck măn frŏm hĭs chămbĕr loŏks
Ăt thĕ twĭstĕd broŏks ;
Hē căn feĕl thĕ coōl
Brēath ŏf ĕach lĭttlĕ poōl ;
Hĭs fēvĕred brāin
Grŏws cālm ăgāin,
Ănd hē brēathes ă blĕssĭng ōn thĕ rāin.
Henry Wadsworth Longfellow—"Rain in Summer."

(2).

Gŏne, gōne, sŏ soōn !
Nŏ mōre mў hālf-crăzed făncў thĕre
Căn shāpe ă gĭănt ĭn thĕ āir,
Nŏ mōre Ĭ seĕ hĭs strēamĭng hāir,
Thĕ wrīthĭng pŏrtĕnt ŏf hĭs fōrm ;—
Thĕ pāle ănd quĭĕt moōn
Măkes hĕr cālm fōrehĕad bāre,
Ănd thĕ lăst frăgmĕnts ŏf thĕ stōrm,
Lĭke shăttĕred rĭggĭng frŏm ă fĭght ăt sēa,
Sĭlĕnt ănd fĕw, ăre drīftĭng ōvĕr mē.
James Russell Lowell—"Summer Storm."

(3).

Hŏw sweĕt, ăt sĕt ŏf sūn, tŏ vĭew
Thў gōldĕn mīrrŏr sprēadĭng wīde,
Ănd seē thĕ mĭst ŏf măntlĭng blūe
Flŏat rōund thĕ dĭstănt mōuntăin's sĭde.
James Gates Percival—"To Seneca Lake."

(4).

Whĭch ĭs thĕ wīnd thăt brīngs thĕ flōwers?
  Thĕ wĕst-wĭnd, Bĕssĭe; ănd sŏft ănd lòw
Thĕ bĭrdĭes sīng ĭn thĕ sūmmĕr hôurs
  Whĕn thĕ wĕst bĕgīns tŏ blōw.
Edmund Clarence Stedman—"What the Winds Bring."

(5).

Līthe ănd lōng ăs thĕ sērpĕnt trāin,
  Sprīngĭng ănd clĭngĭng frŏm treē tŏ treē,
Nŏw dārtĭng ūpwărd, nŏw dōwn ăgāin,
  Wĭth ă twĭst ănd ă twĭrl thăt ăre strānge tŏ seē;
Nĕvĕr tŏŏk sērpĕnt ă dēadlĭĕr hōld,
  Nĕvĕr thĕ coūgăr a wĭldĕr spring,
Strānglĭng thĕ ōak wĭth thĕ bōă's fōld,
  Spānnĭng thĕ bēach wĭth thĕ cōndŏr's wĭng.
William Gilmore Simms—"The Grape-Vine Swing."

(6).

"Whŏ plāntĕd thĭs ōld ăpplĕ-treē?"
  Thĕ chĭldrĕn ŏf thăt dĭstănt dāy
Thŭs tŏ sŏme āgĕd mān shăll sāy;
  Ănd, gāzĭng ōn ĭts mōssў stĕm,
Thĕ grāy-hăired mān shăll ănswĕr thĕm:
  "Ă pŏĕt ŏf thĕ lānd wăs hē,
Bŏrn ĭn thĕ rūde bŭt gŏŏd ōld tĭmes;
  'Tĭs sāid hĕ māde sŏme quāint ōld rhўmes
Ŏn plāntĭng thĕ ăpplĕ-treē."
William Cullen Bryant—"The Planting of the Apple-Tree."

(7).

Ă sōng fŏr thĕ plānt ŏf mў ōwn nātĭve Wēst,
  Whĕre nātŭre ănd freēdŏm rĕsīde,
Bў plĕntў stĭll crōwned, ănd bў pēace ĕvĕr blĕst,
  Tŏ thĕ cōrn! thĕ greĕn cōrn ŏf hĕr prīde!

In climes of the East has the olive been sung,
And the grape been the theme of their lays;
But for thee shall a harp of the backwoods be strung,
Thou bright, ever beautiful maize!
William W. Fosdick—"The Maize."

(8).

But look! o'er the fall see the angler stand,
Swinging his rod with skillful hand;
The fly at the end of his gossamer line
   Swims through the sun like a summer moth,
Till, dropt with a careful precision fine,
   It touches the pool beyond the froth.
A-sudden, the speckled hawk of the brook
Darts from his covert and seizes the hook.
Swift spins the reel; with easy slip
The line pays out, and the rod, like a whip,
Lithe and arrowy, tapering, slim,
Is bent to a bow o'er the brooklet's brim,
Till the trout leaps up in the sun, and flings
The spray from the flash of his finny wings;
Then falls on his side, and, drunken with fright,
   Is towed to the shore like a staggering barge,
   Till beached at last on the sandy marge,
Where he dies with the hues of the morning light,
While his sides with a cluster of stars are bright.
The angler in his basket lays
The constellation, and goes his ways.
Thomas Buchanan Read—"The Angler."

(9).

O, fruit loved of boyhood! the old days recalling;
When wood-grapes were purpling and brown nuts were falling!
When wild, ugly faces we carved in its skin,
Glaring out through the dark with a candle within!
When we laughed round the corn-heap, with hearts all in tune,
Our chair a broad pumpkin, our lantern the moon,

Tĕllĭng tāles ŏf thĕ fāirў̆ whŏ trăvĕled līke stĕam
Ĭn ă pŭmpkĭn-shĕll cōach, wĭth twŏ rāts fŏr hĕr tĕam !
Thĕn thănks fŏr thў̆ prĕsĕnt !—nŏne sweĕtĕr ŏr bĕttĕr
Ĕ'er smōked frŏm ăn ōvĕn ŏr circlĕd ă plāttĕr !
Fāirĕr hănds nĕvĕr wrōught ăt ă pāstrў̆ mŏre fĭne,
Brīghtĕr ĕyes nĕvĕr wătched ŏ'er ĭts bākĭng, thăn thīne !
Ănd thĕ prāyer, whĭch mў̆ mōuth ĭs toŏ fŭll tŏ ĕxprēss,
Swĕlls mў̆ heart thăt thў̆ shădŏw măy nĕvĕr bĕ less,
Thăt thĕ dāys ŏf thў̆ lŏt măy bĕ lēngthĕned bĕlōw,
Ănd thĕ fāme ŏf thў̆ wŏrth līke ă pŭmpkĭn-vĭne grōw,
Ănd thў̆ life bĕ ăs sweĕt, ănd ĭts lăst sŭnsĕt skў̆
Gōldĕn-tĭntĕd ănd fāir ăs thў̆ ōwn pŭmpkĭn-pīe !
      John Greenleaf Whittier—"The Pumpkin."

Tennyson's "Idyls of the King," Burns's "Cotter's Saturday Night," Allan Ramsay's "Gentle Shepherd," Shenstone's "Pastoral Ballads," are fine examples of pastoral poetry; while Wordsworth, Cowper, and Swinburne abound in this excellent verse. Of our American poets, Longfellow, Whittier, Bryant, John Hay, James Whitcomb Riley, Bret Harte, and Joaquin Miller have poems that will rank with the best of English productions.

THE DIDACTIC.

It has been said no subject is so unpromising it has not been selected by some one as a beautiful theme. Didactic poetry has been oftenest employed in the presentation of the various themes thus selected; for, differing from other poetry, its chief aim and object is instruction. Poetry of this species is accompanied with poetic reflection, illustrations and episodes.

Didactic poems are often seemingly dry and prosaic; they are, however, many of them full of interest, filled with noble thoughts, and when considered as poetical essays, may be classed among our finest literature—considered from a purely moral and didactic standpoint. Many didactic poems, however, are highly ornamental in figurative language and metrical beauty:

The "Essay on Criticism" and "Essay on Man" by Alexander Pope, Cowper's "Task," Wordsworth's "Excursion," Dryden's "Hind and Panther," Campbell's "Pleasures of Hope."

PHILOSOPHICAL.

Far from my dearest friend, 'tis mine to rove
Through bare grey dell, high wood, and pastoral cove,
His wizard course where hoary Derwent takes,
Thro' crags, and forest glooms and opening lakes,
Staying his silent waves, to hear the roar
That stuns the tremulous cliffs of high Lodore,
Where peace to Grasmere's lonely island leads
To willowy hedgrows, and to emerald meads;
Leads to her bridge, rude church, and cottaged grounds,
Her rocky sheepwalks, and her woodland bounds;
Where, bosom'd deep, the shy Winander peeps
'Mid clustering isles, and holy sprinkled steeps;
Where twilight glens endear my Esthwaite's shore,
And memory of departed pleasures, more.
Fair scenes! erewhile I taught, a happy child,
The echoes of your rocks my carols wild;
Then did no ebb of cheerfulness demand
Sad tides of joy from Melancholy's hand;
In youth's wild eye the livelong day was bright,
The sun at morning, and the stars at night,
Alike, when first the valves the bittern fills
Or the first woodcocks roamed the moonlight hills.
In thoughtless gayety I course the plain,
And hope itself was all I knew of pain;
For then, even then, the little heart would beat
At times, while young Content forsook her seat,

And wild impatience, pointing upward, showed,
Where, tipped with gold, the mountain summits glowed.
Alas! the idle tale of man is found
Depicted in the dial's moral round;
With hope Reflection blends her social rays
To gild the total tablet of his days;
Yet still, the sport of some malignant power,
He knows but from its shade the present hour.
Wordsworth—"An Evening Walk."

Six years had passed, and forty ere the six,
When Time began to play his usual tricks:
The locks once comely in a virgin's sight,
Locks of pure brown, displayed th' encroaching white;
The blood, once fervid, now to cool began,
And Time's strong pressure to subdue the man.
I rode or walked as I was wont before,
But now the bounding spirit was no more;
A moderate pace would now my body heat,
A walk of moderate length distress my feet.
I showed my stranger guest those hills sublime,
But said, "The view is poor, we need not climb."
At a friend's mansion I began to dread
The cold neat parlor and the gay glazed bed;
At home I felt a more decided taste,
And must have all things in my order placed.
I ceased to hunt; my horses pleased me less,—
My dinner more; I learned to play at chess.
I took my dog and gun, but saw the brute
Was disappointed that I did not shoot.
My morning walks I now could bear to lose,
And blessed the shower that gave me not to choose.
In fact, I felt a languor stealing on;
The active arm, the agile hand, were gone;
Small daily actions into habits grew,
And new dislike to forms and fashions new.
I loved my trees in order to dispose;
I numbered peaches, looked how stocks arose;
Told the same story oft,—in short, began to prose.
George Crabbe—"Tales of the Hall."

MEDITATIVE.

I was a stricken deer, that left the herd
Long since; with many an arrow deep infixed
My panting side was charged, when I withdrew,
To seek a tranquil death in distant shades.
There was I found by one who had himself
Been hurt by the archers. In his side he bore,
And in his hands and feet, the cruel scars.
With gentle force soliciting the darts,
He drew them forth, and healed, and bade me live.
Since then, with few associates, in remote
And silent woods I wander, far from those
My former partners of the peopled scene;
With few associates, and not wishing more.
Here much I ruminate, as much I may,
With other views of men and manners now
Than once, and others of a life to come.
I see that all are wanderers, gone astray
Each in his own delusions; they are lost
In chase of fancied happiness, still wooed
And never won. Dream after dream ensues;
And still they dream, that they shall still succeed;
And still are disappointed. Rings the world
With the vain stir. I sum up half mankind,
And add two-thirds of the remaining half,
And find the total of their hopes and fears
Dreams, empty dreams.
William Cowper—"The Task."

THE EPIC.

The epic or heroic poem is the longest of all poetical compositions, consisting of a recital of great and heroic events. These events are represented as being told by the hero or some participant in the scenes. There should be a plot of interest and many actors therein; added to which are numerous episodes, incidents, stories, scenes, pomp and machinery. This latter term signifies the introduction of supernatural beings, or, as Mr. Pope said, "a term invented by the critics to signify that part which the deities, angels or demons are made to act in a poem, without which no poem can be admitted as an epic." Fiction, invention and imagination are all used to an unlimited extent, and all recounted in the most elevated style and language.

Epic poetry is subdivided into two classes,— the Great Epic and the Mock Epic. The Great Epic poem has for its subject some grand heroic action. English literature possesses the greatest of all epics—Milton's "Paradise Lost;" the Greek literature furnishes the "Iliad" of Homer, while Roman literature gives us the "Æneid" of Virgil, and modern Italian literature gives us Dante's "Divine Comedy." None of our poets of late years have attempted a great epic poem, and few civilized races have produced more than one. Milton's "Paradise Lost," by many of our men of letters, is considered noble in style, unrivaled in language, artistic in construction. Ages have come and gone, yet Milton's grand epic is still considered a work of consummate art.

> All was false and hollow; though his tongue
> Dropped manna, and could make the worse appear
> The better reason, to perplex and dash
> Maturest counsels; for his thoughts were low;
> To vice industrious, but to nobler deeds
> Timorous and slothful: yet he pleased the ear,
> And with persuasive accent thus began.
> *Milton*—"Paradise Lost."

THE MOCK EPIC.

The Mock Epic is a caricature of the Great Epic. Pope's "Rape of the Lock," and "The Battle of the Frogs and Mice," from an unknown Greek original, attributed to Homer, are notable examples familiar to the reader. Mr. Pope says of the "Rape of the Lock." "It will be in vain to deny that I have some regard for this piece, yet you may bear me witness it was intended only to divert a few young ladies who have good sense and good humor enough to laugh not only at their sex's little, unguarded follies, but at their own."

And now, unveiled, the toilet stands displayed,
Each silver vase in mystic order laid.
First, robed in white, the nymph intent, adores,
With head uncovered, the cosmetic powers.
A heavenly image in the glass appears,
To that she bends, to that her eyes she rears;
Th' inferior priestess, at her altar's side,
Trembling begins the sacred rites of pride.
Unnumbered treasures ope at once, and here
The various offerings of the world appear;
From each she nicely culls with curious toil,
And decks the goddess with the glittering spoil.
This casket India's glowing gems unlocks,
And all Arabia breathes from yonder box.
The tortoise here and elephant unite,
Transformed to combs, the speckled and the white.
Here files of pins extend their shining rows,
Puffs, powders, patches, Bibles, billet-doux.
Now awful beauty puts on all its arms;
The fair each moment rises in her charms,
Repairs her smiles, awakens every grace,
And calls forth all the wonders of her face;
Sees by degrees a purer blush arise,
And keener lightnings quicken in her eyes.
The busy sylphs surround their darling care,
These set the head, and those divide the hair,
Some fold the sleeve, whilst others plait the gown;
And Betty's praised for labors not her own.
    Pope—"The Rape of the Lock."

METRICAL ROMANCE.

The Romance is a narrative of love and heroic adventure. It possesses many of the qualities of the Epic poem and ranks next in the order of poetry. It is a tale in verse but little less elevated than the Epic. The passion of love which does not appear in the Grand Epic is usually the leading feature of the Romance, and instead of the machinery of the Epic we have ghosts, witches, elves, fairies, fire worshipers, veiled prophets, and the peri. Metrical romances, for the mere pleasure of reading, give greater delight than any other species. We have many romances in rhyme, both ancient and modern, and it is not difficult to find examples. The "Fairy Queen" by Spenser, written in that peculiar stanza which now bears his name—the Spenserian—is an elegant romance, the "Canterbury Tales" by Geoffrey Chaucer, Scott's "Lady of the Lake" and "Marmion," Keats' "Eve of St. Agnes," Thomas Moore's "Lalla Rookh," Lord Lytton's "Lucile," and Longfellow's "Evangeline" are among the best romances and metrical tales.

They glide, like phăntŏms, īntŏ thē wĭde hāll!
Līke phăntŏms tō thĕ īrŏn pōrch thĕy glīde,
Whĕre lāy thĕ pōrtĕr īn ŭnēasў sprāwl,
Wĭth ā hŭge ēmptў flāgŏn bў hĭs sīde:
Thĕ wăkefŭl bloōdhoŭnd rōse ănd shoōk hĭs hīde,
Bŭt hĭs săgāciŏŭs eўe ăn īnmăte ōwns;
Bў ōne, ănd ōne, thĕ bōlts fŭll ēasў slīde;
Thĕ chāins līe sīlĕnt ōn thĕ foōtwŏrn stōnes;
Thĕ kēy tŭrns, ănd thĕ doōr ŭpōn ĭts hīngĕs grōans.
Keats—"The Eve of St. Agnes."

A metrical tale of exquisite beauty is one of Mr. Charles Algernon Swinburne's latest productions—a story of Arthurian days, entitled "Tale of Balen." It is preëminently melodious, being wonderful in musical expressions, and harmonious in words, and withal a singular grace and rare simplicity of style. Notice the beautiful rhythm of the following stanza:

> Swift from his place leapt Balen, smote
> The liar across his face, and wrote
> His wrath in blood upon the bloat
> Brute cheek that challenged shame for note
>   How vile a king born knave may be.
> Forth sprang their swords, and Balen slew
> The knave ere well one witness drew
> Of all that round them stood, or knew
>   What sight was there to see.

The following is another beautiful stanza from the poem. It is a nine line stanza, composed of a quatrain and a five line stanza. The first four lines of the stanza are fourfold rhymes, the fifth and ninth lines rhyme, while the sixth, seventh and eighth lines of the stanza are threefold or triple rhymes. It is an elegant stanza, brisk and spirited in style —iambic measure:

> As thought from thought takes wing and flies,
> As month on month with sunlit eyes
> Tramples and triumphs in its rise,
> As wave smites wave to death and dies,
>   So chance on hurtling chance like steel
> Strikes, flashes, and is quenched, ere fear
> Can whisper hope, or hope can hear,
> If sorrow or joy be far or near
>   For time to hurt or heal.

METRICAL HISTORY.

The Historical poem is a narrative of public events. Dryden's "Annus Mirabilis" is a noble example. Macaulay's "Lays of Ancient Rome" may also be classed under this head; so, too, ballads descriptive of battles may be classed as metrical history.

THE DRAMA.

It is to Greece we must give praise for the invention of the Drama. It was first invented and exhibited at the festivals of the god Dionysus. The ancient Greek writers tell us that the drama originated in the choral song. Aristotle tells us it had its origin in the singers of dithyramb. While the drama had its origin in pantomimic dances and choral singing, it was slowly purified from its extraneous mixtures. While lyric poetry by means of musical expression by language of mental emotions aims to represent human actions, the drama consists of an impersonal representation by the dramatist or an animated conversation of various individuals from whose speech the movements of the story is to be gathered; thus it is constructed on the one hand with dialogue, and on the other with every other species of poetry. The movements and thoughts of the drama are so lively and the expectation of the issue so vivid that this class of poetry surpasses all others in interest and intensity. The drama from Greece was introduced into Rome and from there into other parts of Europe, where after years of decline, change, and struggle, with the vicissitudes of the age, about the middle of the sixteenth century it extricated itself from its ancient fetters. In the early years of Christianity actors were denied baptism, and the decree of the church was followed by an edict of the Emperor Julian. The drama, however, was finally appropriated by the clergy, and plays known as Miracle Plays and Moralities followed as a result. The Passion Plays of Germany had their origin in this manner. "The Passion of Our Saviour" is still in existence and played at Ammergau and is said to be the only miracle play which has survived. It is played by about five hundred peasants instructed by the village priest, who conducts it morally and reverently, and it is largely attended by the peasants of Bavaria and all parts of Tyrol. These plays originated in Europe about the beginning of the eleventh century and most of them had their ending about the middle of the fifteenth century, and with their decline the drama proper began to flourish.

The drama is divided into two classes, the Tragedy, and Comedy. The first known tragedy of England was the joint production of Mrs. Norton and Lord Buckhurst, and was known variously as "Ferrex and Porrex" or as "Gorbudoc." It was written about 1562. The first comedy was written about the middle of the sixteenth century, 1551, by Nicholas Udall, and was entitled "Ralph Roister Doister." Blank verse was first introduced into dramatic composition in "Ferrex and Porrex," but the play was dull and heavy and not a success. Between this time and the advent of Shakespeare, Christopher Marlowe was the best-known writer of the drama. The plays of "Edward II." and "Dr. Faustus" were said to contain passages unsurpassed by even Shakespeare. It was Marlowe who first introduced blank verse upon the public stage. We pass Shakespeare's predecessors, Lyle, Kyd, Marlowe, Peele, Greene, Lodge, Nash, Chettle and Munday, who were all writers of more or less note in their day and time; the drama in their time, though far from being in a crude state, lacked much of being in a state of full development. Shakespeare was a man of broad vision ; his genius as the poet of the drama was then, as it has remained since, unsurpassed. At first he began to retouch and rewrite some of the old plays of his predecessors. Described as an actor and unknown as a writer, with times and conditions favorable to the development of the English drama he was quick to discover the material at hand, which soon made his fame—a fame that still shines brighter than that of any other poet living or dead. He devoted himself to English and Roman history, and as a result his historic dramas reached a perfection that has never before nor since been attained. Shakespeare was a great poetical genius ; he used blank verse with the skill of the consummate master that he was, and his tragedies and his comedies established themselves for all time to come as examples of the highest type. His historic themes became the perennial models of the modern historic drama. The influence of the diction and versification of Shakespeare cannot be overrated ; in his characterizations he has never been equaled, while his plays furnish models in every phase of human life and are a mirror of humanity. Goethe and Schiller contributed to the German drama. Goethe's "Faust," "Ipigenia" and "Tasso" are masterpieces of the art of dramatic poetry. Schiller contributed "Don Carlos," "Wallenstein" and "William Tell" as masterpieces of his genius, a genius bright as electric light, illuminating the pathway of those to follow who seek the field of literature. Sir Edward Bulwer-Lytton contributed to the modern English drama the "Lady of Lyons" and "Richelieu," both of which found great favor. Sheridan gave an impulse to the genteel comedy that is felt to the present day.

THE TRAGEDY.

Tragedy is earnest and serious, and deals with the great and sublime actions of life. It is generally written in blank heroic verse. Its diction should be elevated. The calamitous side of life with tragic events is placed before the public gaze with a view to arouse pity, fear, or indignation, or it may be of noble deeds in connection with life's events. The subjects of tragedy are various. Shakespeare has given to the world "King Lear," "Othello," "Macbeth," "Hamlet," "Julius Cæsar," "Romeo and Juliet," and many other plays of great merit which the reader may well refer to with profit. "Virginius" is a fine example of the tragedy.

THE COMEDY.

Directly the opposite of tragedy is comedy, which seeks to represent all the follies and foibles of human life, and has only an eye to the ridiculous and ludicrous. Its humor, however, should always be refined and its ending be ever happy. Comedy deals largely in satire, and its caricatures are often grotesque.

THE DIVISIONS OF THE DRAMA.

These constitute acts, which are in turn subdivided into scenes. The regular drama is limited to five acts. The first should present the intrigue, the second should develop it, the third should be filled with incidents forming its complication, the fourth should prepare the means of unraveling, the fifth should unravel the plot.

THE FARCE.

It is a short play in which ridiculous qualities and actions are greatly exaggerated for the purpose of exciting laughter. The dialogues and characters are usually taken from inferior ranks.

THE TRAVESTY, OR BURLESQUE.

It is a humorous dramatic composition where things high and low are commingled. Common thoughts and topics are invested with artificial dignity, and the forms and expressions of serious drama are imitated in language of a ludicrous character.

THE MELODRAMA.

The melodrama is a combination of the tragic and comic interspersed with song and music and gorgeous scenery. Its drama is genteel comedy and is perhaps more popular with the theater-going world than any other species of drama. Oliver Goldsmith's "She Stoops to Conquer," Sheridan's "Critic" and Jefferson's "Rip VanWinkle" are excellent illustrations.

THE BURLETTA.

It is a musical drama of a comic nature.

THE PROLOGUE.

An introduction in verse to be recited before the representation of the drama.

Imagine yourself then, good Sir, in a wig,
Either grizzle or bob—never mind, you look big.
You've a sword at your side, in your shoes there are buckles,
And the folds of fine linen flap over your knuckles.
You have come with light heart, and with eyes that are brighter,
From a pint of red Port, and a steak at the Mitre ;
You have strolled from the Bar and the purlieus of Fleet,
And you turn from the Strand into Catherine Street ;
Thence climb to the law-loving summits of Bow,
Till you stand at the Portal all play-goers know.
See, here are the 'prentice lads laughing and pushing,
And here are the seamstresses shrinking and blushing,
And here are the urchins who, just as to-day, Sir,
Buzz at you like flies with their "Bill o' the Play, Sir?"
Yet you take one, no less, and you squeeze by the chairs,
With their freights of fine ladies, and mount up the stairs ;
So issue at last on the House in its pride,
And pack yourself snug in a box at the side.
Austin Dobson—Prologue to Abbey's Edition of "She Stoops to Conquer."

THE EPILOGUE.

An address in verse to the audience at the conclusion of the drama. It is usually intended to recapitulate the chief incidents, and draws a moral from them.

THE ENVOY.

It is a sort of postscript appended to poetical compositions to enforce or recommend them.

Good-bye to you, Kelley, your fetters are broken
Good-bye to you, Cumberland, Goldsmith has spoken !
Good-bye to sham Sentiment, moping and mumming,
For Goldsmith has spoken and Sheridan's coming ;
And the frank Muse of Comedy laughs in free air
As she laughed with the Great Ones, with Shakespeare, Molière !
Austin Dobson—Envoy to Abbey's Edition of "She Stoops to Conquer."

THE SUBJECTIVE DRAMA.

The drama of the human soul, teaching the lessons of human struggle to the higher stages of life. Goethe's masterpiece, "Faust," is a high type of this species of the drama. Life is made up of incessant toils and struggles to nobler ends. This poem is grand, bringing together as it does, the tragedies and the comedies of human life into a perfect state of reconciliation.

THE OPERA.

The opera is a dramatic composition set to music and sung on the stage, accompanied with musical instruments and enriched with magnificent dresses, machinery, dancing, and songs. Thus made up of music, dancing, decoration, and poetry, it is intended to please the sight, and must be judged more from the standpoint of its being able to secure popular applause and favor than from any real intrinsic literary merit. To the opera of the present day more of its success frequently lies in its decorations and pantomimic character than to the parts sung or spoken. The opera of today is patterned after the French, Italian, and German.

THE SATIRE.

The satire in character is allied to the didactic, and is intended to reform the abuses it attacks. The satirical poem is a composition in which wickedness or folly is ridiculed, censured, and held up to reprobation ; hence it is an invective poem. Satirical poetry is divisible into three classes, Moral, Personal and Political. Of the first class, Pope's "Moral Essays" and the satires of Horace furnish fine examples.

> Tŏ rēst, thĕ cūshiŏn ănd sŏſt dēan ĭnvīte,
> Whŏ nēvĕr mēntiŏns hĕll tŏ ēars pŏlīte.
> > *Pope*—"Moral Essays."

> 'Tĭs ēdŭcātiŏn fŏrms thĕ cōmmŏn mĭnd ;
> Jŭst ăs thĕ twĭg ĭs bĕnt thĕ treē's ĭnclīned.
> > *Idem.*

Satirical poetry is also used for the purpose of exposing the weaknesses, the absurdities or vices of men. Derision, irony, mockery, sarcasm, or burlesque may be employed. Of these personal satires, excellent examples may be found in Dryden's "MacFlecknoe," it being a personal attack on a rival dramatist. "English Bards and Scotch Reviewers," by Lord Byron, is perhaps the greatest of all personal satires. Being attacked by critics and held up to ridicule, he replied in a way that gave evidence of his mighty genius and in turn ridiculed nearly all critics and poets of the author's day and time.

> Stĭll mūst Ĭ hēar?—shăll hōarse Fĭtzgĕrăld bāwl
> Hĭs creēkĭng coŭplĕts ĭn ă tăvĕrn hăll,
> Ănd Ĭ nŏt sīng, lĕst, hăplў̄, Scŏtch rĕviēws
> Shoŭld dūb mĕ scrībblĕr, ănd dĕnoŭnce mў̄ mūse?
> Prĕpāre fŏr rhўme—Ĭ'll pūblĭsh, rĭght ŏr wrōng :
> Foŏls āre mў̄ thĕme, lĕt sătĭre bĕ mў̄ sŏng.
> > *Byron*—"English Bards and Scotch Reviewers."

> Sŏ thĕ strŭck ēaglĕ, strĕtched ŭpŏn thĕ plāin,
> Nŏ mōre throŭgh rōllĭng cloŭds tŏ sōar ăgāin,
> Viĕwed hĭs ŏwn fĕathĕr ŏn thĕ fātăl dărt,
> Ănd wīnged thĕ shăft thăt quĭvĕred ĭn hĭs hēart.
> > *Idem.*

> As soon
> Seek roses in December,—ice in June;
> Hope constancy in wind, or corn in chaff.
> Believe a woman, or an epitaph,
> Or any other thing that's false, before
> You trust in critics.
>
> *Idem.*

The "Dunciad," by Alexander Pope, is an excellent satire of this kind, one in which he vilifies all writers by whom he had been vilified. Under the same head we may be allowed to class James Russell Lowell's "A Fable for the Critics," one of the finest productions of its kind in the English language, of a very different nature, however, from the satires of Dryden, Byron and Pope. Lowell's satire was written for the purpose of provoking friendly rivalry, and not for the purpose of giving offense. His portraits and caricatures were, however, droll, and the colors were laid on with no sparing hand; yet the tone of "A Fable for the Critics" was so good-natured that no one ought to have taken offense, although some of his thrusts left embittered memories.

> There comes Poe with his Raven, like Barnaby Rudge,
> Three-fifths of him genius and two-fifths sheer fudge,
> Who talks like a book of iambs and pentameters,
> In a way to make people of common sense damn meters,
> Who has written some things quite the best of their kind,
> But the heart somehow seems all squeezed out by the mind,
> Who—but hey-day! What's this? Messieurs Matthews and Poe,
> You must not fling mud-balls at Longfellow so,
> Does it make a man worse that his character's such
> As to make his friends love him (as you think) too much?
> Why, there is not a bard at this moment alive
> More willing than he that his fellows should thrive;
> While you are abusing him thus, even now
> He would help either one of you out of a slough;

You may say that he's smooth and all that till you're hoarse,
But remember that elegance also is force ;
After polishing granite as much as you will,
The heart keeps its tough old persistency still ;
Deduct all you can that still keeps you at bay,—
Why, he'll live till men weary of Collins and Gray.
I'm not over-fond of Greek meters in English,
To me rhyme's a gain, so it be not too jinglish,
And your modern hexameter verses are no more
Like Greek ones than sleek Mr. Pope is like Homer ;
As the roar of the sea to the coo of a pigeon is,
So, compared to your moderns, sounds old Melesigenes ;
I may be too partial, the reason, perhaps, o't is
That I've heard the old blind man recite his own rhapsodies,
And my ear with that music impregnate may be,
Like the poor exiled shell with the soul of the sea,
Or as one can't bear Strauss when his nature is cloven
To its deeps within deeps by the stroke of Beethoven ;
But, set that aside, and 'tis truth that I speak,
Had Theocritus written in English, not Greek,
I believe that his exquisite sense would scarce change a line
In that rare, tender, virgin-like pastoral, Evangeline.
     Lowell—" A Fable for the Critics."

Satires of a political nature are written in the interest of some great political party, or its candidates. Dryden's "Absalom Achitophel," Butler's " Hudibras," and Lowell's " What Mr. Robinson Thinks," are all first-class political satires. The satire of Lowell is from his "Bigelow Papers." It was not an ephemeral production, as such satires usually are, but was well received then and has ever since been appreciated by a reading public. Mr. Lowell has written this satire in the Yankee dialect, and has thus helped to preserve this quaint type of New England speech.

Gŭvĕnĕr B. ĭs ă sēnsĭblĕ mān ;
 Hĕ stāys tŏ hĭs hōme ăn' lŏŏks ārtĕr hĭs fōlks ;
 Hĕ drāws hĭs fŭrrĕr ĕz strāit ĕz hĕ cān,—
 Ănd īntĕr nŏbŏdў's tātĕr-pătch pōkes ;—
 Bŭt Jŏhn P.
 Rŏbĭnsŏn hē
Sĕz hē wŭnt vōte fĕr Gŭvĕnĕr B.
 James Russell Lowell—"What Mr. Robinson Thinks."

THE DIALECTIC.

People of the same country do not always speak the same language. In our own country we have many varieties or peculiar forms of the English. These peculiarities of speech may be termed dialectics. America having a more diversiloquent population than any other race on the globe, there are necessarily more dialectics. These varieties are found in all parts of the country. In New England we have the Yankee dialect ; in the South we have the Negro dialect ; on the Western plains we have a dialect peculiar to the cowboy, the mountaineer and the miner ; in the interior we have a dialect peculiar to a large class of Westerners which has received the euphonious name of the Hoosier dialect. "Unzer Fritz" in America has produced what is known as the German dialect, while Patrick has given to us a mixture of his brogue, which is known as the Irish dialect ; on our western coast John Chinaman has given us a mixture of his tongue, and we have what is known as the Chinese dialect. Is it a wonder America is a land where dialectic poetry flourishes? England has dialects peculiar to her own province. So, too, the Welsh and the Scotch. The Scotch dialect Burns has immortalized, and beauty teems in every line of his Lowland Scotch. The peculiar charm which attaches to the dialect of the Irish-American, and the native talent and wit possessed by the Irish people, together with the "bulls" and mistakes that necessarily happen in conversations, has made the Irish dialect quite a favorite in this country, and much excellent as well as amusing poetry is the result. Our German cousin has ever furnished amusement for men like Charles Follen Adams, a Massachusetts poet, who has made a decided success with his favorite dialect—the German. Riley's poems in Hoosier dialect are inimitable, unsurpassable and never-dying. The provincialisms of our Western folk are as indelibly fixed by Riley as was the Scottish by Burns. James Russell Lowell was the author of good dialectic poetry, and many others of our brightest and best authors have indulged in the temptation. Bret Harte is still another one of those peculiar geniuses that have touched the chord-strings of the human heart; and his dialectic poems are the best of their kind, describing the dialect of the far West and the peculiarities of its multigenerous inhabitants. Dialectic poetry has gained so great a prominence in the literature of today that we have concluded to classify it under a distinct head, although it embraces many species or varieties of poetry.

GERMAN DIALECT.

Charles Follen Adams has furnished some Anglo-Teutonic verse that will ever be appreciated by the reading public. Adams is a Boston business man who has, during his leisure moments, for recreation and pastime, written of the troubles and trials of the Strauss family. He has demonstrated himself a master of the art.

> I dōn'd văs prēachĭng vōmăn's rīghdts,
>   Ŏr ānȳdĭng līke dŏt,
> Ŭnd Ī līkes tŏ seē ăll hēoplĕs
>   Shŭst gŏndēntĕd mĭt dhĕir lŏt;

Budt I vants to gondrădict dŏt shap
Dŏt māde dĭs leēdlĕ shōke :
"Ă vōmăn vās dĕr glingĭng vīne,
Ŭnd mān dĕr shtŭrdy ōak."

   Adams—"Der Oak und der Vine."

You vouldn't dĭnk mīne frau,
 If you shŭst look ăt hĕr nŏw,
Vhĕre dĕr wrinklĕs ōn hĕr prōw
  Lōng hăf beēn,
Văs dĕr fräulĕin blŭmp ŭnd fāir,
Mĭt dĕr wăfy flāxĕn hāir,
Who dĭd vŏnce mīne heărt ĕnshnāre—
  Mīne Kătrīne.

   Adams—"Mine Katrine."

Dhĕre văs māny qveĕr dĭngs, ĭn dĭs lānd ŏff dĕr freē,
 I neffĕr could qvīte ŭndĕrstănd ;
Dĕr beoplĕs dhĕy āll seĕm sŏ deēfrĕnt tŏ mé
 Ăs dhōse ĭn mīne ōwn fădĕrlānd.
Dhĕy gĕts blĕndy droublĕs, ŭnd indŏ mĭshăps,
 Mītoudt dĕr leăst bĭt ŏff ă cāuse ;
Ŭnd, vould you pĕliĕf ĭd? dhōse meăn Yăngeĕ chăps,
 Dhĕy fīghts mĭt dhĕir mŏdĕr-ĭn-lāws !

   Adams—"Mine Moder-in-Law."

I'm ă prŏkĕn-heărtĕd Deŭtschĕr,
 Vŏt's vĭll'd mĭt criĕf ŭnd shāme.
I dĕlls you vŏt dĕr droŭplĕ ĭsh :
 I doōsn't knŏw my nāme.

You dĭnks dĭs fĕry vŭnny, ĕh ?
 Vĕn you dĕr schtŏry heăr,
You vĭll nŏt vŏndĕr dĕn sŏ mooch,
 Ĭt văs sŏ schtrānge ŭnd queēr.

Mīne mŏdĕr hăd dwŏ leēdlĕ twins ;
 Dĕy văs mĕ ūnd mīne brŏdĕr :
Vĕ lookt sŏ fĕry mooch ălike,
 Nŏ vŏn knĕw vĭch vrŏm tŏdĕr.

Von off der poys was "Yawcob,"
Und "Hans" der oder's name :
But den it made no tifferent ;
Ve both got called der same.

Vell ! von off us got tead,—
Yaw, Mynheer, dot ish so !
But vedder Hans or Yawcob,
Mine moder she don'd know.

Und so I am in drouples :
I gan't kit droo mine hed
Vedder I'm Hans vot's lifing,
Or Yawcob vot is tead !

    Adams—"The Puzzled Dutchman."

IRISH DIALECT.

Poems in this dialect are very popular with the reading world. They are usually very droll, yet full of pith and point. One by Charles Follen Adams will serve to illustrate our meaning.

"The greatest burd to foight," says Pat,
 " Barring the agle, is the duck ;
He has a foine large bill to peck,
 And plinty of rale Irish pluck.

"And, thin, d'ye moind the fut he has?
 Full as broad over as a cup ;
Show me the fowl upon two ligs
 That's able fer to thrip him up !"

    "Pat's Logic."

"Arrah, boys, it's meself that will tell ye,
 And that I can do pretty soon,
Of the incidents strange that befell me,
 When I traveled up to the moon.

I heard that quare sowls did reside there,
  So I in a balloon wint one day,
And as swift as a race-horse did ride there,
  From earth disappearing away.

CHORUS.

" I tell you the truth on my honor,
  How I traveled up in a balloon ;
For sure it's meself, Paddy Connor,
  That journeyed smack up to the moon."
    Anonymous—" Paddy's Balloon Ascension."

"Oh, 'twas Norah M'Frisky I met on the road
  To the Fair of Tralee, as I trotted away ;
On her breast, a *gossoon*, a most beautiful load,
  And the image of Paddy, each gossip did say.
"Arrah, Norah, my honey, is it you I see there?"
  "'Tis, Murtoch, avic, I'm off to the Fair."
" If that's what you're at, Norah, faith its all right ;
We'll set off together, we'll be there at night.
    And we'll drink to the Lynches,
    The beautiful Clinches,
    The Murphys, O'Ryans,
    The Duffys, the Brians,
    The Careys and Learys,
    The Laughlins, O'Shaughlins,
    The Whelans, the Phelans,
    O'Connells, O'Donnells,
    The Fogartys, Doughertys,
    The Burkes and M'Gurks,
    The Nolans and Folans,
    The Kiernans and Tiernans,
    The Rogans and Brogans,
    The Lacys and Caseys,
That keep up the fun and the frolick galore."
        " The Fun at the Fair."

"Wĭd āll cŏndĕscīnshĭn, Ĭ'd tūrn yoŭr ăttīnshĭn
Tŏ whāt Ĭ woŭld mīnshŭn ŏv Ērĭn sŏ greēn ;
Ăn' wĭdoŭt hĕsĭtāshĭn Ĭ'd shōw hŏw thăt nāshĭn
Bĕcāme ŏv crĕāshĭn thĕ gēm ănd thĕ queēn."
                        "The Origin of Ireland."

Ŏh ! Ērĭn, mў coūntrў, thŏugh strāngĕrs măy rōam
Thĕ hills ănd thĕ vāllĕys Ĭ ōnce cālled mў hōme,
Thў lākes ănd thў moūntăins nŏ lōngĕr Ĭ seē,
Yĕt wārmlў ăs ēvĕr mў heārt bĕats fŏr theē,
  Ŏh ! coŭsh lă măchreē ! mў heārt bĕats fŏr theē,
Ērĭn, Ērĭn, mў heārt bĕats fŏr theē.
                Charles Jeffreys—"Oh ! Erin, My Country."

         Trŏth, Nōră! Ĭ'm wādĭn'
         Thĕ grāss ăn' părādĭn'
Thĕ dēws ăt yoŭr dūre, wĭd mў swāte sĕrĕnādĭn',
         Ălōne ănd fŏrsākĕn,
         Whĭlst yoŭ're nĕvĕr wākĭn'
Tŏ tĕll mĕ yoŭ're wĭd mĕ ăn' Ĭ ăm mĭstākĕn !
        James Whitcomb Riley—"Serenade—To Nora."

WESTERN DIALECT.

Some very excellent poems have been written in this dialect by Francis Bret Harte. Mr. Harte is a master of the art of versification.

        Ĭt wăs Aŭgŭst thĕ thĭrd,
          Ănd quĭte sŏft wăs thĕ skīes ;
      Whĭch ĭt mĭght bĕ ĭnfĕrred
        Thăt Ăh Sĭn wăs līkewīse ;
     Yĕt hĕ plāyed ĭt thăt dāy ŭpŏn Willĭam
        Ănd mĕ ĭn ă wāy Ĭ dĕspīse.
    Bret Harte—"Plain Language from Truthful James."

, Săy thēre ! P'r'āps
Sŏme ōn yoŭ chāps
Mīght knōw Jīm Wild ?
Wĕll, nō ŏffēnse :
Thăr āin't nŏ sēnse
In gīttĭn' rīled !
Bret Harte—" Jim."

I've seēn ă grizzlў shōw hīs teēth ;
I've seēn Kĕntŭckў Pēte
Drăw ōut hīs shoōtĕr 'n' ădvīse
Ă "tĕndĕrfoōt" tĕr trēat ;
Bŭt nŭthĭn' ĕvĕr tŭk mĕ dōwn,
'N' māde mў bĕndĕrs shāke,
Līke thăt sīgn ăbōut thĕ dōughnŭts
Līke mў mōthĕr ūsed tĕr māke.
Charles Follen Adams—" Mother's Doughnuts."

Western dialect is still further exemplified by what is termed Hoosier dialect, a speech peculiar to the people of some of the western states, yet of a little different type from those beyond the Rockies. Many excellent poems are written in this dialect. We have made a few selections :

" 'Scūrĭoŭs-līke," săid thĕ treē-tŏad,
" I've twīttĕred fĕr rāin ăll dāy ;
Ănd I gŏt ŭp soōn,
Ănd hōllĕred tĭll noōn—
Bŭt thĕ sŭn, hĭt blāzed ăwāy,
Tĭll I jĕst clŭmb dōwn ĭn ă crāwfĭsh-hōle,
Wĕarў ăt heārt, ănd sĭck ăt sōul !
James Whitcomb Riley—" The Tree-Toad."

Ă thing 'ăt's 'bōut ăs trȳĭn' ās ă hĕalthў măn kĭn meēt
Is sŏme poŏr fĕllĕr's fūnĕrāl ă-jŏggĭn' 'lŏng thĕ streēt :
Thĕ slōw hĕarse ānd thĕ hōssĕs—slōw ĕnoŭgh, tŏ sāy thĕ lēast,
Fĕr tŏ ēvĕn tāx thĕ pātiĕnce ōf thĕ gĕntlĕmăn dĕcēased !

Thĕ slŏw scrŭnch ŏf thĕ grăvĕl—ānd thĕ slŏw grĭnd ŏf thĕ wheēls,—
Thĕ slŏw,-slŏw gō ŏf ĕv'rў̆ wōe 'ăt ĕv'rў̆bōdў̆ feēls!
Sŏ Ĭ rūthĕr līke thĕ cōntrăst whĕn Ĭ hēar thĕ whĭplăsh crăck
   Ă quĭckstĕp fĕr thĕ hōssĕs,
                        Whēn thĕ
                              Hēarse
                                   Cŏmes
                                        Băck!
    James Whitcomb Riley—"When the Hearse Comes Back."

"Pŏur ŭs ōut ănōthĕr, Dăddў̆," sāys thĕ fĕllĕr, wărmĭn' ŭp,
Ă-spēakĭn' 'crōst ă săucĕrfŭl, ăs Ŭnclĕ tŭck hĭs cŭp,—
"Whĕn Ĭ seēd yĕr sĭgn ŏut yāndĕr," hē wĕnt ōn, tŏ Ŭnclĕ Jāke,—
"'Cŏme ĭn ănd gĭt sŏme cōffeĕ like yĕr mōthĕr ūsed tŏ māke'—
Ĭ thōught ŏf mў̆ ōld mōthĕr, ănd thĕ Pōsĕў̆ cōuntў̆ fārm,
Ănd mē ă lĭttlĕ kĭd ăgĭn, ă-hăngĭn' ĭn hĕr ārm,
Ăs shĕ sĕt thĕ pōt ă-bĭlĭn', brōke thĕ ĕggs ănd pōured 'ĕm ĭn"—
Ănd thĕ fĕllĕr kĭnd ŏ' hāltĕd, wĭth ă trĭmblĕ ĭn hĭs chĭn.
    James Whitcomb Riley—"Like His Mother Used to Make."

Hĕ's fĕr thĕ pōre măn ĕver' tīme! Ănd ĭn thĕ lăst cămpāign
Hĕ stŭmped ōld Mōrgăn Cōuntў̆, through thĕ sūnshĭne ănd thĕ rāin,
Ănd hĕlt thĕ bănnĕr ŭp'ărds frōm ă-trāilĭn' ĭn thĕ dŭst,
Ănd cŭt loōse ŏn mŏnōpŏlīes ănd cŭss'd ănd cŭss'd ănd cŭss'd!
Hĕ'd tĕll sŏme fŭnnў̆ stŏrў̆ ĕver' nŏw ănd thĕn, yoŭ knōw,
Tĕl, blāme ĭt! ĭt wŭz bĕttĕr 'n ă jăck-ŏ'-lāntĕrn shōw!
Ănd Ĭ'd gŏ fŭrdĕr, yĭt, tŏ-dāy, tŏ hēar ōld Jăp nŏrāte
Thăn ānў̆ hīgh-tōned ōrătŏr 'ăt ĕver stŭmped thĕ Stāte!
        James Whitcomb Riley— "Jap Miller."

    Nōthĭn' ĕvĕr mādē wĕ māddĕr
    Thăn fĕr Păp tŏ stŏmp ĭn, lāyĭn'
    Ŏn ă' ĕxtră fōre-stĭck, sāyĭn'
      "Grōun'hŏg's ōut ănd seēd hĭs shăddĕr!"
    James Whitcomb Riley — "Old Winters on the Farm."

Rĕc'lĕct thĕ wŏrtĕr drăppĭn'
  Ĭn thĕ trŏff sŏ stĭll 'nd clāir,
'Nd wĕ'd hŭnkĕr dōwn 'nd drĭnk ĭt,
  Stĭll ă drăppĭn' ĭn ŏur hāir ;
Rĕc'lĕct yĭt hōw ĭt tāstĕd,
  Sŏrtĕr soōthĭn' līke 'nd sweēt,—
Ĕf ă fĕllĕr jĕst coŭld būy ĭt
  Yoŭ coŭld tăp mĕ fĕr ă trēat.
        Joe S. Reed—"Stirrin' Off."

CHINESE DIALECT.

Mr. Harte has given us a specimen of this dialect in "The Latest Chinese Outrage," a poem in anapestic rhythm of unusual merit in descriptive resources, metrical beauty and amusing incidents. We select the fourth stanza.

Thĕn wĕ āxed fŏr ă pārlĕy. Whĕn ŏut ŏf thĕ dĭn
Tŏ thĕ frŏnt cŏmes ă-rŏckĭn' thăt hēathĕn, Ăh Sīn !
"Yoŭ ōwe flŏwtў dŏlleĕ—mĕ wāsheĕ yoŭ cămp,
Yoŭ cātcheĕ mў wāsheĕ—mĕ cātcheĕ nŏ stămp ;
Ŏne dōllăr hăp dōzĕn, mĕ nŏ cātcheĕ yĕt,
Nŏw thăt flŏwtў dŏlleĕ—nŏ hāb?—hŏw căn gĕt ?
Mĕ cātcheĕ yoŭ pĭggeĕ—mĕ sēlleĕ fŏr cāsh,
Ĭt cātcheĕ mĕ līceĕ—yoŭ cātcheĕ nŏ 'hāsh' ;
Mĕ bĕllў goŏd Shĕrĭff—mĕ lĕbbeĕ whĕn căn,
Mĕ āllee sāme hālp pĭn ăs Mĕlĭcăn mān !
    Bŭt Mĕlĭcăn mān,
    Hĕ wāsheĕ hĭm pān
    Ŏn bŏttŏm sīde hĭlleĕ
    Ănd cātcheĕ—hŏw căn ?"

SOUTHERN DIALECT.

The dialect peculiar to the South is known as the Negro dialect. Many excellent poems are written in this dialect, many of them quaint and laughable. We have selected an admirable poem and give it entire, entitled "De 'Sperience of de Reb'rend Quacko Strong":

> Swing dăt gāte wĭde, 'Pōstlĕ Pētĕr,
>   Rĭng dĕ bĭg bĕll, bĕat dĕ gŏng,
> Sāints ănd mārtўrs dĕn wĭll meĕt dăr
>   Brŭddĕr, Rĕb'rĕnd Quāckŏ Strŏng!
>
> Sŏund dăt bŭglĕ, Āngĕl Gābr'ĕl!
>   Tĕll dĕ ĕldĕrs lŏud ăn' lŏng,
> Cl'ār ŏut dĕm hĭgh sĕats ŏb hĕabĕn,
>   Hĕre cŏmes Rĕb'rĕnd Quāckŏ Strŏng!
>
> Tŭrn dĕ guārd ŏut, Gĕn'răl Mīchaĕl,
>   Ārms prĕsĕnt, dĕ lĭne ălŏng,
> Lĕt dĕ bănd plăy "Cŏnk'rĭn Hĕrŏ"
>   Fŏr dĕ Rĕb'rĕnd Quāckŏ Strŏng.
>
> Dĕn bĭd Mōsĕs brĭng dĕ crŏwn, ăn'
>   Pālms, ăn' wĕddĭn' gŏwn ălŏng!
> Wĭd prŏcĕssĭŏn tō dĕ lāndĭn',
>   Hĕre's dĕ Rĕb'rĕnd Quāckŏ Strŏng.
>
> Jōsĕph, mārch dŏwn wĭd yoŭr brĕd'rĕn,
>   Trĭbes, ăn' bănnĕrs mŭsterĭn' strŏng;
> Speĕch ŏf wĕlcŏme frŏm ŏle Ābrăm,
>   Ānswĕr, Rĕb'rĕnd Quāckŏ Strŏng.
>
> Tŭne yoŭr hărp-strĭngs tight, Kĭng Dāvĭd,
>   Sĭng yoŭr goŏd Ŏle Hŭndrĕd sŏng,
> Lĕt dĕ sĕrŏphs dānce wĭd cȳmbăls
>   'Rŏund dĕ Rĕb'rĕnd Quāckŏ Strŏng.
>
> Āngĕls hĕar mĕ yĕll Hŏsānnĕr,
>   Hĕar my dŭlcĕm spĕritoŏl sŏng;
> Hăllĕlūyĕr! Ĭ'm ă-cōmĭn',
>   Ĭ'm dĕ Rĕb'rĕnd Quāckŏ Strŏng.

Māke dăt whīte rŏbe rădděr spācioŭs,
  Ănd thĕ wāist bĕlt strōrdn'rў lōng,
'Cāuse 'twĭll tāke sŏme roŏm ĭn glōrў
  Fōr dĕ Rēb'rĕnd Quāckŏ Strōng.

Whāt! Nō ŏne āt dĕ lāndĭn'!
  'Pēars līke sŭff'n' 'nŭdděr's wrŏng;
Guĕss Ĭ'll gīb dăt sleēpў Pētĕr
  Fīts—frŏm Rēb'rĕnd Quāckŏ Strōng.

Whāt ă nārrăr littlĕ gātewăy!
  Mў! dăt gāte ăm hărd tŏ mōve,
"Whō ăm dāt?" săys 'Pōstlĕ Pētĕr
  Frŏm dĕ părăpēt ăbŏve.

Ŭnclĕ Pētĕr, dŏn't yoŭ knōw mĕ—
  Mĕ ă shīnĭn' līght sŏ lōng?
Whў dĕ bĕrrў nĭggĕrs cāll mĕ
  Goōd ŏle Rēb'rĕnd Quāckŏ Strōng.

Dūn'nŏ mĕ! whў! Ĭ've cŏnvărtĕd
  Hŭndrĕds ŏ' dărkĭes ĭn ă song,
Dūn'nŏ mĕ! nŏr yĕt mў māssă!
  Ĭ'm dĕ Rēb'rĕnd Quāckŏ Strōng!

Ŏle Nĭck's cōmĭn'! Ĭ căn feēl ĭt
  Gĕttĭn' wărmĕr āll ăboūt.
Oh, mў goŏd, kĭnd Kĕrnĕl Pētĕr,
  Lĕt mĕ ĭn, Ĭ'm āll toŏ stoŭt

Tō gŏ 'lōng wĭd Mājŏr Sātăn
  Ĭntŏ dăt wărm clīmăte 'mŏng
Fīre ăn' brĭmstŏne. Hēar mĕ knŏckĭn',
  Ŏle chŭrch mĕmbĕr, Quāckŏ Strōng.

Dăt loŭd nŏise ăm cōmĭn' nēarĕr,
  Drĕfflĕ smĕll līke pŏwdĕr smōke;
'Nŭddĕr screēch! Goŏd hēabĕn hĕlp mĕ—
  Lōrd, fŏrgīb dĭs poŏr ŏle mōke.

Allers was so berry holy,
  Singin' and prayin' extra long;
Now de debble's gwine to catch me,
  Poor ole nigger, Quacko Strong.

Hi! dat gate swings back a little,
  Mighty squeezin' to get froo!
Ole Apollyon howlin' louder,
  Everything around am blue.

Bang de gate goes! an' Beelzebub,
  Bunch ob wool upon his prong,
Goes along widout de soul ob
  Missabul sinner, name ob Strong.

  Anonymous.

Few prettier selections can be made than the following:

A PLANTATION LULLABY.

Mammy's little pickaninny gwine to go to sleep—
  Hush a by-by, hush a by.
Doan' yo' hear de coon-dog bayin' loud an' deep?
  Hush a by-by, hush a by.
Mock-birds' notes a-callin', doan' yo' hear 'em sing?
Pappy's gone a huntin', an' a possum home'll bring.
There's wotermelons coolin' in the shadders o' de spring.
  Hush a pickaninny, an' a by-by.

There's sweet pertaters bilin' an' a ham bone to boot,
  Hush a by-by, hush a by.
Pappy's got a graveyard rabbit's left hind foot,
  Hush a by-by, hush a by.
So hush a pickaninny while de sout' winds moan,
Go to sleep so mammy can go lieb yo' all alone,
Fer she's goin' to make yo'r pappy a big co'n pone.
  Hush a pickaninny, an a by-by.

  Roy Farrell Greene.

YANKEE DIALECT.

The Yankee dialect is peculiar to our New England States. It has a quaintness about it that makes it very pleasant reading. James Russell Lowell has given to the world the finest specimens of this dialect. We select a poem entitled "The Courtin'," which in the excellence of its description is not exceeded:

    God mākes sĕch nights, ăll whīte ăn' still
        Fŭr 'z yoū căn loŏk ŏr līstĕn,
    Moōnshĭne ăn' snōw ŏn fiēld ăn' hill,
        Ăll silĕnce ān' ăll glīstĕn.

    Zĕklĕ crĕp' ŭp quīte ūnbĕknōwn,
        Ăn' pĕcked ĭn thrū' thĕ wīndĕr,
    Ăn' thēre sŏt Hūldȳ ăll ălōne,
        'Ĭth nō ŏne nīgh tŏ hēndĕr.

    Ă fīreplăce fĭlled thĕ roōm's ŏne side
        Wĭth hālf ă cōrd ŏ' woŏd ĭn;—
    Thĕre wārn't nŏ stōves (tĕll cōmfŏrt dīed)
        Tŏ bāke yĕ tō ă pūddĭn'.

    Thĕ wā'nŭt lōgs shŏt spārklĕs ōut
        Tōwărds thĕ poōtiĕst, blĕss hĕr!
    Ăn' leētlĕ flāmes dănced ăll ăboūt
        Thĕ chinȳ ōn thĕ drēssĕr.

    Ăgĭn thĕ chĭmblĕy croōk-nĕcks hūng,
        Ăn' ĭn ămōngst 'ĕm rŭstĕd
    Thĕ ōle queĕn's ārm thĕt Grān'thĕr Yoūng
        Fĕtched bāck fıŏm Cōncŏrd būstĕd.

    Thĕ vĕrȳ roōm, cŏz shē wăs ĭn,
        Seĕmed wārm frŏm floōr tŏ ceĭlĭn'.
    Ăn' shē loŏked fūll ăs rōsȳ ăgĭn
        Ĕz thĕ āpplĕs shē wăs peēlĭn'.

'Twăs kīn' ŏ' kīngdŏm-cōme tŏ loŏk
  Ŏn sēch ă blĕssĕd crē'tŭr',
Ă dŏgrŏse blūshĭn' tō ă broŏk
  Ăin't mŏdĕstĕr nŏr sweētĕr.

Hĕ wăs ā sĭx foŏt ŏ' măn, Ă Ī,
  Clĕan grĭt ăn' hûmăn nātŭr';
Nŏne coŭldn't quĭckĕr pītch ă tōn
  Nŏr drŏr ă fŭrrĕr strāightĕr.

Hĕ'd spârked ĭt with fŭll twĕntў gāls,
  Hĕ'd squīred 'ĕm, dānced 'ĕm, drūv 'ĕm,
Fŭst thĭs ŏne, ăn' thĕn thĕt, bў spĕlls,—
  Ăll ĭs, hĕ coŭldn't lōve 'ĕm.

Bŭt 'lōng ŏ' hĕr hĭs vĕins 'oŭld rŭn
  Ăll crĭnklў like cŭrled māplĕ,
Thĕ side shĕ brĕshed fĕlt fŭll ŏ' sŭn
  Ĕz ā soŭth slōpe ĭn Ăp'ĭl.

Shĕ thŏught nŏ v'īce hĕd sēch ă swĭng
  Ĕz hĭs'n ĭn thĕ chŏir;
Mў! whĕn hĕ māde Ŏle Hŭndrĕd rĭng
  Shĕ *knōwed* thĕ Lōrd wăs nĭghĕr.

Ăn' shĕ'd blŭsh scârlĭt, rĭght ĭn prāyer,
  Whĕn hĕr nĕw meĕtĭn'-bŭnnĕt
Fĕlt sŏmehŏw thrû' ĭts crŏwn ă pāir
  Ŏ' blūe eўes sŏt ŭpŏn ĭt.

Thĕt nĭght; Ĭ tĕll yĕ, shĕ loŏked *sŏme!*
  Shĕ seĕmed tŏ've gŭt ă nĕw sŏul,
Fŏr shĕ fĕlt sârtĭn-sūre hĕ'd cōme,
  Dŏwn tŏ hĕr vĕrў shōe-sōle.

Shĕ heĕred ă foŏt, ăn' knōwed ĭt, tū,
  Ă-răspĭn' ŏn thĕ scrāpĕr,—
Ăll wāys tŏ ŏnce hĕr feĕlĭn's flĕw
  Lĭke spârks ĭn bŭrnt-ŭp pāpĕr.

Hĕ kĭn' ŏ' l'ītĕred ōn thĕ mãt,
  Sŏme dōubtflĕ ō' thĕ sēklĕ;
Hĭs heãrt kĕp' gōĭn' pĭtў-pãt,
  Bŭt hĕr'n wĕnt pĭtў Zēklĕ.

Ăn' yĭt shĕ gĭn hĕr cheēr ă jĕrk
  Ĕz thōugh shĕ wīshed hĭm fŭrdĕr,
Ăn' ōn hĕr ãpplĕs kĕp' tŏ wŏrk,
  Pãrĭn' ăwāy līke mŭrdĕr.

"Yoŭ wānt tŏ seē mў Pā, Ĭ s'pōse?"
  "Wăl—nō—Ĭ cōme dăsīgnĭn'"—
"Tŏ seē mў Mã? Shĕ's sprĭnklĭn' clō'es
  'Ăgĭn tŏ-mōrrĕr's ī'nĭn'."

Tŏ sāy whў gãls ăct sō ŏr sō,
  Ŏr dōn't, 'oŭld bē prĕsūmĭn';
Mĕbbў tŏ mēan *yĕs* ăn' săy *nō*
  Cŏmes nătĕrăl tŏ wŏmĕn.

Hĕ stoōd ă spĕll ŏn ōne foŏt fŭst,
  Thĕn stoōd ă spĕll ŏn t'ōthĕr,
Ăn' ōn whĭch ōne hĕ fĕlt thĕ wŭst
  Hĕ coŭldn't hă' tōld yĕ, nŭthĕr.

Săys hē, "Ĭ'd bĕttĕr cãll ăgĭn";
  Săys shē, "Thĭnk līkelў Mĭstĕr";
Thăt lãst wŏrd prĭcked hĭm like ă pĭn,
  Ăn'—wãl, hĕ ŭp ăn' kĭst hĕr.

Whĕn Mā bĭmebў ŭpōn 'ĕm slĭps,
  Hŭldў sŏt pāle ĕz āshĕs,
Ăll kĭn' ŏ' smĭlў rōun' thĕ lĭps
  Ăn' tēarў rōun' thĕ lãshĕs.

Fŏr shē wăs jĕs' thĕ quĭĕt kĭnd
  Whŏse nātŭrs nĕvĕr vãrў,
Līke strēams thăt keĕp ă sŭmmĕr mĭnd
  Snŏw-hĭd ĭn Jēnoŏãrў.

The blood clost roun' her heart felt glued
　　Too tight for all expressin',
　Tell mother see how metters stood,
　　An' gin 'em both her blessin'.

Then her red come back like the tide
　　Down to the Bay o' Fundy,
An' all I know is, they was cried
　　In meetin' come nex' Sunday.
　　　　　　　　　　James Russell Lowell.

THE SCOTCH DIALECT.

　The Scotch is a very popular dialect. From the time it was first brought into general notice and rendered ever-enduring by the sweetest of Scotland's singers, Robert Burns, it has always been read with delight by the public. We give the following selections.

　　Thou hast sworn by thy God, my Jeanie,
　　　By that pretty white hand o' thine,
　　And by a' the lowing stars in heaven,
　　　That thou wad aye be mine !
　　And I hae sworn by my God, my Jeanie,
　　　And by that kind heart o' thine,
　　By a' the stars sown thick owre heaven,
　　　That thou shalt aye be mine !
Allan Cunningham—"Thou Hast Sworn by Thy God, My Jeanie."

　　He was a gash and faithful tyke,
　　As ever lap a sheugh or dike.
　　His honest, sonsie, baws'nt face,
　　Aye gat him friends in ilka place.
　　His breast was white, his touzie back
　　Weel clad wi' coat o' glossy black ;
　　His gaucy tail, wi' upward curl,
　　Hung o'er his hurdies wi' a swirl.
　　　　　　　　　Burns—"Twa Dogs."

My hēid ĭs lĭke tŏ rēnd, Wĭllĭe,
   My hĕart ĭs lĭke tŏ brēak ;
Ĭ'm weârĭn' ăff mў fēet, Wĭllĭe,
   Ĭ'm dўĭn' fōr yoŭr sāke !
Ŏ, lāy yoŭr chēek tŏ mīne, Wĭllĭe,
   Yoŭr hănd ŏn mў briĕst-bāne,—
Ŏ, sāy yĕ'll thĭnk ŏn mē, Wĭllĭe,
   Whĕn Ĭ ăm dēid ănd gāne !

William Motherwell—" My Heid is Like to Rend, Willie."

Shoŭld āuld ăcquāintănce bē fŏrgōt,
   Ănd nĕvĕr brōught tŏ mīn' ?
Shoŭld āuld ăcquāintănce bē fŏrgōt,
   Ănd dāys ŏ' lăng sўne ?

      CHORUS.

Fŏr āuld lăng sўne, mў dĕar,
   Fŏr āuld lăng sўne,
Wĕ'll tāk ă cūp ŏ' kīndnĕss yĕt,
   Fŏr āuld lăng sўne.

Robert Burns—"Auld Lang Syne."

CHILD DIALECT.

Listening to the dialect of children has ever furnished us some of our happiest hours, as well as most pleasing affections. Simple and artless, it is nevertheless engaging to both old and young. Mr. Riley's "Rhymes of Childhood" and "A Child World" are rare, grand gifts to mankind. A selection from "Maymie's Story of Red Riding Hood" is here given :

      Ăn' nĕn Rĭdĭng Hoōd
Shĕ sāy "Ŏh-mē-ŏh-mў ! Drān'mă ! whăt bĭg
Whīte lōng shărp teēth yoŭ dŏt !"
      Nĕn ōld Wŏlf sāys :
" Yĕs — ăn' thĕy're thătăwāy "—ăn' drōwled —
" Thĕy're thătăwāy," hĕ sāys, " tŏ ēat yoŭ wĭv ! "

An' nen he 'ist jump at her,—
          But she scream'—
An' scream', she did—so 's 'at the Man
'At wuz a-choppin' wood, you know,—he hear,
An' come a-runnin' in there wiv his ax ;
An', 'fore the old Wolf know, what he 's about,
He split his old brains out an' killed him s' quick
It make' his head swim !—An' Red Riding Hood
She wuzn't hurt at all !
          An' the big Man
He tooked her all safe home, he did, an' tell
Her Ma she's all right an' ain't hurt at all
An' old Wolf's dead an' killed—and ever'thing !—
So her Ma wuz so tickled an' so proud,
She gived him all the good things t' eat they wuz
'At's in the basket, an' she tell him 'at
She 's much oblige', an' say to "call adin."
An' story's honest truth—an' all so, too !
                    James Whitcomb Riley.

    My Pa he 'ist fished an' fished !
    An' my Ma she said she wished
    Me an' her was home ; an' Pa
    Said he wished so worse 'n Ma.
        James Whitcomb Riley—"The Fishing Party."

NONSENSE.

    " A little nonsense now and then
    Is relished by the wisest men."

    The writing of a nonsensical verse is a pleasure indulged in by some of our most excellent writers. The rhymes of our childhood—Mother Goose's Melodies—are familiar to almost every one, and it made very little difference what the wording of them was so that the measure and rhythm were perfect ; in fact, Mother Goose has some of the most complex lines to be found in poetry.* Where, however, the measure and rhythm are perfect, words make but very little difference in writing what are termed nursery rhymes, and nonsensical songs. "The Owl and the Pussy Cat," one of Lear's "Nonsense Songs," is one of the best of its kind extant. Lear has a book in which many good songs of this species may be found. They will repay the reading where one has any desire for the quaint. Billowy are the metrical waves of this nonsensical song; leaping and bounding, billow upon billow, leaping higher on the middle or line rhymes, the waves surge and lash each other in beautiful sounds to the end of the stanza; all nonsense, it is true, and yet pleasing in the highest degree to the ear.

> The ŏwl ănd thĕ pūssȳ-căt wĕnt ŏut tŏ sēa
>   Ĭn ă beāūtĭfŭl pēa-greĕn bōat ;
> Thĕy tŏŏk sŏme hŏnĕy, ănd lŏts ŏf mōnĕy
>   Wrăpped ŭp ĭn ă fīve-pŏund nōte.
> Thĕ ŏwl lŏŏked ŭp tŏ thĕ moŏn ăbŏve,
>   Ănd sāng tŏ hĭs līght gŭitār,
> "Ŏ pūssȳ, Ŏ pūssȳ, Ŏ pūssȳ, mȳ lŏve,
>   Whăt ă beāūtĭfŭl pūssȳ yŏu āre, yŏu āre !—
>   Whăt ă beāūtĭfŭl pūssȳ yŏu āre ! "
>
> Pŭssȳ sāid tŏ thĕ ŏwl, " Yŏu ēlĕgănt fōwl,
>   Hŏw chārmĭnglȳ sweēt yŏu sīng !
> Cŏme, lĕt ŭs bĕ mărriĕd—toŏ lōng wĕ hăve tărriĕd;
>   Bŭt whăt shăll wĕ dō fŏr ă rĭng ? "
> Sŏ thĕy sāiled ăwāy fŏr ă yēar ănd ă dāy,
>   Tŏ thĕ lănd whĕre thĕ bōng-treĕ grŏws,
> Ănd thĕre ĭn thĕ woŏd ă pĭggȳ-wĭg stoŏd,
>   Wĭth ă rĭng ĭn thĕ ĕnd ŏf hĭs nōse, hĭs nōse—
>   Ă rĭng ĭn thĕ ĕnd ŏf hĭs nōse.

---

* Mary Goose, wife of Isaac Goose, the author of "Mother Goose's Melodies," lived and died in Boston, Massachusetts, and was buried in Old Christ's Church Cemetery.

THE ART OF POETRY.

"Dĕar pig, ăre yoŭ willĭng tŏ sēll fŏr ŏne shillĭng
Yoŭr ring?" Săid thĕ piggў, "Ĭ will";
Sŏ thĕy toŏk ĭt ăwāy, ănd wĕre mărriĕd nĕxt dāy,
Bў thĕ tūrkĕy whŏ lives ŏn thĕ hill.
Thĕy dined ŭpŏn mince, ănd slicĕs ŏf quince,
Whĭch thĕy āte wĭth ă rūncĭblĕ spoŏn,
Ănd hānd ĭn hānd ŏn thĕ gōldĕn sānd
Thĕy dānced bў thĕ light ŏf thĕ moŏn, thĕ moŏn—
Thĕy dānced bў thĕ light ŏf thĕ moŏn.
Edward Lear—"The Owl and the Pussy Cat."

James Whitcomb Riley has some excellent verses of this species. Mr. Riley delights in amusing mankind, and few authors have been more prolific in writing poems that cause men to forget troubles and laugh heartily at the eccentricities of life. We make two selections:

Ă littlĕ Dŏg-Wōggў
Ŏnce wālked roŭnd thĕ Wōrld:
Sŏ hĕ shŭt ŭp hĭs hōuse; ănd, fŏrgĕttĭng
Hĭs twō pŭppў-chĭldrĕn
Lŏcked ĭn thĕre, hĕ cūrled
Ŭp hĭs tāil ĭn pĭnk bōmbăzĭne nēttĭng,
Ănd sĕt ōut
Tŏ wălk rōund
Thĕ Wōrld.
James Whitcomb Riley—"The Little Dog-Woggy."

Dāintў Bābў Āustĭn!
Yoŭr Dăddў's gŏne tŏ Bŏstŏn
Tŏ seē thĕ King
Ŏf Oŏ-Rĭnktŭm Jĭng
Ănd thĕ whāle hĕ rŏde ăcrŏst ŏn!
James Whitcomb Riley—"The King of Oo-Rinktum-Jing."

THE VERSICLE.

A little verse, a metrical toy. Poets of all ages—past as well as present, have taken delight in writing these momentary thoughts suggested by the occasion of passing incidents. Many of them, however, are very bright and deserve a place in the household of poetry. Our magazines and newspapers furnish a never-ending amount of them. We make the following selections :

WHAT SHE DIDN'T KNOW.

"That darling girl knew everything,
  Knew Hebrew, Latin, Greek—
Yes, several other languages
  With fluency could speak.

"Of music, art, embroidery,
  She had a thorough knowledge,
And many other things besides
  That girls are taught at college.

"The only thing she didn't know
  (Nor could the maid conceal
Her ignorance of that) was how
  To cook a decent meal.

"But did that make the maiden less
  Desirable to me?
No, she was rich, and could afford
  To hire a cook, you see."

YOUTH AT CHRISTMAS.

"Oh, would I were young," the old man sighs
  When the Christmas songs are sung.
The old woman never a word replies —
  She still claims she is young."

TOMMIE'S GIRL.

"She is cheerful, warm-hearted and true,
 And is kind to her father and mother;
She studies how much she can do
 For her sweet little sister and brother.

"If you want a companion for life,
 To comfort, enliven, and bless,
She is just the right sort of a wife,
 My girl with a calico dress."

A SURPRISE.

"I met her strolling on the street,
 We walked together up the hill,
She was a maiden very neat,
 Who made my heart stand still,
When in a manner hard to beat
 She shyly said, 'I know you're sweet.'

"Such words I knew not how to meet,
 She was not wont to talk that way,
But happiness I found was fleet
 For very soon I heard her say,
 'I think it faces toward the street.'
 And then I knew she meant my suite."

IN COLLEGE CAP AND GOWN.

"My sweetheart is a student in a famous female college,
 And though I do not think she'll win particular renown
In any special study, or be noted for her knowledge,
 I'm certain that she's charming in her college cap and gown.
That the costume's fascinating there's no reason for concealing,
 I think my love most beautiful when in it she appears,
But when I steal a kiss from her, how funny is the feeling
 When the edges of the mortar board are tickling my ears."

Jĕnnĭe kĭssed mĕ whĕn wĕ mĕt,
    Jŭmpĭng frŏm thĕ chāir shĕ sāt ĭn ;
Tīme, yoŭ thiēf, whŏ lōve tŏ gĕt
    Sēcrĕts ĭntŏ yoŭr līst, pŭt thāt ĭn.
Sāy Ĭ'm wēarȳ, sāy Ĭ'm sād,
    Sāy thăt hēalth ănd wēalth hăve mĭssed mĕ ;
Sāy Ĭ'm grōwĭng ōld, bŭt ādd—
            Jĕnnĭe kĭssed mĕ.
                        Leigh Hunt.

Thĕ lāw lŏcks ŭp thĕ māu ŏr wōmăn
    Whŏ stēals ă goōse frŏm ōff thĕ cōmmŏn ;
But lēts thĕ greātĕr vīlliăn loōse,
    Whŏ stēals thĕ cōmmŏn frōm thĕ goōse.
                        E. Elliott.

Whĕn fīrst ĭn Cēliă's ēar Ĭ pōured
    Ă yĕt ŭnprāctĭced prāyer,
Mȳ trĕmblĭng tōngue sĭncēre ignōred
    Thĕ āids ŏf "sweēt" ănd "fāir."
Ĭ ōnlȳ sāid, ăs ĭn mĕ lāy,
    Ĭ'd strĭve hĕr "wŏrth" tŏ rēach ;
Shĕ frōwned ănd tūrned hĕr ēyes ăwāy—
    Sŏ mŭch fŏr trŭth ĭn speēch.

Thĕn Dēliă cāme. Ĭ chănged mȳ plăn ;
    Ĭ prāised hĕr tŏ hĕr făce ;
Ĭ prāised hĕr feātŭres,—prāised hĕr făn,
    Hĕr lăp-dŏg ănd hĕr lăce ;
Ĭ swōre thăt nŏt tĭll Tīme wĕre dēad
    Mȳ pāssiŏn shoŭld dĕcāy ;
Shĕ, smīlĭng, găve hĕr hănd, ănd sāid
    'Twĭll lāst, thĕn, fŏr ă Dāy.
                Austin Dobson—"A Love Song."

Yoŭ sleēp ŭpŏn yoŭr mōthĕr's brĕast.
        Yoŭr rāce bĕgŭn,
Ă wĕlcŏme, lōng ă wĭshed-fŏr Guĕst,
        Whŏse āge ĭs Ōne.

A baby-boy, you wonder why
　　You cannot run;
You try to talk—how hard you try!
　　You're only One.

Ere long you won't be such a dunce;
　　You'll eat your bun,
And fly your kite, like folk, who once
　　Were only One.

You'll rhyme and woo, and fight and joke,
　　Perhaps you'll pun!
Such feats are never done by folk
　　Before they're One.

Some day, too, you may have your joy,
　　And envy none;
Yes, you, yourself, may own a Boy,
　　Who isn't One.
　　　　Frederick Locker—"A Rhyme of One."

A MEAN LOVER.

"I love to make my Mabel cry,
　　By jealous taunts and jeers.
For then I get a chance to try
　　And kiss away her tears."

LEGAL WHISKERS.

"As o'er their wine and walnuts sat,
Talking of this and then of that,
Two wights well learned in the law—
That is, well skilled to find a flaw—
Said one companion to the other,
'How is it, most respected brother,
That you have shaven away
Those whiskers which for many a day
Have ornamented much your cheek?
Sure, 'twas an idle, silly freak.'

Tŏ whōm thĕ ōthĕr ānswĕr gāve,
With loōk hălf mērrў ănd hălf grāve,
' Thŏugh ōthĕrs bē bў whĭskĕrs grāced,
Ă lāwyĕr cān't bĕ toō bărefāced.' "

CONCLUSION.

And now we bring to a close a subject full of never-ending interest to the student of general literature — poetry, the art divine. Endeavoring to make its study practical, we have followed it step by step, exemplifying its measures by quotations from our great authors. It is a theme inexhaustible, and yet one may become familiar with its elements and science.

Were you to ask how to excel, the answer would be : if nature has endowed you with the natural gift, cultivate it by a careful study of authors whose works are preëminent. Longfellow, Lowell, Holmes, Whittier, and Bryant are a galaxy of names that will ever adorn American literature, and whose works should be read and thoroughly analyzed by every student of literature and art. England and Scotland have had a long line of poets whose works are gems of rare art.

Every one would commend the works of Tennyson and Burns. They were poets who possessed the faculty divine. The world acknowledges them as two of the grandest of any age. Yet there are those of our own time who are living, toiling, struggling writers for fame, present as well as future, that are models of excellence and elegance. Dobson, Lang, Gosse, and Swinburne may be cited. Read, and you may find yourself in touch with some one or all of them. Of our present-day American authors, Stedman, Aldrich, Riley, Harte, Hay, Carleton, and Stoddard, have each earned a well-deserved fame. But be not mere imitators, read and study the works of great authors, and then mold and fashion your talent after a style of your own. There is a peculiar something in the writings of our poets that has a distinctiveness of its own plainly perceptible. Spontaneity in writing may be, and often is, genius assisting her own true children on and on, to nobler and greater deeds, giving them clearer vision — a direct insight. But let it not be supposed that genius alone makes men great. The lives of the best authors reveal the fact that men of genius are men who are untiring workers. Great poems are not mere accidents of genius. The great beehive of poetry is not inhabited by drones. The honey gathered from every flower is the result of their toil and industry. Care, precision, and painstaking methods are the royal roads to success. How beautifully William Cullen Bryant has expressed in these lines the poet's art :

> Thĕ sĕcrĕt woŭldst thŏu knŏw
>   Tŏ toŭch thĕ heărt ŏr fīre thĕ bloŏd ăt wĭll?
> Lĕt thīne ŏwn eȳes ŏ'erflŏw ;
>   Lĕt thȳ lĭps quīvĕr with thĕ pāssionăte thrĭll ;
> Sĕize thĕ greăt thŏught, ĕre yĕt ĭts pōwer bĕ păst,
> Ănd bīnd, ĭn wŏrds, thĕ fleĕt ĕmōtiŏn făst.
> "The Poet."

INDEX OF AUTHORS.

	PAGE
Adams, Charles Follen,	304, 305, 306, 309
Adams, John Quincy,	153
Adams, Sarah Flower,	252
Aldrich, Thomas Bailey,	140, 152, 153, 159, 179, 180, 202, 221, 222, 256
Alkaios,	171
Allston, Washington,	226
Armstrong, John,	181
Arnold, Edwin,	12
Arnold, Matthew,	90, 115
Aytoun, William Edmonstoune,	216
Baer, Libbie C.,	65
Baillie, Joanna,	97
Barham, Richard Harris,	188
Barlow, Joel,	225
Baxley, Isaac R.,	64
Bayly, Thomas Haynes,	159
Beaumont, Francis,	225
Beattie, James,	99, 178, 182
Beddoes, Thomas Lovell,	84
Bennett, S. Filmore,	253
Bennett, William Cox,	72
Bethune, George Washington,	25
Bible,	4
Bishop, Sir Henry,	240
Blackstone, Sir William,	155
Bowles, William Lisle,	114
Bradbury, W. H.,	254
Branch, Mary Bolles,	71
Brennan, Joseph,	25, 164
Brooks, Maria Gowen,	82

INDEX OF AUTHORS.

	PAGE
Brown, Frances,	249
Browning, Elizabeth Barrett,	84, 195
Browning, Robert,	55
Bruce, Michael,	135
Bryant, William Cullen, 16, 81, 100, 101, 134, 155, 157, 160, 249, 263, 267, 268, 283, 285, 328.	
Brydges, Samuel Egerton,	111
Buckingham, Duke of, (George Villiers),	82
Burns, Robert, 4, 11, 16, 40, 45, 46, 48, 49, 50, 79, 96, 100, 169, 197, 207, 222, 256, 263, 268, 278, 279, 285, 318, 319.	
Butler, Samuel,	148, 302
Byron, Lord, 13, 29, 48, 76, 98, 101, 183, 203, 204, 208, 209, 223, 255, 256, 300.	
Carey, Henry,	90
Cary, Alice,	55
Cary, Phœbe,	91
Campbell, Thomas, 6, 10, 11, 15, 16, 19, 55, 156, 187, 188, 217, 221, 224, 226, 260, 286.	
Carleton, Will,	21, 22, 163, 168
Carpenter, J. E.,	244
Catullus,	174
Chalkhill, John, (Izaac Walton),	138, 166
Chatterton, Thomas,	86
Chaucer, Geoffrey,	11, 42, 190, 291
"Chevy Chase,"	260
Churchill, Charles,	156
Claribel,	244
Clark, Willis G.,	225
Cobb, Henry N.,	87
Coit, John O.,	65
Coleridge, Samuel Taylor,	13, 27, 47, 55, 73, 204, 278
Collins, William,	214, 278
Cooke, Philip Pendleton,	93
Cornwall, Barry, (B. W. Proctor),	55
Cotton, Charles,	130
Cowley, Abraham,	208
Cowper, William,	3, 168, 171, 183, 263, 285, 286, 288
Crabbe, George,	287

INDEX OF AUTHORS.

	PAGE
Craik, Dinah Maria Mulock,	72, 88, 89, 99
Cunningham, Allan,	216, 318
Dana, Richard Henry,	80, 192
Daniel, Samuel,	94
Dante,	289
Darwin, Erasmus,	200
Davies, Sir John,	92
Dickens, Charles,	105
Dobson, Austin,	117, 119, 122, 123, 125, 129, 132, 298, 325
Doddridge, Philip,	199
Drayton, Michael,	218
Dryden, John,	3, 135, 257, 286, 293, 300, 302
Durbin, Charles,	61
Eastman, Charles Gamage,	54
Edwards, Amelia B.,	55
Elliot, Ebenezer,	278, 325
Emerson, Ralph Waldo,	212, 272
Emmett, Dan. D.,	246
Falconer, William,	59
Field, Eugene,	62, 150, 152, 193
Fletcher, Giles,	194
Fontenelle, Bernard le Bovier,	229
Fosdick, William W.,	283
Foster, Stephen Collins,	240
Franc, G.,	254
Gates, Ellen N. H.,	141
Gay, John,	138
Gaylord, Willis,	56
Gilder, Richard Watson,	108
Goethe, Johann Wolfgang von,	141, 150, 256, 295
Goldsmith, Oliver,	156, 182, 183, 196, 212
Gosse, Edmund,	128
Goose, Mary,	321
Gray, Thomas,	106, 147, 182, 206, 219, 224, 263, 266, 273
Greene, Roy Farrell,	314
Hale, Sarah J.,	105
Hall, Charles S.,	246
Harte, Francis Bret,	28, 87, 90, 167, 170, 218, 285, 308, 309, 311

INDEX OF AUTHORS.

	PAGE
Harvey, James,	213
Hastings, Thomas,	254
Hay, John,	11, 178, 257, 261, 285
Heber, Reginald,	145, 253
Heine, Heinrich,	256
Hemans, Felicia,	12, 180, 213
Henryson, Robert,	131
Herbert, George,	50
Herrick, Robert,	15, 77, 148, 149, 151, 178, 190, 191
Hervey, Thomas Kibble,	55
Heywood, Thomas,	106
Hill, Thomas,	190
Hogg, James,	152, 162
Holmes, Oliver Wendell,	51, 64, 147, 158, 201, 260, 262, 263
Homer,	217, 289
Hood, Thomas,	10, 31, 54, 55, 77, 89, 93, 113, 161, 191, 198, 260
Horace,	58, 226
Howe, Julia Ward,	247
Howells, William Dean,	64
Hoyt, Ralph,	55, 78
Hunt, Leigh,	325
Hunter, Anne,	146
Hugo, Victor,	149
Ingelow, Jean,	85
Jeffreys, Charles,	308
Johnson, Samuel,	180
Jones, Sir William,	203
Jonson, Ben,	279
Josephus,	4
Keats, John	103, 111, 181, 195, 212, 277, 291
Keeling, Elsa D. E.,	67
Kingsley, Charles,	81, 86, 144, 171, 173
Kinney, Coates,	25, 142, 225
Knox, William,	28
Körner, Charles Theodore,	80
Larcom, Lucy,	140, 143, 168, 170
Landon, Letitia Elizabeth,	224
Lang, Andrew,	116, 125, 130, 154

	PAGE
Lanier, Sidney,	44, 255
Lear, Edward,	321
Linley, G.,	244
Locker-Lampson, Frederick,	112, 325
Lockhart, Burton W.,	64
Lockhart, John Gibson,	221
Logan, Margaret B.,	122
Longfellow, Henry Wadsworth,	8, 12, 13, 14, 15, 35, 41, 44, 45, 55, 73, 74, 81, 110, 164, 171, 173, 194, 199, 207, 220, 222, 263, 281, 285, 291
Lowell, James Russell,	257, 263, 282, 301, 302, 303, 315, 317
Lowry, Rev. Robert,	253
Lytton, Sir Edward Bulwer,	295
Lytton, Robert Bulwer,	291
Macaulay, Lord,	258, 293
Macdonald, George,	11, 160
Mace, Frances Laughton,	252
Mackay, Charles,	14, 104, 145
Manners, Lady Frances,	56
Marlowe, Christopher,	294
Matthews, James Newton,	167
McCabe, Charles C.,	247
McCarthy, H.,	246
Marsh, Simeon B.,	254
Merrick, James,	179
Miller, Joaquin,	285
Milton, John,	48, 104, 109, 134, 198, 201, 219, 226, 266, 277, 289
Montgomery, James,	79, 134, 248
Moore, Thomas,	72, 239, 263, 291
Morris, Ida G.,	53
Motherwell, William,	166, 319
Moultrie, John,	78
Nelson, S.,	244
Norton, Caroline E.,	96, 113
O'Conner, Joseph	179
Osgood, Frances Sargent,	55, 68
Ossian,	3
Palgrave, Francis Turner,	193
Parnell, Thomas,	213

	PAGE
Parsons, Thomas W.,	43
Patmore, Coventry,	55
Payne, John Howard,	4, 240
Percival, James Gates,	194, 282
Perry, T. S.,	55
"Piers Plowman,"	195
Pike, Albert N.,	246
Pickering, Henry,	192, 223
Pinkney, Edward Coate,	93
Poe, Edgar Allan,	10, 18, 38, 68, 76, 146, 175, 192
Pope, Alexander,	2, 3, 27, 37. 58, 59. 177, 192, 197, 202, 206, 222, 286, 290, 300.
Powell,	54
Procter, Adelaide Anne,	75, 95, 218
Proctor, Bryan W., (Barry Cornwall),	104
Quarles, Francis,	11, 77
Ramsay, Allan,	285
Randall, James R.,	246
Read, Thomas Buchanan,	4, 55, 87, 284
Reed, Joe S.,	311
Riley, James Whitcomb,	67. 159, 263, 264. 265, 266, 285, 308, 309, 310, 319, 320, 322.
Roberts, Sarah,	79
Robinson, Maria Durey,	248
Rogers, Alexander,	94
Rouget de Lisle, Claude Joseph,	41
Russell, Henry,	242
Sappho,	172
Saxe, John Godfrey,	60, 70, 95, 97, 204
Schiller, J. C. F. von,	256, 261, 295
Scott, Lady Jane,	242
Scott, Sir Walter,	51, 163, 169, 183, 220, 291
Sedley, Sir Charles,	99
Shakespeare, William,	48, 78, 103, 112, 187, 192, 194, 195, 196, 206, 207, 215.
Shelley, Percy Bysshe,	70, 102
Shenstone, William,	214, 285
Shepherd, N. G.,	14

INDEX OF AUTHORS.

	PAGE
Shillaber, P. B.,	75
Shirley, James,	94
Sibley, Charles,	83
Sidney, Sir Philip,	69
Sigourney, Lydia H.,	151
Simms, William Gilmore,	283
Smith, Charlotte,	71
Smith, James,	198
Southey, Robert,	153, 161, 163, 171, 172, 207, 219, 225
Spenser, Edmund,	11, 181, 291
Stedman, Edmund Clarence,	73, 96, 143, 179, 205, 221, 283
Still, John,	196
Stoddard, Richard Henry,	55, 203
Stoddart, Thomas Tod,	88
Suckling, Sir John,	70, 189
Swinburne, Algernon Charles,	123, 124, 127, 142, 171, 172, 175, 285, 291, 292.
Taylor, Bayard,	55
Tennyson, Alfred,	12, 15, 28, 35, 38, 43, 47, 55, 59, 71, 76, 85, 90, 139, 146, 159, 162, 171, 173, 174, 202, 204, 205, 213, 214, 218, 256, 262, 263, 266, 285.
Thackeray, William Makepeace,	169
Thomson, James,	178, 182, 190, 197
Toplady, Rev. A. M.,	254
Tusser, Thomas,	48, 49
Udall, Nicholas,	294
Vaughan, Henry,	194
Virgil,	216, 289
Voiture, Vincent,	121
Waller, Edmund,	74
Walford, Rev. W. H.,	254
Walton, Izaak,	44
Watts, Isaac,	26, 157, 172, 254
Weir, Harrison,	106
Wesley, Charles,	251, 254
White, Joseph Blanco,	115
White, Henry Kirke,	74
Whitman, Walt,	3

	PAGE
Whittier, John Greenleaf,	12, 14, 28, 35, 44, 72, 210, 263, 284, 285
Wilcox, Ella Wheeler,	16, 110, 193, 205
Willis, Nathaniel Parker,	35
Winner, Septimus,	245
Wither, George,	57
Wolfe, Charles,	180
Wolfe, James,	277
Wordsworth, William,	37, 47, 54, 158, 285, 286

INDEX OF SUBJECTS

	PAGE		PAGE
Accent,	6, 19	Construction of the Stanza,	63
Acrostics,	56	Couplet,	11
Alcaics,	171	Cretic,	26
Allegory,	199	Dactyl,	24
Alliteration,	42	Dactylic Dimeter,	10
Amatory Ode,	256	Dactylic Rhythm,	160
Amphibrach,	26	Dialect,	303
Amphimacer,	26	Didactic	235, 285
Anapest,	24	Dimeter Measure,	138, 150, 160, 166.
Anapestic Rhythm,	165		
Anapestic Tetrameter,	10	Drama,	236, 293
Anaphora,	201	Echo,	218
Antithesis,	202	Ecphonesis	206
Apheresis,	187	Eight Line Stanza,	92
Apocope,	188	Elegy,	262
Apostrophe,	200	Ellipsis,	191
Assonantal Rhyme,	44	Empire of Poetry,	229
Ballad,	258	Enallage,	193
Ballade, The	116	Envoy,	298
Blank Verse,	133	Epanalepsis,	203
Burlesque,	297	Epenthesis,	188
Burletta,	297	Epic,	235, 288
Cento Verse,	54	Epigram,	203
Chant,	221	Epilogue,	298
Chant Royal,	118	Epitaph,	278
Child Dialect,	319	Epizeuxis,	204
Chinese Dialect,	311	Erotesis,	205
Classification,	235	Farce,	297
Comedy,	296	Feminine Rhyme,	45
Consonantal Rhyme,	45	Figures of Etymology,	187

INDEX OF SUBJECTS.

	PAGE		PAGE
Figures of Rhetoric,	199	Nonsense,	320
Figures of Speech,	187	Objective Poetry,	236
Figures of Syntax,	191	Octometer Measure,	146, 159
Five Line Stanza,	69	Odd Rhyme,	50
Foreign Words and Expressions,	60	Ode,	254
German Dialect,	304	Onomatopœia,	218
Hearing,	208	Opera,	299
Hendecasyllables,	174	Pantoum,	131
Heptameter Measure,	144, 158	Paragoge,	189
Heroic Ode,	257	Paraleipsis,	220
Hexameter Measure,	143, 157, 164, 170, 172.	Pastoral,	235, 281
		Pentameter Measure,	142, 155
Hyperbaton,	197	Personification,	220
Hyperbole,	208	Pleonasm,	198
Iambic Pentameter,	11	Poetical Licenses,	177
Iambic Rhythm,	147	Poetry as an Art,	1
Iambus,	23	Poetic Pauses,	36
Imitation of Classical Measures,	171	Prologue,	297
Inverse Rhyme	49	Prosthesis,	190
Inversion,	197	Quantity,	6
Interrogation,	205	Quatrain,	12
Irish Dialect,	306	Refrain,	221
Irony,	210	Rhythm,	30
Kinds of Poetry,	229	Rhythmic Combinations,	65
Litotes,	211	Rhyme,	40
Lyric,	235, 237	Rondeau,	120
Masculine Rhyme,	45	Rondel,	123
Measures Exemplified,	136	Roundel,	124
Melodrama,	297	Sacred Ode,	255
Meter,	18	Sacred Songs,	248
Metonymy,	212	Sapphics,	172
Metrical History,	293	Satire,	236, 299
Metrical Romance,	291	Scansion,	33
Middle Rhyme,	46	Secular Songs,	238
Mock Epic,	289	Sectional Rhyme,	48
Monometer Measure,	137, 148, 165	Selection of Words,	58
Moral Ode,	255	Sestine,	126
Nine Line Stanza,	98	Seven Line Stanza,	82

INDEX OF SUBJECTS.

	PAGE		PAGE
Scotch Dialect,	318	Triolet,	129
Simile,	222	Triple Rhyme,	46
Six Line Stanza,	75	Tragedy,	296
Sonnet,	107	Travesty,	297
Southern Dialect,	311	Trimeter Measure,	139, 151, 167
Spondee,	26	Triplet,	12
Stanza,	11	Trochaic Rhythm,	136
Subjective Poetry,	236	Trochaic Tetrameter,	10
Subjective Drama,	299	Trope,	223
Syllepsis,	198	Trochee,	23
Synæresis,	190	Verse,	10
Synecdoche,	223	Versicle,	323
Syncope,	190	Villanelle,	124
Task Rhyme,	50	Virelay,	130
Ten Line Stanza,	102	Vision,	226
Tetrameter Measure, 140, 152, 163, 168.		Western Dialect,	308
		Yankee Dialect,	315
Tmesis,	191		

www.ingramcontent.com/pod-product-compliance
Lightning Source LLC
Chambersburg PA
CBHW020245240426
43672CB00006B/647